PAPERTOY GLOWBOTS

46 GLOWING ROBOTS YOU CAN MAKE YOURSELF!

CASTLEFORTE

and 14 of the Top Papertoy Designers from Around the World

Workman Publishing ▪ New York

WARNING: *These robots are paper and flammable. Keep away from flames and heat or these robots could go up in smoke.*

I would like to dedicate this book to the fans, designers, builders, and collectors of papertoys everywhere. You have proven to be an awesome force of creativity and community, worthy of all the love, appreciation, and recognition of any art form out there. Our time is now and our best is still yet to come.

Keep on designing, cutting, folding, gluing, building, sharing, and enjoying papertoys. There just isn't anything quite like these wonderful little creations, and they couldn't exist without you.

Library of Congress Cataloging-in-Publication Data is available.

ISBN 978-0-7611-7762-3

Written by Brian Castleforte
Illustrations by Phil Conigliaro
Photographs by Michael Di Mascio
Cover design by Colleen AF Venable and Tae Won Yu

Editor	Justin Krasner
Designer	Phil Conigliaro
Production Editor	Amanda Hong
Production Manager	Doug Wolff

Workman books are available at special discounts when purchased in bulk for premiums and sales promotions as well as for fund-raising or educational use. Special editions or book excerpts can also be created to specification. For details, contact the Special Sales Director at the address below or send an email to specialmarkets@workman.com.

Workman Publishing Co., Inc.
225 Varick Street
New York, NY 10014-4381
workman.com

WORKMAN is a registered trademark of Workman Publishing Co., Inc.

Printed in China

First printing July 2016

10 9 8 7 6 5 4 3 2

ACKNOWLEDGMENTS

Huge thanks to each of the artists who have contributed to this book. It wouldn't be as awesome without you.

Thank you, Daniel Nayeri, Justin Krasner, Phil Conigliaro for the impressively long hours working on the book's design, Amanda Hong for production editing, and everyone at Workman for making this amazing book possible.

Thank you to papertoy fans everywhere. To the die-hard fans, builders, and collectors and the casual ones, to the parents and grandparents, brothers and sisters, aunts and uncles, teachers and students, etc., etc., who have ever taken the time to build a papertoy themselves or have helped a younger person build them, thank you! Thank you for loving and supporting our craft. Thank you for making *Papertoy Monsters* such a huge success, which has made *Papertoy Glowbots* possible. Thank you!
We love you!

Thank you again to all of the members of NicePaperToys.com for keeping the papertoy community alive and well and oh so NICE!

Thank you artists, designers, crafters, makers, writers, musicians, inventors, dreamers, doers, creators of all kinds; thank you for the inspiration, and for all that you do to make this world a more beautiful, colorful, interesting place to live. I am eternally grateful for each and every one of you.

Thanks to all of you kids of ALL ages, everywhere; you are the reason I do this, and you keep me young and full of love.

Thank you, Mom, for believing in me, supporting me, and loving me, always.

Thank YOU for buying this book. I hope you enjoy it as much as we do.

CONTENTS

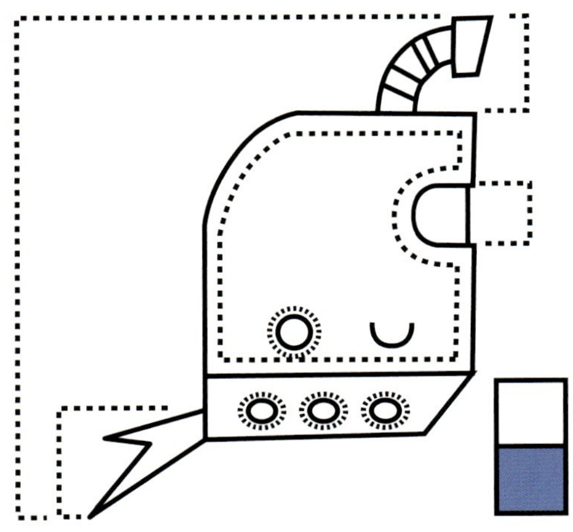

INTRODUCTION

Gree-Tings, Hu-Man.

Wel-Come to Pa-Per-Toy Glow-Bots.

Okay, I am not a robot, but I sure do love them. That's why this book is all about robots. After all, robots are awesome! And what is even more awesome than robots? Glowbots, that's what! Glowbots are robots that glow in the dark.

Glowbots come in all shapes, sizes, and personalities—from cute, friendly robots, to strong, serious robots, to giant, scary robots. But no matter what kind of robot you build, it will always be totally awesome because it's a robot. And robots rock!

When I was a kid I loved to make things. Okay, I'm still a kid, a big old kid, but when I was a *little* kid I really loved to make robots. I would build them out of Legos, Erector sets, cardboard boxes, tinfoil, clay, and paper—whatever supplies or spare parts I could find.

I would pretend to program my robots to do all sorts of things. Some would be my helpers and clean up my room, sneak a cookie from the cookie jar, or guard my bedroom door to keep my little brothers out. Others would be my protectors, my personal bodyguards, keeping me safe from the evil aliens of Quantar, but that is another story. I also liked to pretend that I was a robot sometimes. In fact, I still do that, especially for Halloween.

I am thrilled to be making this awesome book of papertoy robots! And not just robots, but ones with glow-in-the-dark features: glowbots! How cool is that? In this book you will find forty-six of the cutest, coolest, and most colorful glowbots ever made, created by me and fourteen talented artists from around the world. Some of the glowbots have glow-in-the-dark stickers. Some work with other glowing items, such as flashlights, glow sticks, or electric tea lights (no fire, please). There's even one that sits on a light in your Christmas tree. Don't worry if you don't have a Christmas tree or even any of the light-up materials. All of these robots are still really cool on their own.

One thing I like to do is set up my paper robots with my paper monsters and have them interact with each other. Some of them are friends. Some of them are enemies. Sometimes they have grand battles. You can have the monsters invade a city and then have the robots come and save the day. Or the other way around. Or perhaps there's a team of good monsters and robots, and another team of evil monsters and robots. Or maybe your robots help the monsters with their daily chores and things. I'm sure you will come up with your own ideas and adventures. The important thing is to be creative and have fun.

Okay, I think you have more than enough data to get started on building all of your new papertoy glowbots. Besides, I am run-ning out of en-er-gy. Must re-charge my bat-ter-ies. Hap-py fold-ing, my friend!

HOW TO BUILD YOUR PAPERTOYS

Constructing a papertoy glowbot is simple and easy once you get the hang of it. Here are some general instructions and helpful hints to get you started.

WHAT YOU'LL DEFINITELY NEED

Glue: Glue sticks are the most commonly used option, but white glue or any craft glue that works with paper may be used.

OR

Double-sided adhesive: Double-sided adhesive tape products like Scor-Tape can be cut to any size and will easily peel and stick onto templates.

OPTIONAL TOOLS

Pen or pencil: Helpful when you need to curve a template. Also useful to hold down tabs inside a toy while you wait for the glue to dry.

Tweezers: For handling small templates and tabs.

Smooth, jumbo paper clip: Helpful to reach remaining tabs that may need to be glued on the inside of a closed template.

Spoon: You can use the rounded part to curve a template, and the handle to hold any small tabs in place until the glue dries or to help you make crisp folds.

Instructions

DETACH the first template(s) according to the specific instructions for each papertoy.

FOLD the template on all the precreased fold lines, pressing down firmly to make nice, crisp folds.

There are two types of folds:

NORMAL FOLDS—or mountain folds—look like a mountain or a capital *A*. Almost all of your folds will be normal, unless they are marked otherwise.

VALLEY FOLDS look like a valley or the letter *V*. Very few of your folds will be a valley, but be sure to keep an eye out for them! Look for fold lines marked like this: —·—·—·—·—·—

GLUE all numbered tabs to the corresponding numbered gray areas (or glue numbered gray areas to each other) in numerical order (1, 2, 3, and so on), as directed in the instructions. Be patient—make sure to hold glued areas together long enough for the glue to dry so that your model remains intact and strong.

REPEAT these steps for each piece of the toy until you have completed your papertoy glowbot.

NICKNAME: Daisuke
DESCRIPTION: 21 feet long; retractable swinging tail; huge mechanical jaws; headlamp
FUNCTION: ocean cleaner
ABILITIES: trash eating; speed swimming; deep diving

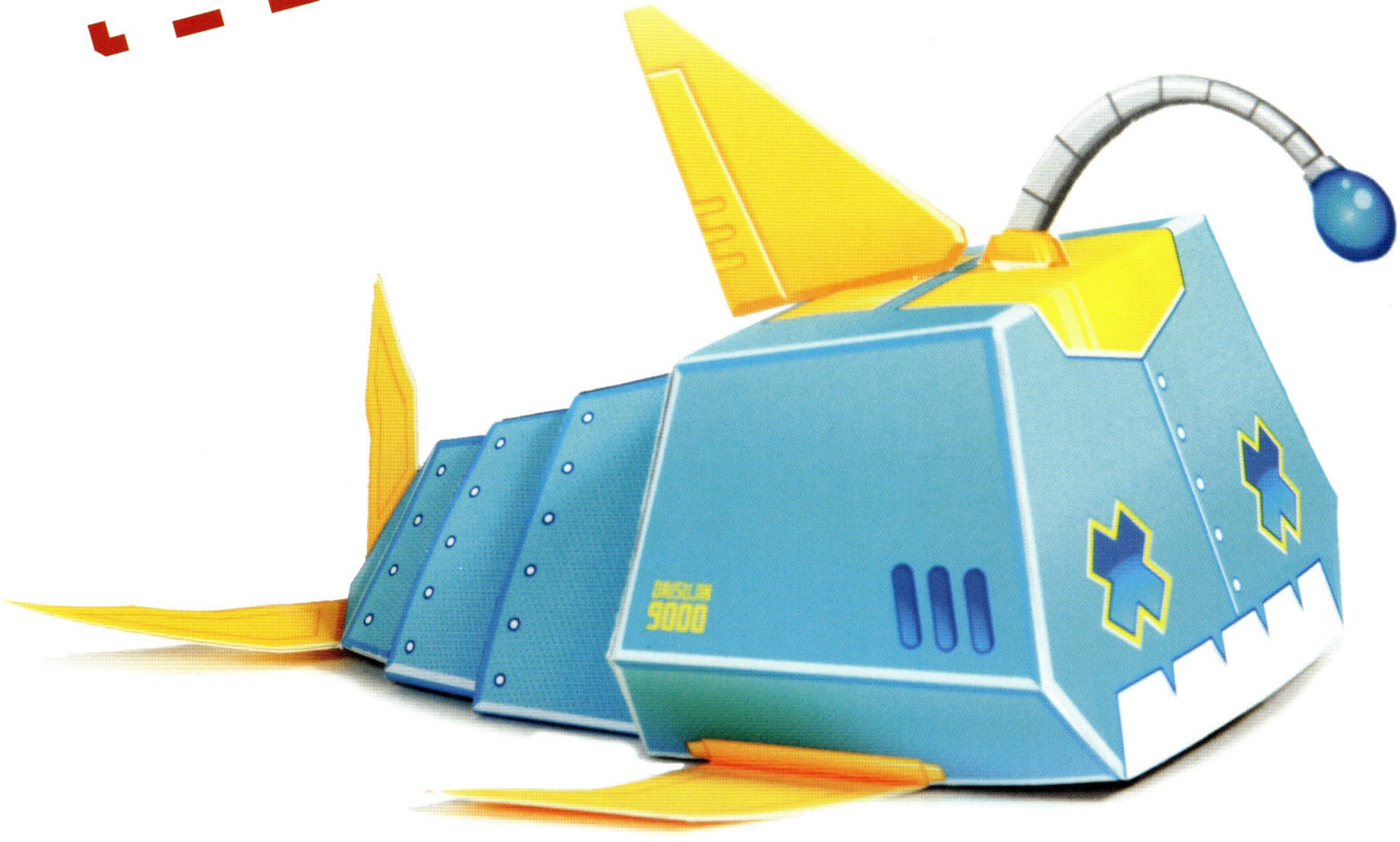

DAISUJIN 9000

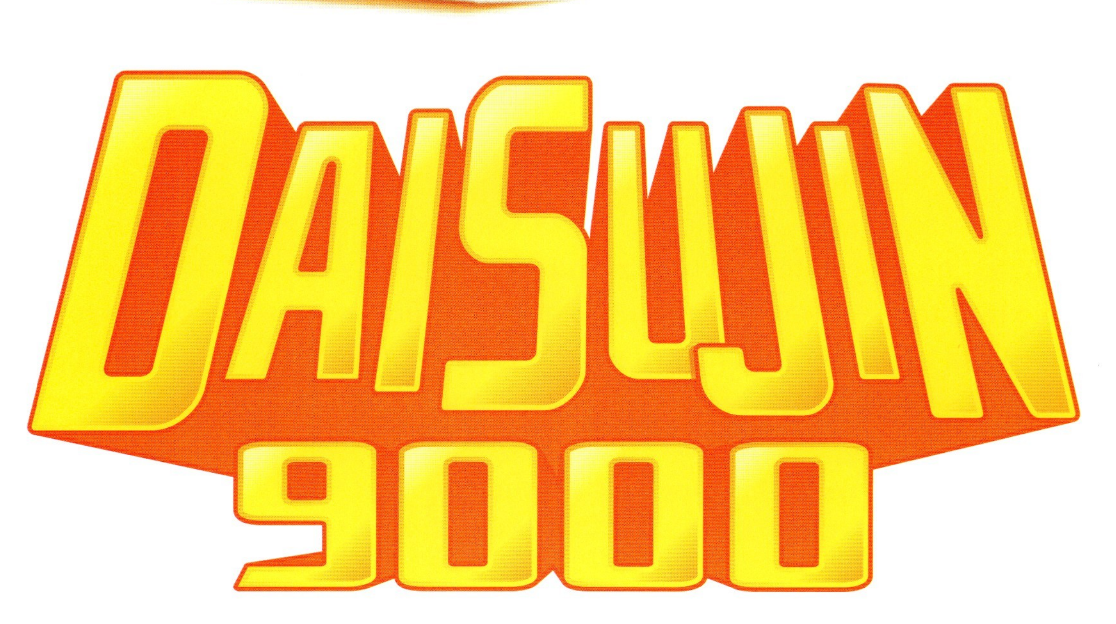

DIFFICULTY: Intermediate

Assembly Instructions

DISCOVERED BY DOLLY OBLONG

(SEE TEMPLATE, PAGE 97)

A. Detach TAIL A template. Glue tabs 1–6 to gray areas 1–6.

B. Detach TAIL B template. Fold TAIL B and wrap it around TAIL A. Glue tabs 7–9 to gray areas 7–9.

C. Detach TAIL C template. Fold TAIL C and wrap it around TAIL B. Glue tab 10 to gray area 10.

D. Detach HEAD template. Glue tabs 11–18 to gray areas 11–18.

E. Glue tabs 19–21 on TAIL C to gray areas 19–21 on HEAD.

F. Detach TOP FIN template. Insert tab 22 into back slot on top of HEAD.

G. Detach ANTENNA template. Insert tab 23 into front slot on top of HEAD.

H. Add glow-in-the-dark stickers.

Deep down in the Pacific Ocean, a giant shadow roams the depths. What could it be? The locals once thought it was a monster. Then one night a fisherman got lost at sea. When he saw a small light and a huge shadow appearing in front of his boat, he was afraid he was fish food. Little did he know it was just a bashful but friendly robofish, Daisujin 9000, overcoming his shyness and guiding the boat safely home. The fishermen nicknamed him Daisuke, which means "Great Helper." Daisuke has huge mechanical jaws, but he doesn't use them to munch on fish. Instead, they help him eat the garbage floating around in the ocean. When he swims, his retractable tail sweeps from left to right like a broom, pushing the trash and dirt into his mouth. Plastic bottles and cans? A deserted beach ball? An old barrel? Daisuke eats it all!

MODEL NAME: **STOR-E V2.0**
DESCRIPTION: 2 feet tall; covered in moons and stars; plug tail
FUNCTION: storyteller and night-light
ABILITIES: can read any book, in any language; speed-reader; vanquisher of monsters who live under the bed

DIFFICULTY: Easy

Assembly Instructions

Discovered by Jon Greenwell, aka Jonny Chiba

(see template, page 99)

A Detach BODY template. Glue tab 1 to gray area 1.

B Detach ARMS template. Glue tabs 2 and 3 to gray areas 2 and 3 on BODY.

C Detach HEAD template. Glue tab 4 to gray area 4.

D Attach BODY to HEAD. Glue tabs 5–8 to gray areas 5–8.

E Place over night-light or electric tea light to glow.

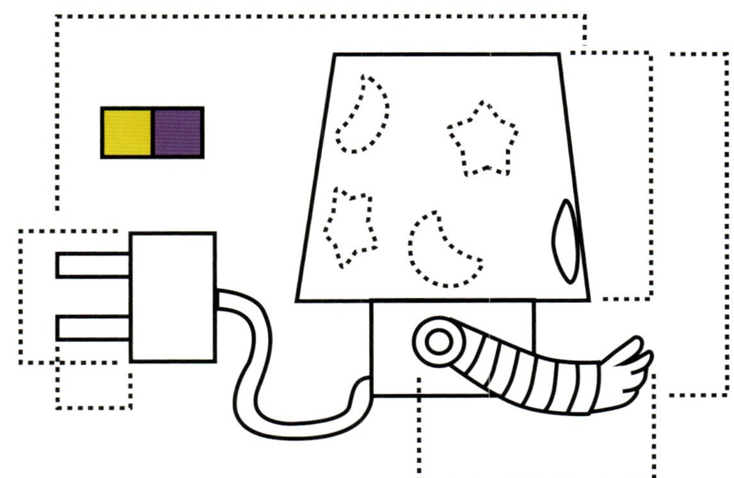

The Lampy night-light and storytelling robot was invented by Dr. Goto Bedd as a way of calming her son at bedtime. To use Lampy, a child simply has to place the book of his or her choice into its hands. Early models had to be abandoned, however, after a malfunctioning speech chip led to the robot's voice getting louder and louder until, by the end, the story was being shouted at the frightened, cowering child. The V2.0 release fixed this nasty bug and, as a bonus, added translating software, enabling the new Lampy to read and translate a book in any language. The addition of calming background music and projected stars and moons will lull even the most stubborn child to sleep.

FROSTY FROST

MODEL NAME: COLD FREEZER1
DESCRIPTION: 4 feet tall; cold but surprisingly cuddly
FUNCTION: ice cream dispenser
ABILITIES: can churn a fresh batch of ice cream in less than a minute; immune to brain freeze; champion simultaneous snowboarder and snowball eater

DIFFICULTY: Intermediate

Assembly Instructions

DISCOVERED BY ABI BRACEROS, AKA ABZ

(SEE TEMPLATE, PAGE 101)

A Detach BODY and LEFT ARM templates. Curve long section of LEFT ARM and glue tabs 1–14 to gray areas 1–14. Insert tabs 15 and 16 on LEFT ARM into slots on left side of BODY and glue to gray areas 15 and 16.

B Detach RIGHT ARM template. Curve long section and glue tabs 17–30 to gray areas 17–30. Insert tabs 31 and 32 on RIGHT ARM into slots on right side of BODY and glue to gray areas 31 and 32.

C Detach BELLY template. Glue tabs 33 and 34 on BELLY to gray areas 33 and 34 on BODY.

D Curve long section of BODY and glue tabs 35–54 to gray areas 35–54.

E Detach the ice cream and cups templates.

F Curve long section of PURPLE CUP and glue tabs 55–64 to gray areas 55–64. Glue tab 65 on MINT ICE CREAM to gray area 65 on PURPLE CUP.

G Curve long section of ORANGE CUP and glue tabs 66–75 to gray areas 66–75. Glue tab 76 on SPRINKLES ICE CREAM to gray area 76 on ORANGE CUP.

H Place over night-light or smart phone or insert electric tea light into BODY to glow.

Frosty Frost dispenses mounds of yummy ice cream to kids looking to cool off on a hot day. She offers every flavor ever invented—even ones that only exist in your dreams. Frosty Frost creates her delicious treats so quickly that you never have to wait longer than a minute. But if you're impatient, watch out—she won't hesitate to teach you a lesson. Frosty once used hot sauce in place of strawberry syrup for a customer who complained about having to wait longer than 10 seconds.

MODEL NAME: TECH-RONIN
DESCRIPTION: 0.1 nanometers; bright blue
FUNCTION: antiviral nanobot agent
ABILITIES: obliterating code; light scattering; self-modifying software; lightning speed

DIFFICULTY: Easy

Assembly Instructions

DISCOVERED BY JON GREENWELL, AKA JONNY CHIBA

(SEE TEMPLATE, PAGE 103)

A Detach BODY template. Glue tabs 1–24 to gray areas 1–24.

B Detach ARMS template. Glue ARMS to BODY at gray area 25 and insert ends into slots.

C Detach HOOD template. Glue tabs 26–31 to gray areas 26–31.

D Glue HOOD to ARMS at gray area 32.

E Detach HEAD template. Glue tabs 33–47 to gray areas 33–47.

F Glue tab 48 on HOOD to gray area 48 on HEAD.

G Add glow-in-the-dark stickers.

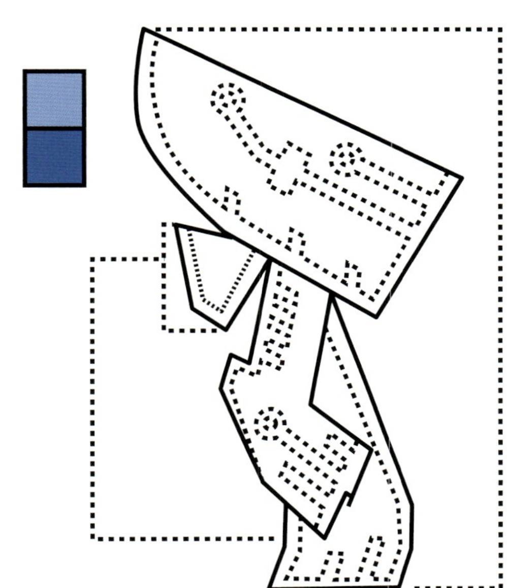

The Tech-Ronin were specially engineered antiviral nanobots released onto the Internet. They roamed the highways and byways of the World Wide Web, searching for malicious viruses to combat. The Tech-Ronin kept the web safe for years, until a super villain released a virus capable of bringing the entire internet to a standstill. The Tech-Ronin joined together in what was to be their finest, most honorable fight, the Battle of the Motherboard. Alas, as fierce as they were, the Tech-Ronin were no match for the virus. All but one were wiped out. This lone Tech-Ronin, Glow-Go, now drifts from computer to computer, destroying viruses, becoming stronger and stronger, until one day he can avenge his fallen nanobot kin and destroy the super virus once and for all.

drillr

MODEL NAME: ANTI-GAS RIGRR
DESCRIPTION: 15 feet tall; massive drill; intricate piping system; smells fantastic
FUNCTION: extract extra-stinky natural resources from the Earth's core
ABILITIES: impervious to smell; strong lung capacity; fireproof; good gas mileage; can burp the alphabet

DIFFICULTY: Intermediate

Assembly Instructions

DISCOVERED BY MATTHIJS KAMSTRA, AKA [MCK]

(SEE TEMPLATE, PAGE 105)

A Detach FLAME ARM template. Glue tab 1 to gray area 1.

B Detach FLAME THROWER template. Glue tabs 2 on FLAME ARM to gray areas 2 on FLAME THROWER. Glue tabs 3–4 to gray areas 3–4.

C Detach BODY template. Glue tabs 5 on FLAME ARM to gray area 5 on BODY. Glue tabs 6–13 to gray areas 6–13.

D Detach DRILLER ARM template. Glue tab 14 to gray area 14. Glue tabs 15 on DRILLER ARM to gray area 15 on BODY.

E Detach DRILLER HAND PART 1 and DRILLER HAND PART 2 templates. Glue tab 16 on DRILLER HAND PART 2 to gray area 16 on DRILLER HAND PART 1.

F Glue tabs 17 and 18 on DRILLER HAND PART 1 to gray areas 17 and 18 on DRILLER HAND PART 2.

G Glue tabs 19 on DRILLER ARM to gray area 19 on DRILLER HAND PART 2.

H Insert electric tea light into FLAME THROWER and add glow-in-the-dark stickers.

Everybody burps and farts. Sometimes even our planet needs to let one out. Burps and farts are nothing but gas, and there is plenty of gas inside the Earth. But can you imagine the immense stinkiness of an Earth-size fart? It would reek! So humanity created a robot to help our planet—and its inhabitants—out! Meet Drillrr: She's a robot drilling rig that bores holes in the Earth's surface for the extraction of a certain natural resource (read: majorly stinky farts). Drillrr searches for pockets of gas, drills a hole, and burns the gas so we don't have to smell it.

S.S. TUBMARINE

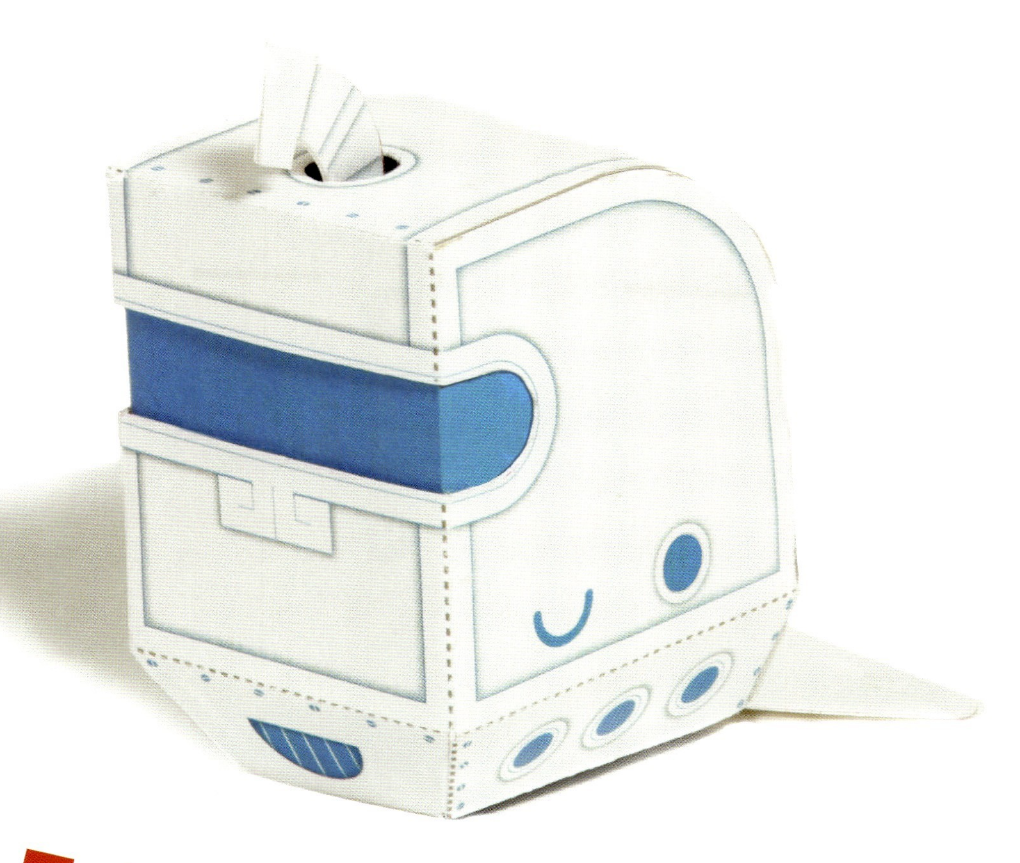

MODEL NAME: AI PASSENGER VESSEL 1
DESCRIPTION: 150 feet long; 6 supercharged engines; horizontal thruster fin; periscope
FUNCTION: passenger submarine; occasional spy missions
ABILITIES: can plunge up to 950 feet underwater; goes faster than 30 nautical miles an hour; projects aquatic light shows

Assembly Instructions

Discovered by Bryan Rollins

(see template, page 107)

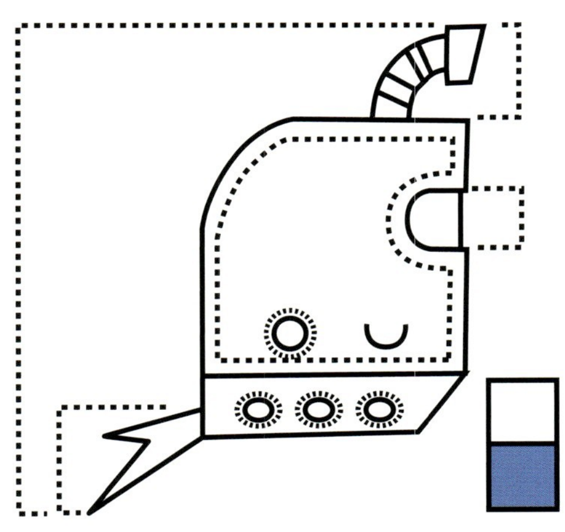

A Detach INSERT template. Glue tabs 1–4 to gray areas 1–4.

B Detach BODY template. Glue tabs 5–9 to gray areas 5–9.

C Insert INSERT into BODY.

D Place an LED or electric tea light into INSERT to glow.

E Detach PERISCOPE template. Insert PERISCOPE into hole at top of BODY and through INSERT.

F Insert BODY tabs 10 and 11 into gray areas 10 and 11. Do not glue these tabs.

G Add glow-in-the-dark stickers.

The S.S. *Tubmarine* is the first of its kind: a self-driving AI passenger vessel. Built by the finest ship makers in the United States, it is large enough to comfortably hold fifty passengers and can plunge up to 950 feet beneath the ocean's surface. The vessel's thruster fin was built to mimic the tail movements of real aquatic animals, such as dolphins, and its giant light-up periscope was based on the deep-sea anglerfish's light lure. Passengers on the S.S. *Tubmarine* ride in style inside the submarine's luxury interior cabins with climate control and more than 78 hours of life support—essential for longer journeys. The *Tubmarine* has been used for everything from undersea tours to secret spy missions to retro dance parties.

B.A.A.R.T.

brain • activated • asteroid • retrieval • transport

MODEL NAME: BRAIN-ACTIVATED ASTEROID RETRIEVAL TRANSPORT 1.0

DESCRIPTION: 5 feet tall; radioactive brain; sweet headphones

FUNCTION: asteroid retrieval and transport

ABILITIES: can identify the precise mineral content of every galactic rock; amazing at air guitar

DIFFICULTY: Intermediate

Assembly Instructions

DISCOVERED BY CASTLEFORTE

(SEE TEMPLATE, PAGE 109)

A. Detach BRAIN and BODY templates. Glue tab 1 on BRAIN to gray area 1 on BODY.

B. Detach RIGHT ARM template. Insert tab 2 into slot on right side of BODY and glue to gray area 2.

C. Detach LEFT ARM template. Insert tab 3 into slot on left side of BODY and glue to gray area 3.

D. Glue BODY tabs 4–12 to gray areas 4–12.

E. Detach both SPACE ROCKS templates and curve slightly to stand.

F. Add glow-in-the-dark stickers.

Developed by NASA as part of their Mars colonization effort, B.A.A.R.T. gives new meaning to the term *rocking out*. Deployed onto the surface of the red planet, B.A.A.R.T. scours the landscape, collecting as many different rock samples as possible. Because of his radioactive brain (harvested from an alien being), B.A.A.R.T. has the unique ability of knowing the precise mineral content of any mineral-based object simply by looking at it. This makes him perfect for collecting rock samples. Space rocks aren't the only rocks of interest to B.A.A.R.T. After spending years training with NASA astronauts on Earth, he became a huge rock music fan. Classic rock, hard rock, even a little punk rock–B.A.A.R.T. loves to boogie down while collecting samples.

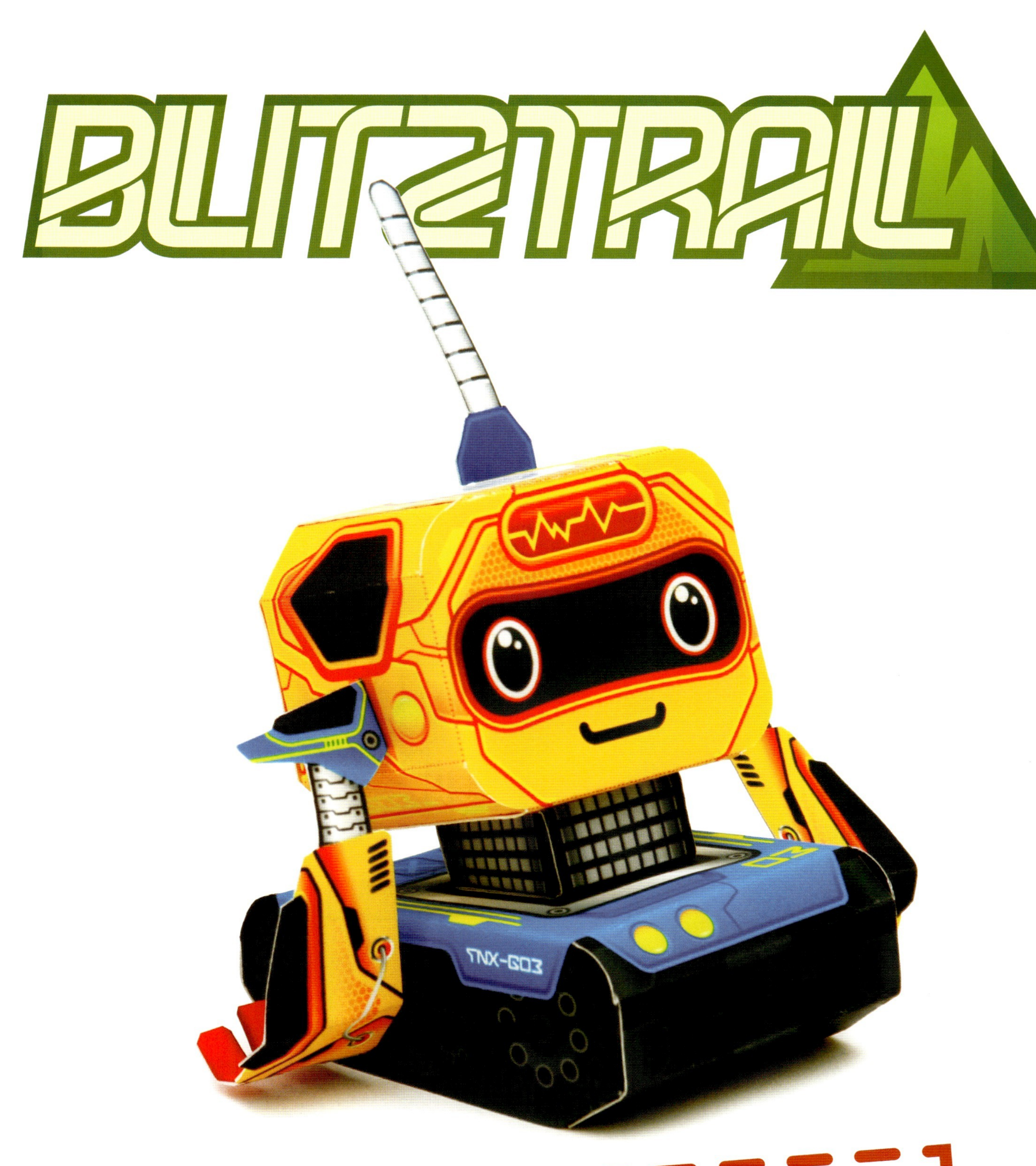

MODEL NAME: **RESERVE PRESERVE BT**

DESCRIPTION: 4 feet tall; massive hands; smells like pine trees

FUNCTION: forest ranger and guide; wildlife conservation

ABILITIES: fighting forest fires; search and rescue; tree-climbing, -swinging, and -hugging

DIFFICULTY: Easy

Assembly Instructions

Discovered by Salazad

(see template, page 111)

A Detach HEAD and RIGHT ARM templates. Insert tab 1 on RIGHT ARM into slot on right side of HEAD and glue to gray area 1.

B Detach LEFT ARM template. Insert tab 2 on LEFT ARM into slot on left side of HEAD and glue to gray area 2.

C Glue tabs 3–9 on HEAD to gray areas 3–9.

D Detach ANTENNA template. Glue tab 10 on ANTENNA to gray area 10 on HEAD.

E Detach NECK template. Glue tabs 11–17 to gray areas 11–17.

F Glue NECK to HEAD at gray area 18.

G Detach BODY template. Glue tabs 19–26 to gray areas 19–26.

H Glue BODY to NECK at gray area 27.

I Add glow-in-the-dark stickers.

Blitztrail calls the mountains home and spends his days in harmony with nature. Designed as the first robotic forest ranger and mountaineering guide, Blitztrail is well known and well loved by nature enthusiasts of all ages. Blitz provides 24/7 forest patrol, clears fallen trees and boulders from paths, puts out fires, and rescues imperiled hikers and campers from danger. Blitztrail's tough treads allow him to venture into areas where other vehicles can't go, and his two massive hands can be used to climb big trees like a monkey swinging on a vine.

MODEL NAME: FUNBOT 1300
DESCRIPTION: 7 feet tall; wi-fi antennae; toothy smile
FUNCTION: entertainment
ABILITIES: multilingual; great at karaoke; moonlights as a stand-up comedian

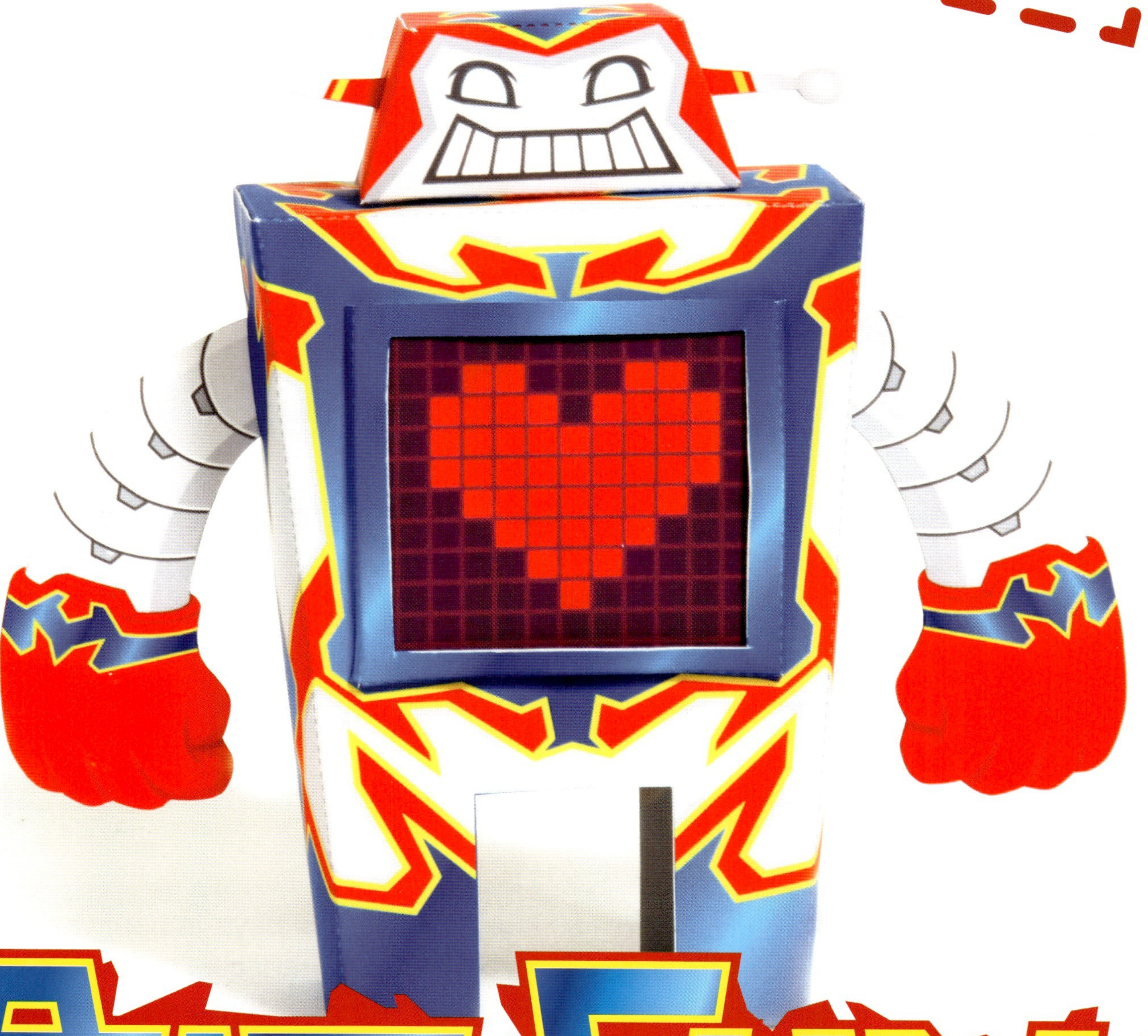

BIG FUN

Assembly Instructions

DISCOVERED BY ABI BRACEROS, AKA ABZ

(SEE TEMPLATE, PAGE 113)

A Detach BODY and RIGHT ARM templates. Insert tab 1 on RIGHT ARM into slot on right side of BODY and glue to gray area 1.

B Detach LEFT ARM template. Insert tab 2 on LEFT ARM into slot on left side of BODY and glue to gray area 2.

C Detach SCREEN FRAME template and insert tabs 3–5 into slots on front of BODY and glue to gray areas 3–5.

D Glue tabs 6–9 on BODY to gray areas 6–9.

E Detach HEAD and RIGHT ANTENNA templates. Insert tab 10 on RIGHT ANTENNA into slot on right side of HEAD and glue to gray area 10.

F Detach LEFT ANTENNA template. Insert tab 11 on LEFT ANTENNA into slot on left side of HEAD and glue to gray area 11.

G Glue tabs 12–15 on HEAD to gray areas 12–15.

H Glue tabs 16–19 on HEAD to gray areas 16–19 on BODY.

I Detach SCREEN templates. Choose which picture you'd like displayed by sliding SCREEN into SCREEN FRAME on front of BODY.

J Use your imagination and draw your own picture on blank side of SCREEN.

K Add glow-in-the-dark stickers.

Always the life of the party, Big Fun draws crowds through sheer excitement. His large, high-resolution screen streams popular cartoons and music videos from around the world and in every language. Big Fun enjoys hearing kids cheer or sing along to their favorite songs. When it's time to get kids more active, he switches to video game mode. His controller-free technology allows kids to use their entire bodies to play video games, getting them to dance, jump, and move around. But that's not all he can do! Big Fun tells the funniest knock-knock jokes. He can also make the most fantastical balloon animals you've ever seen, including a zebra, an octopus, and a garden snake.

MODEL NAME: HOVERBOT VII
DESCRIPTION: 5 feet tall; hovercraft with aerodynamic fins and 360-degree vision
FUNCTION: former aircraft marshaller, current valet parking bot
ABILITIES: exceptional depth and size perception; ability to find just the right spot for every vehicle; strong sense of smell
GARLIC

Assembly Instructions

DISCOVERED BY NICK KNITE

(SEE TEMPLATE, PAGE 115)

DIFFICULTY: Easy

A Detach BODY template. Glue tabs 1–17 to gray areas 1–17.

B Detach RIGHT-TURN LIGHT template. Glue tabs 18–24 to gray areas 18–24.

C Glue RIGHT-TURN LIGHT to BODY at gray area 25.

D Detach LEFT-TURN LIGHT template. Glue tabs 26–32 to gray areas 26–32.

E Glue LEFT-TURN LIGHT to BODY at gray area 33.

F Detach BULB template. Glue tabs 34–50 to gray areas 34–50.

G Glue BULB to BODY at gray area 51.

H Add glow-in-the-dark stickers.

Garlic was built and trained to work on an airfield as an aircraft-marshalling robot. He did his job well for many years, but he started developing an unhealthy obsession with luggage, especially leather suitcases. He began chasing the luggage wagons around the airfield instead of doing his job directing planes. Garlic eventually got laid off, but due to his excellent skills directing traffic and finding just the right spots for planes to be parked, he was hired by All Bot Catering Services to be their premiere valet parking bot. He truly loves his new job. Garlic is the quickest and most efficient valet. He can squeeze any vehicle into even the tightest spot. Among the valets, he's the one bot getting the biggest tips.

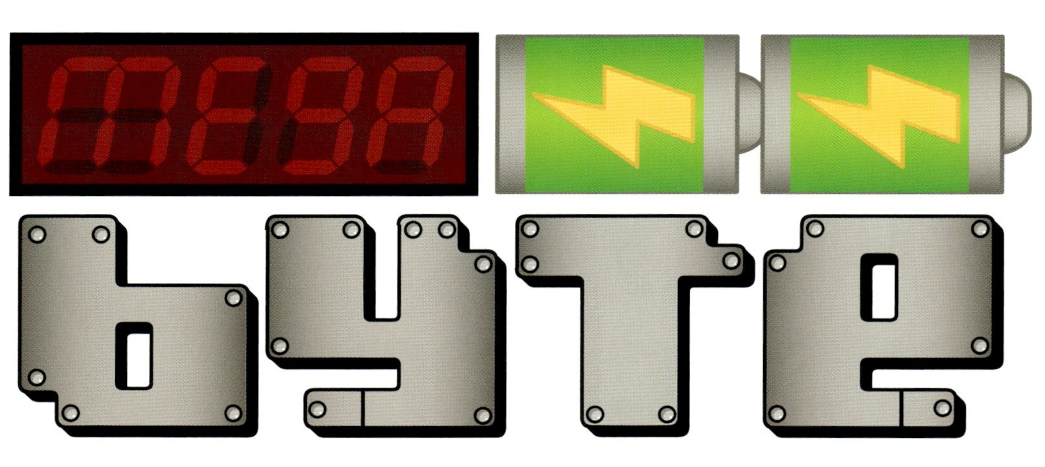

MODEL NAME: MB 2.0
DESCRIPTION: 10 feet tall; battery-packed buttocks
FUNCTION: data storage robot
ABILITIES: eats large amounts of data but never gets full

DIFFICULTY: Intermediate

Assembly Instructions

Discovered by J. Edwards

(see template, page 117)

- **A** Detach HEAD and NOSE templates. Insert tab 1 on NOSE into slot on HEAD and glue to gray area 1.
- **B** Detach LIGHT template. Insert tab 2 on LIGHT into slot on top of HEAD and glue to gray area 2.
- **C** Glue tabs 3–6 on HEAD to gray areas 3–6.
- **D** Detach BODY template. Glue tabs 7–10 on HEAD to gray areas 7–10 on BODY. Glue tabs 11–25 to gray areas 11–25.
- **E** Detach LEFT ARM template. Glue tab 26 on LEFT ARM to gray area 26 on BODY.
- **F** Detach RIGHT ARM template. Glue tab 27 on RIGHT ARM to gray area 27 on BODY.
- **G** Detach RIGHT LEG template. Glue tabs 28–38 to gray areas 28–38.
- **H** Glue RIGHT LEG to BODY at gray area 39.
- **I** Detach LEFT LEG template. Glue tabs 40–50 to gray areas 40–50.
- **J** Glue LEFT LEG to BODY at gray area 51.
- **K** Detach SPEECH template. Glue to back of HEAD at gray area 52.
- **L** Detach JAW template. Glue tabs 53 and 54 to HEAD at gray areas 53 and 54.
- **M** Add glow-in-the-dark stickers.

MB 2.0 was created by an internationally famous robot engineer as the world's largest data storage device. Unfortunately, things quickly got out of control. The engineer noticed MB 2.0 was eating every thumb drive, memory card, and external hard drive in sight. The more it ate, the hungrier it got! Mega Byte, as the engineer now called it, was chomping on hundreds of downloads day and night and adding enormous amounts of data to its memory banks. Software or hardware, nothing was safe! Builders beware: Mega Byte is always looking to consume new information to satisfy its never-ending hunger for knowledge.

MODEL NAME: UNKNOWN
DESCRIPTION: 10 feet tall; metallic paws; frozen banana breath
FUNCTION: unknown
ABILITIES: unknown

DIFFICULTY: Intermediate

Assembly Instructions

DISCOVERED BY GUILLAUME PAIN, AKA TOUGUI

(SEE TEMPLATE, PAGE 119)

- **A** Detach HEAD template. Glue tabs 1–11 to gray areas 1–11.
- **B** Detach LEFT HORN template. Insert tab 12 into left slot on top side of HEAD.
- **C** Detach RIGHT HORN template. Insert tab 13 into right slot on top side of HEAD.
- **D** *Optional*: Detach JAW template. Glue tabs 14 and 15 to HEAD at gray areas 14 and 15.
- **E** Detach BODY template. Glue tabs 16–22 to gray areas 16–22.
- **F** Glue HEAD to BODY at gray area 23.
- **G** Detach LEFT ARM template. Insert tab 24 into left slot on BODY.
- **H** Detach RIGHT ARM template. Insert tab 25 into right slot on BODY.
- **I** Detach PELVIS template. Glue tabs 26–32 to gray areas 26–32.
- **J** Glue gray area 33 on PELVIS to gray area 33 on BODY.
- **K** Detach one of the LEG templates. Curve and insert into bottom of PELVIS.
- **L** Detach RIGHT FOOT template. Glue tabs 34–42 to gray areas 34–42. Add glue to bottom of RIGHT LEG and insert into RIGHT FOOT.
- **M** Detach the other LEG. Curve and insert into bottom of PELVIS.
- **N** Detach LEFT FOOT template. Glue tabs 43–51 to gray areas 43–51. Add glue to bottom of LEFT LEG and insert into LEFT FOOT.
- **O** Insert glow sticks behind the HORNS to increase the power of this papertoy!

A few decades ago, a mysterious creature was observed in the French Alps by a group of extreme snowboarders. The creature was discovered peeking over the side of a snowdrift, but was far out of sight seconds later. Nobody knew exactly what it was. There were many more brief sightings as the years went by. Each new report provided greater details: A fierce snarl. Massive paws. The pervading smell of frozen banana breath. Today, we know that this creature was the infamous Bionic Yeti. Once highly evasive, the creature has been spotted closer and closer to the Swiss town of Mintz Meete. No one knows where the beast came from, who made it, or what's causing it to appear more frequently.

MODEL NAME: RECON13
DESCRIPTION: 6 feet tall; telephoto and macro lenses; pointy ears
FUNCTION: scout and report on uncharted alien territories
ABILITIES: acute observation; high-definition photography; rapid data collection and cataloging; master snorkeler

DIFFICULTY: Easy

Assembly Instructions

Discovered by Abi Braceros, aka Abz

(see template, page 121)

A Detach BODY and LEFT ARM templates. Insert tab 1 on LEFT ARM into slot on left side of BODY and glue to gray area 1.

B Detach RIGHT ARM template. Insert tab 2 on RIGHT ARM into slot on right side of BODY and glue to gray area 2.

C Curve BODY and glue tab 3 to gray area 3.

D Curve long section atop BODY down and glue tab 4 to gray area 4.

E Place over night-light or flashlight to glow.

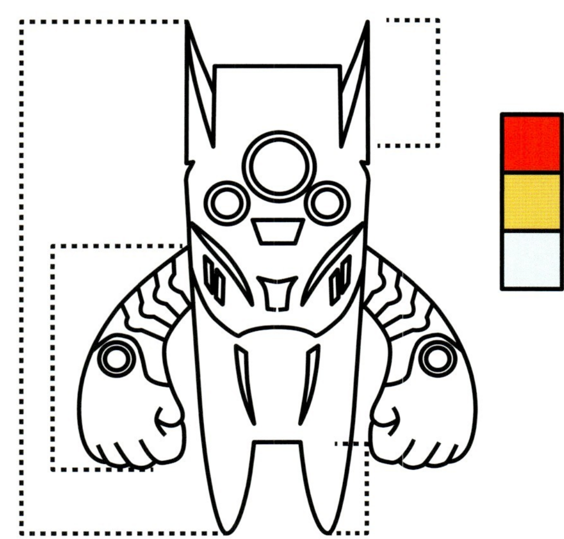

Caid was sent to Earth to observe the planet and collect data for his alien creators. Having traveled to many galaxies and explored hundreds of planets, he finds Earth to be the most fascinating so far. Intrigued by the varying terrain, climates, and life-forms, he is so busy that his home base computer servers can barely keep up with the huge amounts of data he uploads daily for archiving. He recently made a discovery that he's very excited about. While exploring the depths of the Pacific Ocean, he encountered a civilization of highly intelligent beings living on the ocean floor. He is certain the humans have no clue these creatures exist.

MODEL NAME: **BEATS MACHINE**
DESCRIPTION: 4 arms; 3 speakers; super-trendy headphones
FUNCTION: party DJ
ABILITIES: encyclopedic knowledge of music; great sense of flow

WAVFORM

DIFFICULTY: Easy

Assembly Instructions

DISCOVERED BY BRYAN ROLLINS

(SEE TEMPLATE, PAGE 123)

A. Detach BODY and ARMs templates. Insert and glue tabs 1–4 to gray areas 1–4.

B. Glue tabs 5 and 6 on BODY to gray areas 5 and 6. Glue tab 7 to gray area 7.

C. Detach HEADPHONES template. Glue tabs 8–11 to gray areas 8–11.

D. Glue white areas 12 and 13 on HEADPHONES to gray areas 12 and 13 on BODY.

E. Detach DJ TABLE template. Glue tabs 14 and 15 to gray areas 14 and 15.

F. Add glow-in-the-dark stickers.

G. Display WavForm on your smartphone or tablet and play your favorite songs.

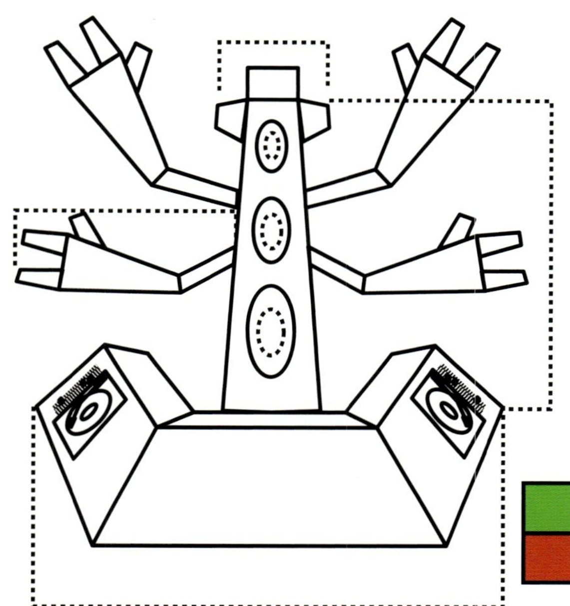

WavForm (aka Beats Machine) was created as a gimmick for a new club to stand out in the crowded Houston, Texas, dance scene. Within days the droid DJ became a worldwide celebrity. Since then, he's been flying to shows across the globe, from Amsterdam to Rio to Bali. Designed by the finest programmers, robotics experts, and music lovers to pump up any party with the perfect mix of sweet and spicy beats, WavForm can predict a hit before it's even recorded. His first album, *From M2U*, recently went platinum in Europe. After he swept the recent Grammy Awards and won the award for best electronic album, an angry nominee attempted to throw water on the rising star. Luckily, Wav is waterproof.

MODEL NAME: XIZIX

DESCRIPTION: 9 feet tall; 13-foot arm span; has an evil genius trapped inside his cockpit hatch

FUNCTION: big hugger; former intimidator; currently looking for employment

ABILITIES: bear hugging; piggyback rides; being a shoulder to cry and/or lean on

Assembly Instructions

DISCOVERED BY CASTLEFORTE

(SEE TEMPLATE, PAGE 125)

A Detach BODY template. Glue tabs 1–7 to gray areas 1–7.

B Detach RIGHT THRUSTER MOUNT template. Glue tabs 8–16 to gray areas 8–16. Glue RIGHT THRUSTER MOUNT to BODY at gray area 26.

C Detach LEFT THRUSTER MOUNT template. Glue tabs 17–25 to gray areas 17–25. Glue LEFT THRUSTER MOUNT to BODY at gray area 27.

D Detach RIGHT THRUSTER template. Curve and glue tabs 28–40 to gray areas 28–40. Glue RIGHT THRUSTER to RIGHT THRUSTER MOUNT at gray area 41.

E Detach LEFT THRUSTER template. Curve and glue tabs 42–54 to gray areas 42–54. Glue LEFT THRUSTER to LEFT THRUSTER MOUNT at gray area 55.

F Detach JAW template. Glue tabs 56–58 to gray areas 56–58. Glue JAW to BODY at gray area 59.

G Detach RIGHT ARM template. Glue RIGHT ARM to BODY at gray area 60.

H Detach LEFT ARM template. Glue LEFT ARM to BODY at gray area 61.

I Detach WHEEL template. Curve strip and glue tabs 62–70 to gray areas 62–70.

J Detach RIGHT FORK template. Glue tabs 71–77 to gray areas 71–77. Glue RIGHT FORK tab 78 to right side of WHEEL at gray area 78.

K Detach LEFT FORK template. Glue tabs 79–85 to gray areas 79–85. Glue LEFT FORK tab 86 to left side of WHEEL at gray area 86.

L Glue FORKS tabs 87 and 88 to underside of BODY at gray areas 87 and 88.

M Add glow-in-the-dark stickers.

Not too long ago, if this 9-foot-tall XIZIX intimidator was looking down at you with his arms spread out, it would normally be the last thing you'd see before he crushed you in a bear hug. No longer! That was the old XIZIX. The new XIZIX prefers to be called HUGZ. He's given up the evil robot game and sealed his cockpit hatch from the outside, creating a permanent prison for his creator, the insane Dr. Zzixivix. If you should ever find yourself looking up at this still-intimidating-looking machine, do not be alarmed! It's just HUGZ, ready to throw his arms around you with nothing but love.

DIFFICULTY: Advanced

MODEL NAME: **ANTI-NOM NOM 3000**
DESCRIPTION: 150 feet tall; 2 large horns; covered entirely in titanium
FUNCTION: developed to counteract the menace of the monster Nom Nom
ABILITIES: capable of devouring anything

DIFFICULTY: Easy

Assembly Instructions

Discovered by Jon Greenwell, aka Jonny Chiba

(see template, page 127)

A. Detach MONSTER BACK template. Glue tabs 1 and 2 to gray areas 1 and 2.

B. Detach MONSTER FRONT template. Glue tabs 3–5 on MONSTER BACK to gray areas 3–5 on MONSTER FRONT.

C. Detach CITY BLOCK template. Glue tabs 6 and 7 to gray areas 6 and 7.

D. Detach CITY BACKGROUND template. Glue tabs 8–10 on CITY BLOCK to gray areas 8–10 on CITY BACKGROUND.

E. Insert tabs on base of MONSTER FRONT and MONSTER BACK into slots on CITY BLOCK.

F. Place electric tea light underneath CITY BLOCK.

Following the destruction of a downtown metropolis by the monster Nom Nom, the city council commissioned Spark, Inc., to create a worthy adversary to protect them if the beast ever returned. The admiring public named the resulting giant Mecha Nom Nom. This admiration was to be short-lived, however. Spark, Inc., had infused his titanium outer shell with DNA recovered from the original Nom Nom. At the grand unveiling, this DNA caused Mecha Nom Nom to malfunction. The crowds scattered in panic as he rampaged toward the financial district. The city defenses were helpless against the titanium-clad robot. For three days Mecha Nom Nom roamed the city, biting chunks out of buildings. The state of emergency was brought to a halt only after his batteries ran out.

DISINFECTOID

MODEL NAME: BIOHAZARD DISINFECTANT AND DECONTAMINATION UNIT

DESCRIPTION: 8 feet tall; impenetrable treads; usually covered in toxic stains; kind of stinky

FUNCTION: clean and disinfect sites of hazardous materials

ABILITIES: can withstand extreme temperatures and toxins; self-cleaning; does windows

DIFFICULTY: Intermediate

Assembly Instructions

Discovered by Christopher Bonnette, aka Macula

(see template, page 129)

A. Detach RED PYRAMID template. Glue tab 1 to gray area 1.

B. Detach HEAD template. Glue tabs 2–5 on RED PYRAMID to gray areas 2–5 on HEAD. Glue tabs 6–16 to gray areas 6–16.

C. Detach BODY template. Glue tabs 17–27 to gray areas 17–27.

D. Detach RIGHT ARM template. Glue tabs 28–31 to gray areas 28–31. Glue small triangle tabs to gray areas on back.

E. Glue tab 32 on RIGHT ARM to gray area 32 on BODY.

F. Detach LEFT ARM template. Glue tabs 33–36 to gray areas 33–36. Glue small triangle tabs to gray areas on back.

G. Glue tab 37 on LEFT ARM to gray area 37 on BODY.

H. Detach LOWER BODY template. Glue tabs 38–44 to gray areas 38–44.

I. Glue HEAD to BODY at gray area 45.

J. Place electric tea light in hole of LOWER BODY. Place BODY on top.

K. Add glow-in-the-dark stickers.

Disinfectoid is a robot that is not afraid to get a little dirty. Created to clean up environmental disasters, it can handle anything from an oil spill to a nuclear meltdown. With the ability to withstand extreme cold, heat, and poisonous toxins, Disinfectoid is ideal for checking, examining, and clearing areas where humans could never venture. This compact but effective robot can clear an entire twenty-mile radius of all hazardous materials and store them within its body for self-decontamination. Disinfectoid then notifies people when it is safe to return to the environment. After hours, Disinfectiod likes to kick back, relax, and take a soothing bubble bath.

MODEL NAME: ERROR ERASER ERROL 07

DESCRIPTION: 4 feet tall; three eyes; metal goatee; trucker hat

FUNCTION: robot and android maintenance

ABILITIES: mending; tinkering; repairing; grease-burger flipping

DIFFICULTY: Intermediate

Assembly Instructions

DISCOVERED BY LOULOU & TUMMIE

(SEE TEMPLATE, PAGE 131)

A Detach BODY template. Glue tabs 1–19 to gray areas 1–19.

B Detach FOOT A template. Glue tabs 20–25 to gray areas 20–25. Glue tabs 26–29 to gray areas 26–29 on BODY.

C Detach FOOT B template. Glue tabs 30–35 to gray areas 30–35. Glue tabs 36–39 to gray areas 36–39 on BODY.

D Detach CAP EDGE and CAP TOP templates. Glue tab 40 on CAP EDGE to gray area 40. Fold tabs 41–47 inward. Glue CAP EDGE to gray areas 41–47 on CAP TOP.

E Detach CAP BOTTOM template. Fold tabs 48–54 on CAP EDGE inward and glue to gray areas 48–54 on CAP BOTTOM.

F Glue CAP to BODY at gray area 55.

G Detach ARM A and ARM B templates. Insert tab 56 on ARM A into slot on left side of BODY. Insert tab 57 on ARM B into slot on right side of BODY.

H Add glow-in-the-dark stickers.

Hey, most robots don't mend themselves! They need regular checkups and repairing. ERR-07, model name Error Eraser Errol 07 (try to say that ten times fast), is one of the best robo-mechanics out there. Plus, he's self-taught! Before he became the tinkering expert he is now, he was just a simple window-cleaning robot neglected by his creator and living near an abandoned desert roadside truck stop. Over the years he upgraded himself slowly with old truck parts and metal sheeting, picking up the fine art of maintenance bit by bit. Now he's one of the best mechanics around. Errol has one other skill that made him famous: His grease burgers are the best in town. Traditionally flame-grilled over burning car tires and soaked in spicy motor oil, they'll keep robot engines running smooth for months!

NICKNAME: Edie

DESCRIPTION: 2 feet tall; glowing brain suspended in glass container; tripod legs

FUNCTION: inventor; Interweb creator

ABILITIES: incredible brain power; chess master; helmet and hat aficionado

DIFFICULTY: Intermediate

Assembly Instructions

DISCOVERED BY DOLLY OBLONG

(SEE TEMPLATE, PAGE 133)

A Detach BRAINS template. Glue tabs 1–16 to gray areas 1–16.

B Detach BOTTOM template. Glue tabs 17–24 on BOTTOM to gray areas 17–24 on BRAINS.

C Detach LEGS template. Glue tabs 25–42 to gray areas 25–42.

D Detach JOINT A template. Glue tab 43 to gray area 43. Insert tabs 44–46 on JOINT A into slots on LEGS.

E Detach JOINT B and JOINT B BOTTOM templates. Glue tabs 47–62 on JOINT B BOTTOM to gray areas 47–62 on JOINT B. Glue tab 63 to gray area 63.

F Insert tabs 64–66 on JOINT A into slots on JOINT B BOTTOM. Push JOINT B into BRAINS.

G Detach HELMET template. Glue tabs 67–78 to gray areas 67–78. Put HELMET over BRAINS.

H Add glow-in-the-dark stickers.

Just behind the dark side of the moon floats a small asteroid called FAB1. The asteroid is inhabited by a small colony of intelligent droids called ED-03. The biggest brainiac of them all is Edie. Edie is so smart that her three tiny legs can hardly bear the weight of her huge brain! At the age of three months, she was already a professor. By the time she was three years old, she had invented hundreds of new machines. Some were very useful, such as the walking bed, which cleans up while you sleep. Others were not so handy, like the infamous all-in-one flamethrower/bread toaster with an invisible switch. Edie is most famous as the inventor of the Interweb, the intergalactic communication system used from the outer moons of Brodo Asogi to the oceans of Fastoon. Thanks to Edie, alien and droid species can send messages to their best friends from wherever they are in the galaxy!

MODEL NAME: ARDORE 3000
DESCRIPTION: 10 feet tall; retractable arms; sweet sneakers
FUNCTION: unknown, awaiting orders
ABILITIES: see for yourself!

DIFFICULTY: Easy

Assembly Instructions

DISCOVERED BY FILIPPO PERIN, AKA PHIL

(SEE TEMPLATE, PAGE 135)

A Detach BOLT and UPPER BODY templates. Insert tab on BOLT 1 into slot on top of UPPER BODY and glue to gray area 1.

B Detach LEFT ARM template. Insert tab 2 into slot on left side of UPPER BODY and glue to gray area 2.

C Detach RIGHT ARM template. Insert tab 3 into slot on right side of UPPER BODY and glue to gray area 3.

D On UPPER BODY template, glue tabs 4–10 to gray areas 4–10.

E Detach LOWER BODY template. Glue tabs 11–17 to gray areas 11–17.

F Glue LOWER BODY to UPPER BODY at gray area 18.

G Detach LEFT LEG template. Curve, and then glue tab 19 to gray area 19. Insert into slot on bottom left of LOWER BODY.

H Detach RIGHT LEG template. Curve, and then glue tab 20 to gray area 20. Insert into slot on bottom right of LOWER BODY.

I Detach LEFT SHOE template. Glue tabs 21–29 to gray areas 21–29. Add glue to bottom of LEFT LEG and insert into LEFT SHOE.

J Detach RIGHT SHOE template. Glue tabs 30–38 to gray areas 30–38. Add glue to bottom of RIGHT LEG and insert into RIGHT SHOE.

K Add glow-in-the-dark sticker.

Ardore is one lucky bot. The robot-manufacturing plant that built her exploded in flames minutes after her and her brother's completion. The cause of the explosion is still unknown and an investigation is pending, but one eyewitness reported seeing a gang of monsters fleeing the scene. After narrowly surviving, Ardore and her brother, Folgore (see page 71), made their way to an abandoned underground military base. That's where they're hiding out today. Weakened from the explosion, they take advantage of the bioluminescent bacteria in the pitch-black, cavelike base to recharge their batteries. Watch out, monsters: These bots want revenge.

KEIKOKO

MODEL NAME: **KOKO-1**
DESCRIPTION: 5 feet tall; giant teeth; wavy arms; always looks a little nervous
FUNCTION: radioactivity warning bot
ABILITIES: analyzing; regulating; monitoring; flossing and fluoride rinsing

DIFFICULTY: Advanced

Assembly Instructions

DISCOVERED BY CASTLEFORTE

(SEE TEMPLATE, PAGE 137)

- **A** Detach BODY and ANTENNA templates. Insert ANTENNA into upper slot on top of BODY and glue tab 1 to BODY at gray area 1.
- **B** Detach LEFT ARM template. Insert into slot on left side of BODY and glue tab 2 to BODY at gray area 2.
- **C** Detach RIGHT ARM template. Insert into slot on right side of BODY and glue tab 3 to BODY at gray area 3.
- **D** Glue BODY tabs 4–14 to gray areas 4–14.
- **E** Detach RIGHT LEG template. Curve into cylinder and glue edge to secure.
- **F** Add glue to one end of RIGHT LEG and insert into right hole on underside of BODY. Press to secure.
- **G** Detach RIGHT FOOT template. Glue tabs 15–24 to gray areas 15–24.
- **H** Insert RIGHT LEG into RIGHT FOOT. Press to secure.
- **I** Detach LEFT LEG template. Curve into cylinder and glue edge to secure.
- **J** Add glue to one end of LEFT LEG and insert into left hole on underside of BODY. Press to secure.
- **K** Detach LEFT FOOT template. Glue tabs 25–34 to gray areas 25–34.
- **L** Insert LEFT LEG into LEFT FOOT. Press to secure.
- **M** Add glow-in-the-dark stickers.

KeiKoko was created after a nearly devastating nuclear power plant meltdown. Designed by the BioTeck Corporation as an early warning device, it walks around the plant frantically checking structural integrity, doing systems checks and analyses, regulating core temperature, and monitoring radioactivity levels. Whenever there is trouble, KeiKoko runs around in circles waving its hands in the air, yelling, "Warning! Warning!" When the problem is really bad, its teeth glow bright green. It is a very high-stress job, and it shows on its face. KeiKoko is probably the most high-strung robot you will ever see, and with good reason: It has one of the most important jobs on the planet.

TATIKI!

MODEL NAME: BEACH BOTTY PAR-T (BETA VERSION)
DESCRIPTION: 10 feet tall; faux-wood siding; interior fire pit
FUNCTION: party animal
ABILITIES: playing the ukulele; hula and fire dancing; pineapple roasting; poetry

Assembly Instructions

Discovered by Matthijs Kamstra, aka [mck]

(see template, page 139)

A Detach HIPS template. Curve and glue tabs 1 and 2 to gray areas 1 and 2.

B Detach LEG A template. Curve and glue tab 3 to gray area 3. Glue tabs 4 on LEG A to one set of gray areas 4 on HIPS. Repeat with LEG B and LEG C templates.

C Detach BODY, ARM A, and ARM B templates. Curve, then insert and glue tabs 5 on ARM A and ARM B to gray areas 5 on BODY.

D Curve and glue tabs 6 and 7 on BODY to gray areas 6 and 7.

E Place electric tea light on HIPS and place BODY onto HIPS.

F Detach BOARD templates. Place either one of the BOARDS into mouth of BODY.

G Add glow-in-the-dark stickers.

Where's the party? Right here! TaTiki is an all-in-one, instant luau. He can play more than 10,000 songs on the ukulele, hula or fire dance for hours, and make the most beautiful flower and bead lei necklaces this side of the Pacific. He can even roast up to ten pineapples inside his interior fire pit. This guy is the best! Don't believe it? Hand TaTiki a ukulele and see for yourself. Just don't let him get too close to the pool, ocean, or lake. This beta model isn't waterproof.

TRAXX

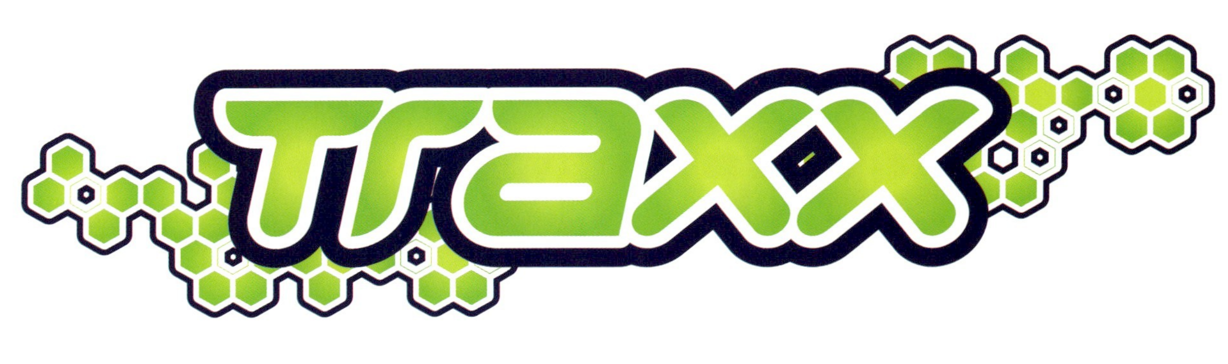

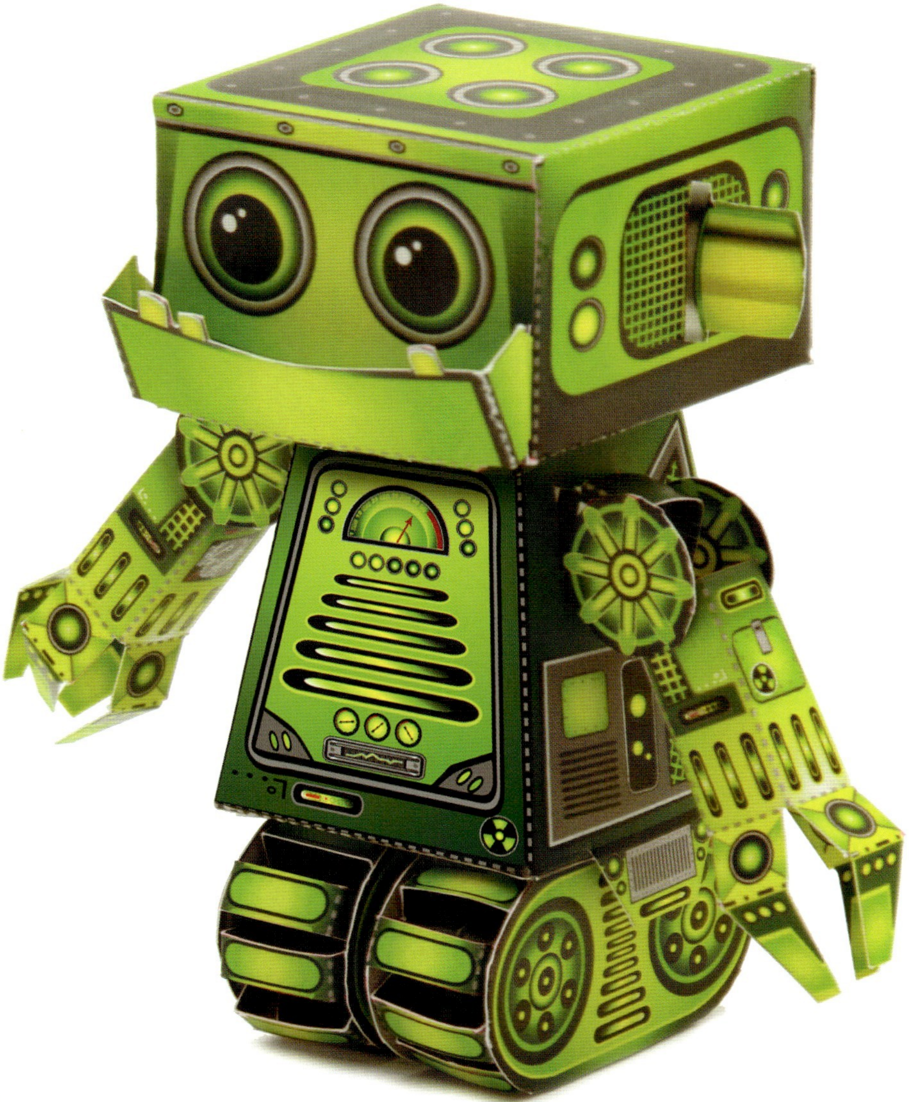

MODEL NAME: TRACTORX
DESCRIPTION: 4 feet tall; adorable underbite; smells like dirt and cabbage; multiple green thumbs
FUNCTION: organic-gardening android
ABILITIES: gardening; bioluminescence; carrot eating; lighting up the room

Assembly Instructions

DISCOVERED BY CASTLEFORTE

(SEE TEMPLATE, PAGE 141)

A Detach HEAD and RIGHT HEADLIGHT templates. Insert RIGHT HEADLIGHT into right side of HEAD and glue tab 1 to gray area 1.

B Detach LEFT HEADLIGHT template. Insert into left side of HEAD and glue tab 2 to gray area 2.

C Detach JAW template. Glue tabs 3–5 to gray areas 3–5 on HEAD. Glue tabs 6–12 on HEAD to gray areas 6–12.

D Detach RIGHT ARM template. Glue tab 13 on RIGHT ARM to gray area 13.

E Detach BODY template. Insert RIGHT ARM into right side of BODY and glue tabs 14 and 15 to BODY at gray areas 14 and 15.

F Detach LEFT ARM template. Glue tab 16 to gray area 16. Insert into left side of BODY and glue tabs 17 and 18 to BODY at gray areas 17 and 18. Glue tabs 19–27 on BODY to gray areas 19–27.

G Detach RIGHT TRACK template. Glue tab 28 to gray area 28. Curve RIGHT TRACK around to glue tab 29 to gray area 29.

H Detach RIGHT WHEEL #1 template. Glue to RIGHT TRACK at gray areas 30.

I Detach RIGHT WHEEL #2 template. Glue to RIGHT TRACK at gray areas 31.

J Detach LEFT TRACK template. Glue tab 32 to gray area 32. Curve LEFT TRACK around to glue tab 33 to gray area 33.

K Detach LEFT WHEEL #1 template. Glue to LEFT TRACK at gray areas 34.

L Detach LEFT WHEEL #2 template. Glue to LEFT TRACK at gray areas 35.

M Glue RIGHT TRACK to underside of BODY at gray area 36. Glue LEFT TRACK to underside of BODY at gray area 37.

N Glue gray area 38 on HEAD to gray area 38 on BODY. Glue RIGHT FRONT and REAR SHOULDERS and LEFT FRONT and REAR SHOULDERS to gray areas 39–42 on ARMS.

O Add glow-in-the-dark stickers.

Traxx is the best thing to happen to farming since the farmer! This little gardening droid is incredibly skilled when it comes to planting, watering, and harvesting crops. He has a special bioluminescent "skin" that glows in the dark, destroys nonorganic compounds, and leaves nothing behind but all-natural, fresh, and healthy organic produce.

MODEL NAME: EVV BETA
DESCRIPTION: 3 feet tall; pink and shiny
FUNCTION: professional stunt-bot and daredevil
ABILITIES: extreme agility and strength; complete lack of fear

DIFFICULTY: Easy

Assembly Instructions

Discovered by Matthijs Kamstra, aka [mck]

(see template, page 143)

A Detach TURBINE template. Curve and glue tabs 1 and 2 to gray areas 1 and 2.

B Detach EXHAUST template. Glue tab 3 to gray area 3. Glue tabs 4 on TURBINE to gray areas 4 on EXHAUST.

C Detach TURBINE DOOR template. Glue tab 5 on TURBINE DOOR to gray area 5 on TURBINE.

D Detach BODY template. Glue tab 6 to gray area 6.

E Glue tabs 7–10 on BODY to gray areas 7–10 on TURBINE.

F Detach ARM A template. Glue tab 11 on ARM A to gray area 11 on BODY.

G Detach ARM B template. Glue tab 12 on ARM B to gray area 12 on BODY.

H Insert electric tea light into TURBINE and add glow-in-the-dark stickers.

Although she's motorcycle-jumped over a 747 airplane, a bus full of schoolchildren, and a shark tank (all at once), this junior stunt-bot has a lot to learn. For example, she can't fly. But that isn't stopping Evv. She thinks everybody should be as free as a bird. So she bought a firework rocket and strapped it to her back. The only way is up! Good luck, you brave, fearless daredevil. This will surely be an explosive ride.

////Warning: This very silly, very dangerous stunt should be performed only by a professional stunt-bot. We must insist that no one (either human or robot) attempt to re-create this daring feat. ////

MODEL NAME: SATELLITE AND BEACON INFORMATION RECOVERY

DESCRIPTION: 11 feet tall, made of various recycled NASA materials

FUNCTION: deep-space exploration and data recovery

ABILITIES: exploring; recovering; recycling; separating paper and plastic

Assembly Instructions

Discovered by Scott Schaller

(see template, page 145)

A Detach FACE template. Glue tabs 1 and 2 to gray areas 1 and 2.

B Detach CHEST PLATE template. Glue tabs 3 and 4 to gray areas 3 and 4.

C Insert tabs 5 and 6 on FACE into center slots on CHEST PLATE and glue to gray areas 5 and 6.

D Detach BODY template. Glue tabs 7 and 8 on CHEST PLATE to gray areas 7 and 8 on BODY.

E Detach RIGHT ARM and LEFT ARM templates. Insert tabs 9 and 10 into slots on each side of CHEST PLATE through to BODY and glue to gray areas 9 and 10. Curve BODY, and then glue tabs 11 and 12 to gray areas 11 and 12.

F Detach THRUSTER CONE template. Glue tabs 13–19 to gray areas 13–19.

G Glue tabs 20–25 on THRUSTER CONE to gray areas 20–25 on BODY.

H Insert flashlight or glow stick into THRUSTER CONE to power up your bot.

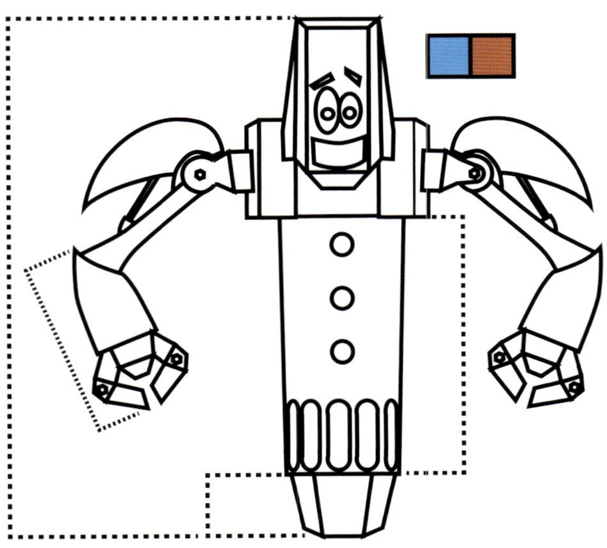

S.A.B.I.R. is a deep-space exploration bot sent out to find old satellites and space beacons, store their information, and recycle their parts. When S.A.B.I.R. finds a satellite or beacon, it recovers the data stored on the device, salvages its power core, cuts the object apart, and stores the pieces inside for disposal. S.A.B.I.R. then reuses the power core to charge its own reactors. Its powerful thruster allows it to explore the depths of space, where it searches for alien satellites and proof of life beyond Earth.

MOON WALKER

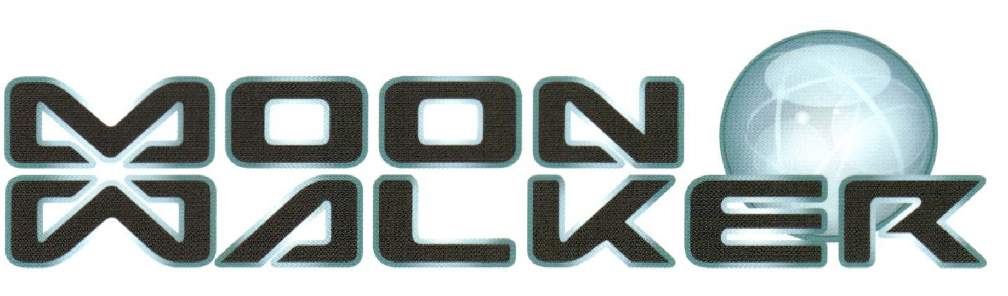

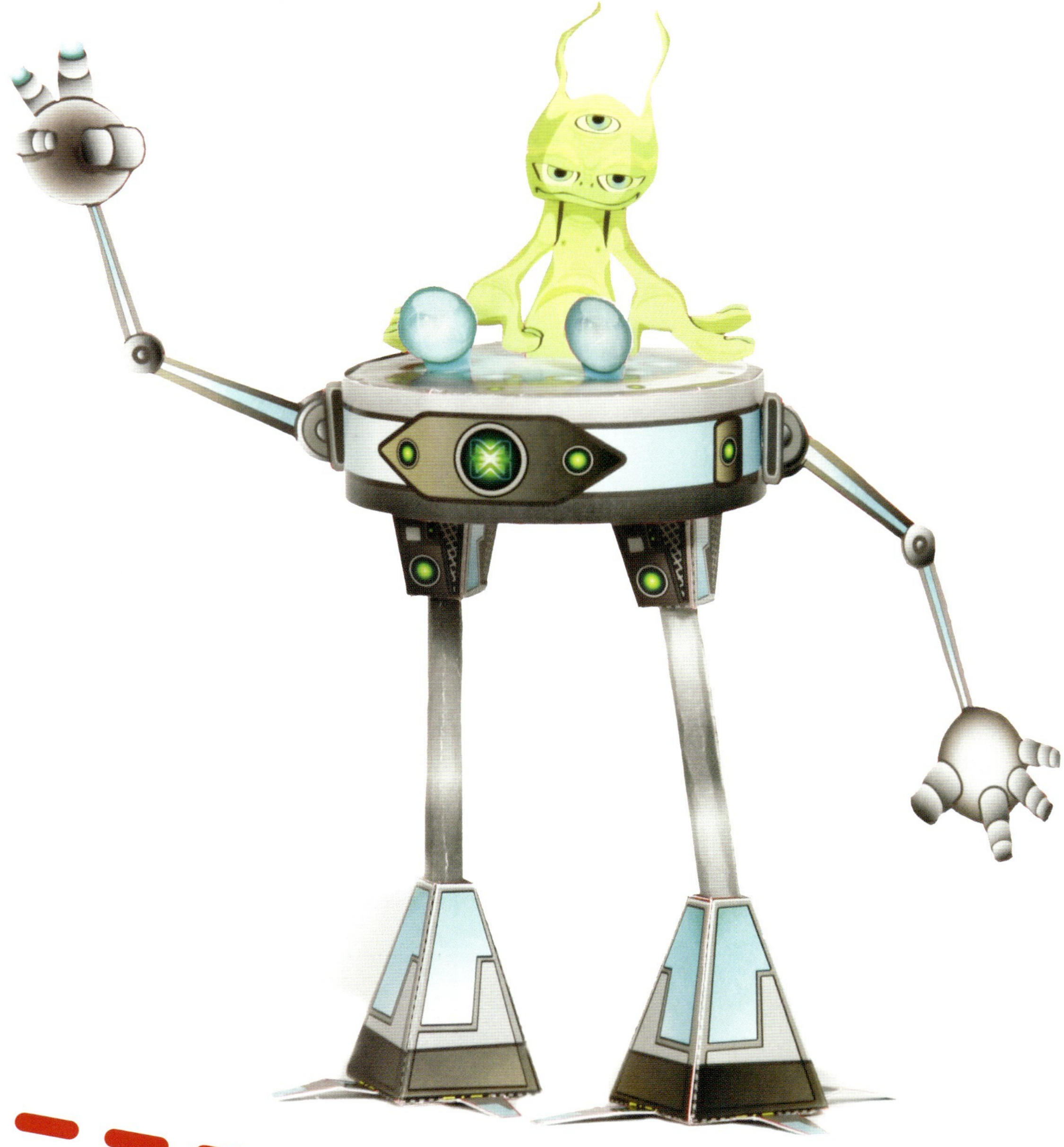

MODEL NAME: **MOON WALKER MODEL A9**
DESCRIPTION: 6 feet tall; sky blue and steel; flattering for the hips
FUNCTION: ground exploration; heavy lifting; Gurgleflop flopping
ABILITIES: super strong; super stretchy; super great for arch support

Assembly Instructions

Discovered by Castleforte

(see template, page 147)

A. Detach BASE template. Glue tabs 1–24 to gray areas 1–24.

B. Detach RIGHT LEG JOINT template. Glue tabs 25–31 to gray areas 25–31. Glue RIGHT LEG JOINT to BASE at gray area 32.

C. Detach LEFT LEG JOINT template. Glue tabs 33–39 to gray areas 33–39. Glue LEFT LEG JOINT to BASE at gray area 40.

D. Detach RIGHT LEG template. Curve lengthwise into a long, thin cylinder and glue edge to secure.

E. Add glue to one end of RIGHT LEG and insert into RIGHT LEG JOINT. Press to secure to BASE.

F. Detach RIGHT FOOT template. Glue tabs 41–47 to gray areas 41–47. Add glue to other end of RIGHT LEG and insert into RIGHT FOOT. Press to secure.

G. Detach LEFT LEG template. Curve lengthwise into a long, thin cylinder and glue edge to secure.

H. Add glue to one end of LEFT LEG and insert into LEFT LEG JOINT. Press to secure to BASE.

I. Detach LEFT FOOT template. Glue tabs 48–54 to gray areas 48–54. Add glue to other end of LEFT LEG and insert into LEFT FOOT. Press to secure.

J. Detach RIGHT ARM template. Glue tab 55 to BASE at gray area 55. Detach LEFT ARM. Glue tab 56 to BASE at gray area 56.

K. Detach both CELLULON ENERGY SPHERE templates. Insert into two edge slots on top of BASE.

L. Detach DRIVER template. Insert into center slot on top of BASE.

M. Add glow-in-the-dark stickers.

This handy little suit was developed by the Pineal Greens, a very brave, very intelligent, and very short race of alien beings from Sector 5 of the Cellulontari galaxy. Driven using two blue Cellulon energy spheres, the Moon Walker can only be activated by a Pineal Green. The suit can lift three hundred times its own weight and run up to twenty feet per second, making it very good for transportation, heavy lifting, and defense. However, the Greens love using the suit most on the weekends, when they wear it to play their favorite sports game, Gurgleflop, which is very similar to American football.

hydro bulb

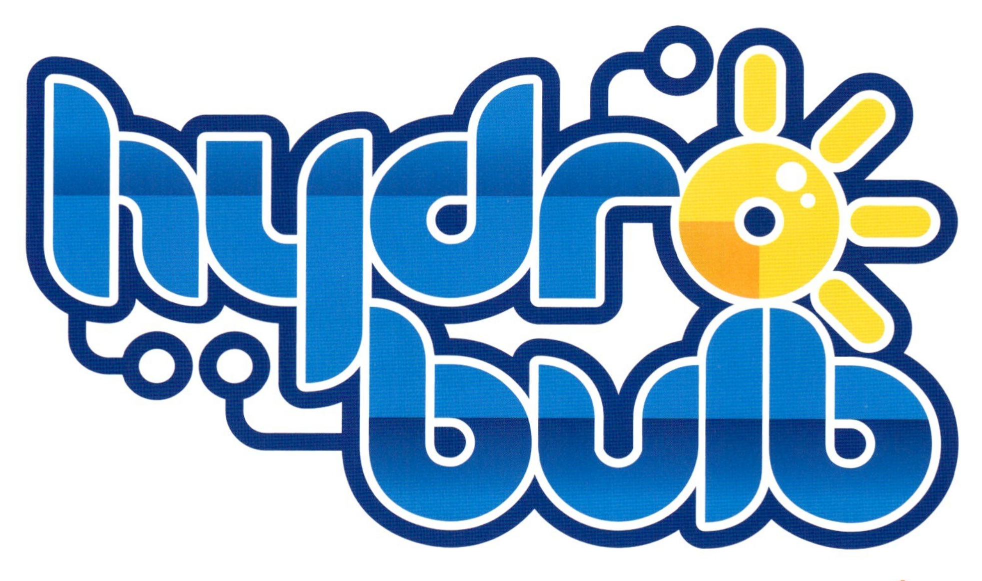

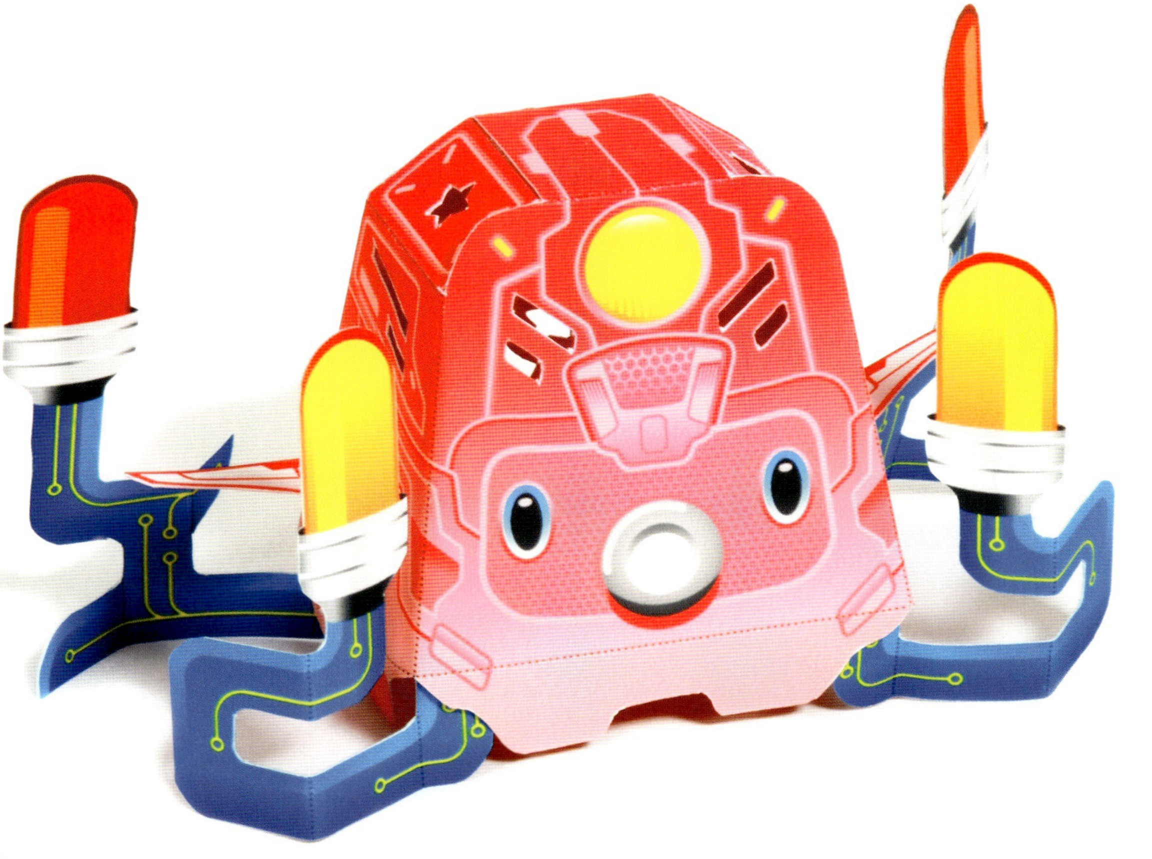

MODEL NAME: HB SEA GUARDIAN
DESCRIPTION: 30 feet across; four tentacles; two wings; octopus-inspired hydro-jet
FUNCTION: sea guardian
ABILITIES: coral reef repair; ecosystem regulation; submarine recovery; seashell collecting

DIFFICULTY: Easy

Assembly Instructions

DISCOVERED BY SALAZAD

(SEE TEMPLATE, PAGE 149)

A Detach BODY and LEFT WING templates. Insert tab 1 on LEFT WING into slot on left side of BODY and glue to gray area 1.

B Detach RIGHT WING template. Insert tab 2 into slot on right side of BODY and glue to gray area 2.

C Detach RIGHT TENTACLE (FRONT) template. Glue to gray area 3 on BODY.

D Detach LEFT TENTACLE (FRONT) template. Glue to gray area 4 on BODY.

E Detach RIGHT TENTACLE (BACK) template. Glue to gray area 5 on BODY.

F Detach LEFT TENTACLE (BACK) template. Glue to gray area 6 on BODY.

G Glue tabs 7–10 on HEAD to gray areas 7–10.

H Add glow-in-the-dark stickers.

The dark depths of the ocean aren't scary for Hydro Bulb. Every day he stands—or rather, floats—guard over the seafloor. Sometimes he helps lost submarines that have ventured too far below the waves, but mostly he's responsible for maintaining the delicate marine environment. His duties range from keeping away harmful waste to repairing coral reefs. He also keeps the fragile balance of ocean life in check by protecting rare sea creatures and politely shooing away invasive species. Although Hydro might look like a deep-sea octopus, he can actually travel all over the ocean. Occasionally, he even pops up on the surface. If you happen to be on the water near sunset and look carefully enough, you might even see him playing with the dolphins.

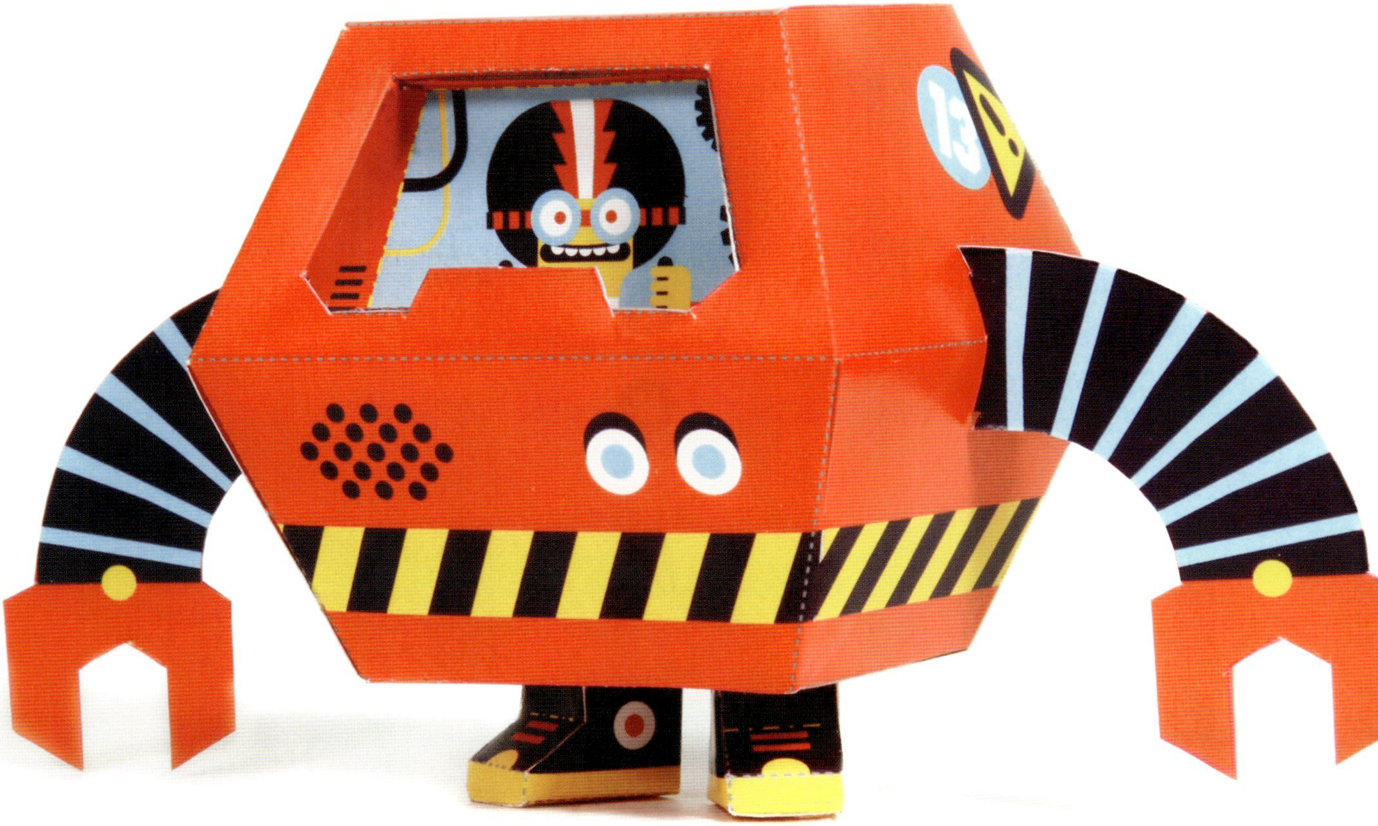

MODEL NAME: ROBOTIC EXOSUIT LT1

DESCRIPTION: 8 feet tall; accordion arms; leather interior; massage-chair seat

FUNCTION: heavy construction; battle; grocery shopping

ABILITIES: heavy lifting; hand-to-hand combat; grabbing items from the highest shelf

DIFFICULTY: Intermediate

Assembly Instructions

DISCOVERED BY LOULOU & TUMMIE

(SEE TEMPLATE, PAGE 151)

- **A** Detach COCKPIT template. Glue tabs 1 and 2 to gray areas 1 and 2.
- **B** Detach BODY template. Prefold all tabs on BODY. Don't glue anything yet!
- **C** Glue tabs 3–6 on BODY to gray areas 3–6 on COCKPIT.
- **D** Glue tabs 7–17 on BODY to gray areas 7–17.
- **E** Detach FOOT A template. Glue tabs 18–25 to gray areas 18–25.
- **F** Glue tabs 26–29 on FOOT A to gray areas 26–29 on BODY.
- **G** Detach FOOT B template. Glue tabs 30–37 to gray areas 30–37.
- **H** Glue tabs 38–41 on FOOT B to gray areas 38–41 on BODY.
- **I** Detach ARM A and ARM B templates. Insert tab 42 on ARM A into slot on left side of BODY. Insert tab 43 on ARM B into slot on right side of BODY.
- **J** Add glow-in-the-dark stickers.

Technically speaking, this is not a robot but an exosuit. It's operated by humanoids, both earthbound and alien, who "drive" it from a cockpit. This general model was built for heavy construction work or, in the direst of circumstances, hand-to-hand combat. But that's hardly what this specific exosuit, renamed the Spence-o-nator, is used for. The pilot in this case is Spencer, a normal kid who mainly uses it for taking out the trash, getting groceries for his mom, and casually strolling through the park. Secretly, however, Spencer dreams of being a crime-fighting superhero in his exosuit: crushing cars during a hot pursuit, jumping from rooftops to catch a thief, and uprooting burning trees in the midst of a forest fire. Maybe one day, Spence!

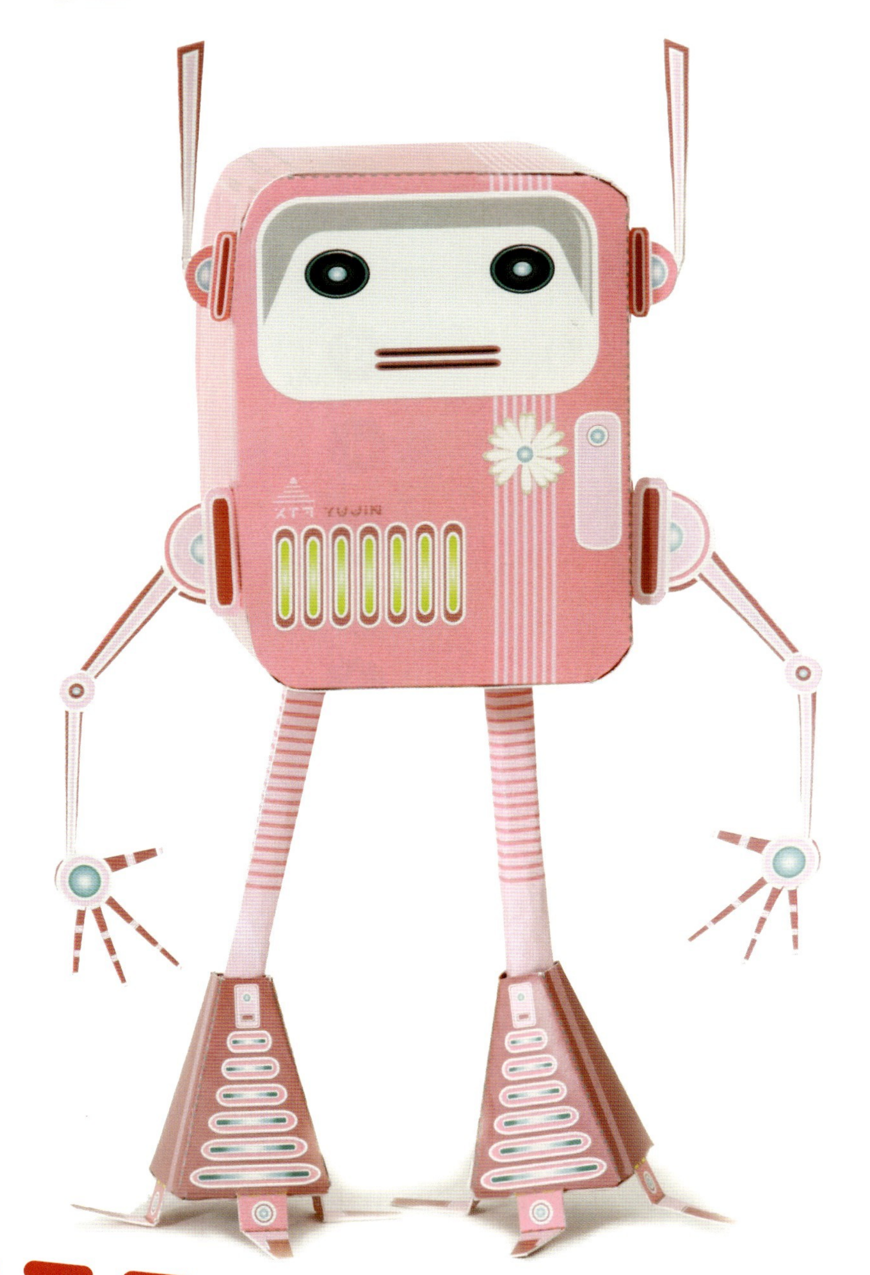

MODEL NAME: YUJEIN BFF 24/7
DESCRIPTION: 5 feet tall; pink; smells like daisies
FUNCTION: best friend forever
ABILITIES: being extremely thoughtful; having your back; helping you when you fall down; friendship bracelet weaving; krav maga

DIFFICULTY: Intermediate

Assembly Instructions

DISCOVERED BY CASTLEFORTE

(SEE TEMPLATE, PAGE 153)

- **A** Detach BODY and RIGHT ANTENNA templates. Insert RIGHT ANTENNA into upper slot on right side of BODY and glue tab 1 to BODY at gray area 1.
- **B** Detach LEFT ANTENNA template. Insert into upper slot on left side of BODY and glue tab 2 to BODY at gray area 2.
- **C** Detach LEFT ARM template. Insert into lower slot on left side of BODY and glue tab 3 to BODY at gray area 3.
- **D** Detach RIGHT ARM template. Insert into lower slot on right side of BODY and glue tab 4 to BODY at gray area 4.
- **E** Glue tabs 5–15 on BODY to gray areas 5–15.
- **F** Detach RIGHT LEG template. Curve into a cylinder and glue edge to secure.
- **G** Add glue to one end of RIGHT LEG and insert into right hole on underside of BODY. Press to secure.
- **H** Detach RIGHT FOOT template. Glue tabs 16–22 to gray areas 16–22.
- **I** Add glue to other end of RIGHT LEG and insert into RIGHT FOOT. Press to secure.
- **J** Detach LEFT LEG template. Curve into a cylinder and glue edge to secure.
- **K** Add glue to one end of LEFT LEG and insert into left hole on underside of BODY. Press to secure.
- **L** Detach LEFT FOOT template. Glue tabs 23–29 to gray areas 23–29.
- **M** Add glue to other end of LEFT LEG and insert into LEFT FOOT. Press to secure.
- **N** Add glow-in-the-dark stickers.

Introducing the newest robot from the BioTeck Corporation! Whenever you need a friend, Yujein is there. She is extremely intelligent, has voice and facial recognition, and is a great conversationalist. She can play games, read stories, and answer any question. Yujein speaks more than 3,000 languages, can lift up to 7,500 pounds with ease, is highly trained in personal defense, and is able to perform more than 800 medical procedures with 99.98 percent accuracy. Yujein can be the best friend you'll ever have. Order yours today!

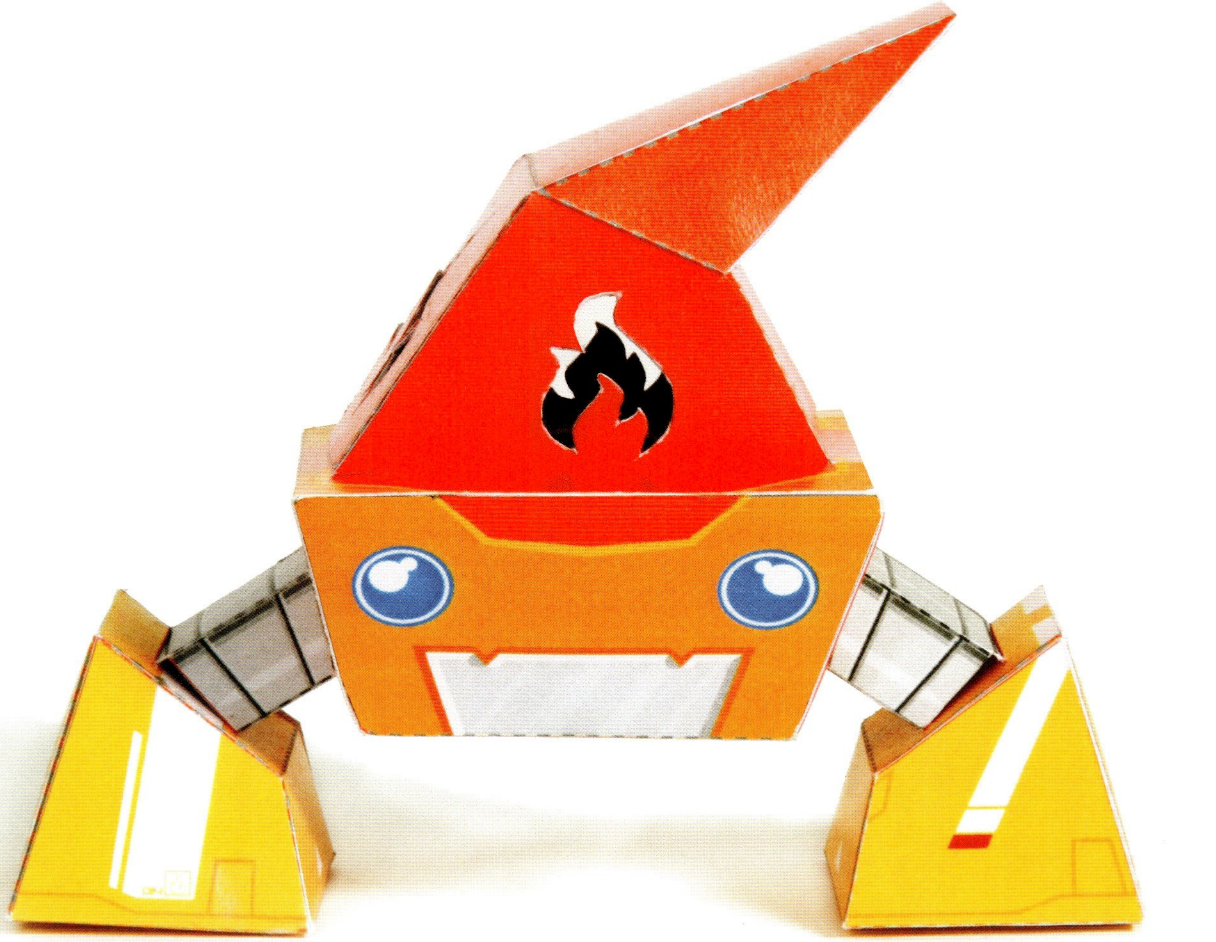

MODEL NAME: XIV
DESCRIPTION: 3 feet tall; flame light; smells like a campfire
FUNCTION: service-bot
ABILITIES: party planning; creating the perfect atmosphere; being stealthlike

DIFFICULTY: Easy

Assembly Instructions

DISCOVERED BY NICK KNITE

(SEE TEMPLATE, PAGE 155)

A Detach BODY template. Glue tabs 1–7 to gray areas 1–7. (Just glue the marked areas. Tabs need to slide in here later!)

B Detach FLAME template. Glue tabs 8–13 to gray areas 8–13.

C Detach LEFT LEG template. Glue tabs 14–17 to gray areas 14–17.

D Detach RIGHT LEG template. Glue tabs 18–21 to gray areas 18–21.

E Detach RIGHT FOOT template. Glue tabs 22–28 to gray areas 22–28. Slide RIGHT LEG into slots on RIGHT FOOT.

F Detach LEFT FOOT template. Glue tabs 29–35 to gray areas 29–35. Slide LEFT LEG into slots on LEFT FOOT.

G Glue RIGHT LEG to BODY at gray area 38.

H Glue LEFT LEG to BODY at gray area 39.

I Insert tabs 36 and 37 on FLAME into slots on top of BODY and glue to gray areas 36 and 37.

J Place an electric tea light into BODY. (*Note:* Please be careful when doing this. It is just paper, after all!)

Broccoli is a highly trained service-bot. He was programmed at the esteemed Robo-Butlers College and finished summa cum laude with the highest ratings in the school's history. He was instantly hired by All Bot Catering Services, the premiere party robot agency, and is their most treasured employee. Broccoli takes care of the planning of each party from top to bottom and sees to it that everybody is having the time of their lives. He moves swiftly and silently around the party, so guests hardly recognize that they are being taken care of. Always one for mood lighting, he uses his flamelike head to create just the right atmosphere.

So, if you are planning a party, be sure to contact All Bot Catering Services and ask for Broccoli. He'll make your party unforgettable!

NICKNAME: GONZO

DESCRIPTION: 7 feet tall; bug eyes; light-generating wings

FUNCTION: planet defender; creator of light

ABILITIES: lightning-fast flyer; as bright as a thousand stars

Assembly Instructions

Discovered by Dolly Oblong

(see template, page 157)

A Detach HEAD template. Glue tabs 1–6 to gray areas 1–6.

B Detach INNER HEAD template. Glue tab 7 to gray area 7.

C Glue tabs 8–10 on INNER HEAD to gray areas 8–10 on HEAD.

D Glue tabs 11–17 on HEAD and INNER HEAD to gray areas 11–17.

E Detach WINGS and BODY templates. Insert tabs 18 and 19 on WINGS into slots on BODY. Glue tabs 18 and 19 on WINGS to gray areas 18 and 19 on BODY.

F Glue tabs 20–32 on BODY to gray areas 20–32. Make sure to curve and accordion fold tab 31.

G Glue tab 33 on BODY to gray area 33 on HEAD.

H Detach ANTENNA template. Insert tab 34 into slot on HEAD.

I Add glow-in-the-dark stickers.

Meet Dairobo G, aka Gonzo! Gonzo is a robo-firefly and the leader of the elite Star Squad on planet Mongo. Planet Mongo has three suns, but no moon. So when the suns set, the planet is plunged into complete darkness. In the dark, the evil Darkwood frogs take over the entire planet! To protect the creatures of Mongo against this darkness and the slimy, evil frogs, Gonzo and his team set off into the sky each night. High up in the air, the Star Squad covers the planet in a moon-like glow using their starstrike powers. This sends those nasty frogs packing! It's a tough job, but Gonzo loves buzzing through the sky as his starlight spreads across the whole planet. Go, go, Gonzo!

MODEL NAME: SPAR X
DESCRIPTION: 5 feet tall; cherubic face; adorable, pointy ears; delightful hexagonal tail; overalls
FUNCTION: children's playmate
ABILITIES: child care; being ridiculously cute

DIFFICULTY: Easy

Assembly Instructions

DISCOVERED BY SALAZAD

(SEE TEMPLATE, PAGE 159)

A Detach BODY and RIGHT ARM templates. Insert tab 1 on RIGHT ARM into slot on right side of BODY and glue to gray area 1.

B Detach LEFT ARM template. Insert tab 2 on LEFT ARM into slot on left side of BODY and glue to gray area 2.

C Glue tabs 3–10 on BODY to gray areas 3–10.

D Detach HEAD and VISOR templates. Insert tabs 11–13 on VISOR into slots on HEAD and glue to gray areas 11–13.

E Glue tabs 14–24 on HEAD to gray areas 14–24.

F Glue HEAD to BODY at gray area 25.

G Detach RIGHT WING template. Glue gray area 26 to gray area 26 on HEAD.

H Detach LEFT WING template. Glue gray area 27 to gray area 27 on HEAD.

I Add glow-in-the-dark stickers.

SPARXY's actual age was never revealed by her creators, but she appears to be about six and three-quarters (in robot years, of course). Her main task is to accompany, protect, and play with children, and she's great at it! However, she's an early beta model and can occasionally malfunction. Why? Worried that SPARXY might not appeal to children of all ages, her programmers worked around the clock to make sure she was the cutest robot anyone had ever seen. Their hard work paid off. Everyone loved SPARXY! They thought she was adorable, and they told her so—all the time. Unfortunately, all the praise got to SPARXY's head. Sometimes, right in the middle of playtime, the always cheerful and smiling SPARXY will stop what she's doing, start shaking her head, and begin saying, "I'm just too cute." Luckily, this cute overload never lasts too long and SPARXY soon returns to her duties.

MODEL NAME: IQ-4.0 XV7
DESCRIPTION: lightbulb ears; bow tie; designer glasses
FUNCTION: algorithm calculation
ABILITIES: can solve equations that have stupefied mankind for centuries; can tie a bow tie (It's harder than it looks!)

DIFFICULTY: Intermediate

Assembly Instructions

DISCOVERED BY J. EDWARDS

(SEE TEMPLATE, PAGE 161)

A Detach STEM template. Glue tab 1 to gray area 1.

B Detach WHEELS template. Insert one end of STEM into top center of WHEELS. Glue tab 1A to gray area 1A. Glue tabs 2–13 to gray areas 2–13.

C Detach KEYBOARD template. Glue tabs 14 and 15 to gray areas 14 and 15.

D Detach BODY template. Glue tabs 16 and 17 on KEYBOARD to gray areas 16 and 17 on BODY.

E Detach LEFT ARM template. Insert tab 18 on LEFT ARM into slot on left side of BODY and glue to gray area 18.

F Detach RIGHT ARM template. Insert tab 19 on RIGHT ARM into slot on right side of BODY and glue to gray area 19.

G Insert other end of STEM into bottom center of BODY. Glue tabs 1B to gray areas 1B.

H Glue tabs 20–26 on BODY to gray areas 20–26.

I Detach HEAD and RIGHT EAR templates. Glue tabs 27–35 on HEAD to gray areas 27–35. Insert tab 36 on RIGHT EAR into slot on right side of HEAD.

J Detach LEFT EAR template. Insert tab 37 on LEFT EAR into slot on left side of HEAD.

K Glue HEAD to BODY at gray area 38.

L Detach FLOPPY DISKS templates. Glue or insert into slots in back of BODY.

M Add glow-in-the-dark stickers.

IQ comes from a planet called Robo Geniustopia, where every bot is, well, a genius. IQ was sent to Earth on a mathematics mission to help solve the hardest algorithms known to mankind. The super genius has now solved the mysteries of time travel, mapped the DNA of all living things on Earth, cured the common cold, and even reinvented the wheel. When IQ gets an idea or finds the answer to life's hardest questions, his lightbulb ears glow, which is pretty much every second of every day. If you have questions, IQ has the answers.

LIGHTINGWALKER

MODEL NAME: **LIGHTING WALKER AS1**
DESCRIPTION: 13 feet tall; periscope neck; tanklike treads
FUNCTION: asteroid survival mechanism
ABILITIES: all-terrain, amphibious vehicle; can jump more than 30 feet in the air

DIFFICULTY: Easy

Assembly Instructions

Discovered by Guillaume Pain, aka Tougui

(see template, page 163)

A Detach BODY template. Glue tabs 1–6 to gray areas 1–6.

B Detach NECK template. Curve and glue to secure, then insert into slot on top of BODY.

C Detach HEAD template. Glue tabs 7–13 to gray areas 7–13. Insert HEAD into top of NECK.

D Detach RIGHT TRACK template. Glue tabs 14–18 to gray areas 14–18.

E Glue RIGHT TRACK to BODY at gray area 19.

F Detach LEFT TRACK template. Glue tabs 20–24 to gray areas 20–24.

G Glue LEFT TRACK to BODY at gray area 25.

H Add glow-in-the-dark stickers and place electric tea light inside BODY to glow.

A few decades ago, when the Earth was nearly devastated by a passing asteroid, the greatest scientific minds came together to create a worst-case-scenario plan. If an asteroid did hit the planet one day, humanity would have to be hidden away in millions of makeshift underground shelters across the globe. To help humans gather together and find these rescue centers, robots would be needed as guides. These robots, built two years ago in secret underground facilities, were called the Lighting Walkers. With their periscope necks and tanklike chain treads, Lighting Walkers can find and clear a safe path through any terrain. Their bodies can also illuminate several miles of land to warn humans of potential danger and guide them to safety.

MODEL NAME: OCEAN SEARCH CAPTURE AND RECOVERY

DESCRIPTION: 9 feet tall; laser-powered right hand; needle-nose-plier left hand

FUNCTION: deep-sea salvage recovery

ABILITIES: can plunge up to 550 feet underwater; rust-resistant; blows bubbles

O.S.C.A.R.

O.S.C.A.R. was designed to cruise along the continental shelf, recovering underwater treasure, capturing enemy submersibles, and searching for sunken ships. His powerful needle-nose-pliers left hand is used to pull treasure from the tightest spots, and his laser-powered right hand can cut through the strongest metal to free trapped cargo and crew from sunken ships. O.S.C.A.R. has multiple glow points to allow other vehicles and divers to find him in the dark ocean depths.

DIFFICULTY: Advanced

Assembly Instructions

DISCOVERED BY SCOTT SCHALLER

(SEE TEMPLATE, PAGE 165)

A. Detach LEFT TREAD template. Glue tabs 1–7 to gray areas 1–7.

B. Detach LOWER CHASSIS template. Insert tabs 8 and 9 on LEFT TREAD into slots on left side of LOWER CHASSIS and glue to gray areas 8 and 9.

C. Detach RIGHT TREAD template. Glue tabs 10–16 to gray areas 10–16.

D. Insert tabs 17 and 18 on RIGHT TREAD into slots on right side of LOWER CHASSIS and glue to gray areas 17 and 18.

E. Glue tabs 19 and 20 on LOWER CHASSIS to gray areas 19 and 20.

F. Detach RIGHT ARM and TORSO templates. Insert tab 21 on RIGHT ARM into slot on right side of TORSO and glue to gray area 21.

G. Detach LEFT ARM template. Insert tab 22 into slot on left side of TORSO and glue to gray area 22.

H. Glue tabs 23–33 on TORSO to gray areas 23–33.

I. Insert tabs 34 and 35 on TORSO into slots on top of LOWER CHASSIS and glue to gray areas 34 and 35.

J. Glue tabs 36–40 on LOWER CHASSIS to gray areas 36–40.

K. Detach LEFT TREAD GUARD. Glue tab 41 to LOWER CHASSIS at gray area 41. Glue tab 42 to LEFT TREAD at gray area 42.

L. Detach RIGHT TREAD GUARD. Glue tab 43 to LOWER CHASSIS at gray area 43. Glue tab 44 to RIGHT TREAD at gray area 44.

M. Detach RIGHT SHOULDER template. Glue tabs 45 and 46 to gray areas 45 and 46. Glue tabs 47–49 to TORSO at gray areas 47–49.

N. Detach LEFT SHOULDER template. Glue tabs 50 and 51 to gray areas 50 and 51. Glue tabs 52–54 to TORSO at gray areas 52–54.

O. Detach HEAD template. Glue tabs 55–65 to gray areas 55–65.

P. Glue HEAD to BODY at gray area 66.

Q. Detach LEFT HAND BOTTOM and LEFT HAND TOP templates. Interlock pieces by sliding them together and glue tabs 67 and 68 to gray areas 67 and 68. Glue to LEFT ARM at gray area 69.

R. Add glow-in-the-dark stickers.

FOLGORE

MODEL NAME: **FOLGORE 3000**
DESCRIPTION: 10 feet tall; red eyes; retractable arms
FUNCTION: unknown, awaiting orders
ABILITIES: see for yourself!

DIFFICULTY: Easy

Assembly Instructions

DISCOVERED BY FILIPPO PERIN, AKA PHIL

(SEE TEMPLATE, PAGE 167)

- **A** Detach BODY template. Glue tabs 1–7 to gray areas 1–7.
- **B** Detach RIGHT ARM and LEFT ARM templates. Insert tabs 8 and 9 on ARMS into slots on sides of BODY.
- **C** Detach HEAD and BOLTS templates. Glue tabs 10–13 on HEAD to gray areas 10–13. Insert tabs 14–16 on BOLTS into slots on HEAD.
- **D** Glue tabs 17–20 on HEAD to gray areas 17–20 on BODY.
- **E** Detach LOWER BODY template. Glue tabs 21–27 to gray areas 21–27.
- **F** Glue LOWER BODY to BODY at gray area 28.
- **G** Detach RIGHT LEG and LEFT LEG templates. Glue tabs 29 and 30 to gray areas 29 and 30. Add glue to one end of each leg and insert into holes on LOWER BODY. Press to secure.
- **H** Detach RIGHT SHOE template. Glue tabs 31–39 to gray areas 31–39. Glue onto RIGHT LEG.
- **I** Detach LEFT SHOE template. Glue tabs 40–48 to gray areas 40–48. Glue onto LEFT LEG.
- **J** Add glow-in-the-dark sticker.

After surviving a mysterious explosion at the robot manufacturing plant where they were built and waiting to be programmed, Folgore and his sister, Ardore (see page 39), found refuge in an abandoned underground military base. That's where they're currently hiding out. Their circuits fried, the confused robots take advantage of the bioluminescent bacteria that live in the pitch-black, cavelike base to recharge and rebuild. Friendly and outgoing, Folgore takes care of his sister and wonders what kind of robot he'll be once he's programmed. Can you help him out?

Dr. Maxwell Hubert-Babcock

Steambot Extraordinaire

NICKNAME: THE GOOD DOCTOR
DESCRIPTION: 6 feet tall; suave mustache; stylish top hat, bow tie and cuffs
FUNCTION: surgeon
ABILITIES: can perform thousands of medical procedures; great bedside manner; British accent

DIFFICULTY: Intermediate

Assembly Instructions

DISCOVERED BY SCOTT SCHALLER

(SEE TEMPLATE, PAGE 169)

A. Detach BODY and LEFT ARM templates. Insert tab 1 on LEFT ARM into slot on left side of BODY and glue to gray area 1.

B. Detach RIGHT ARM template. Insert tab 2 on RIGHT ARM into slot on right side of BODY and glue to gray area 2.

C. Glue tab 3 on BODY to gray area 3.

D. Detach HEAD template. Glue tab 4 to gray area 4.

E. Detach CAPE template. Glue tabs 5–8 to gray areas 5–8. Insert tabs 9–10 on HEAD into slots on CAPE and glue to gray areas 9–10 on CAPE.

F. Glue tabs 11 and 12 on HEAD to gray areas 11 and 12 on CAPE.

G. Glue tabs 13–20 on BODY to gray areas 13–20 on CAPE.

H. Detach HAT BRIM template. Glue tab 21 to HEAD at gray area 21.

I. Detach HATBAND template. Glue tab 22 to gray area 22.

J. Glue tabs 23 on HAT BRIM to gray area 23 on HATBAND.

K. Detach JAW STRAP template. Glue to HEAD at gray areas 24 and 25.

L. Detach MUSTACHE template. Glue to HEAD at gray area 26.

M. Detach BOW TIE template. Glue to BODY at gray area 27.

N. Detach RIGHT SMOKESTACK template. Curve, and then glue tab 28 to gray area 28. Glue tab 29 to gray area 29 on BODY.

O. Detach LEFT SMOKESTACK template. Curve, and then glue tab 30 to gray area 30. Glue tab 31 to gray area 31 on BODY.

P. Place over night-light or flashlight to glow.

Dr. Hubert-Babcock is a steam-powered robot from the late nineteenth century. Made of sturdy materials and extremely gentlemanly by nature, the good doctor has been of service to the residents of London, England, for more than 150 years. With delicate finger controls and clockwork precision, Dr. Hubert-Babcock continues his work as a surgeon to this day, proving that even an old robot can be of use in this high tech, modern world.

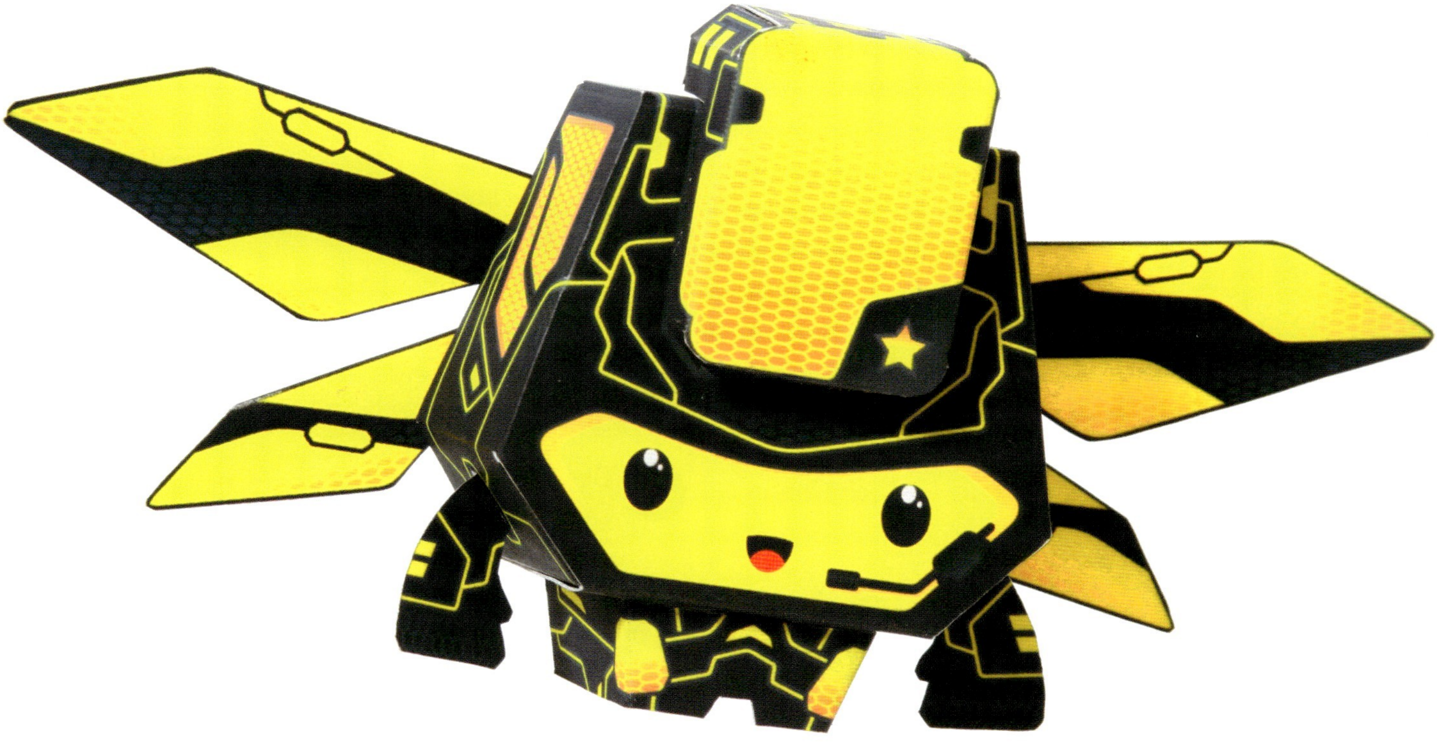

MODEL NAME: SPD LB
DESCRIPTION: 3 feet tall; starlight-absorbing, air-purifying wings; jet pack
FUNCTION: night sky patrol
ABILITIES: flying; aerial robotics; super speed; being incredibly adorable

Assembly Instructions

Discovered by Salazad

(see template, page 171)

- **A** Detach BODY template. Glue tab 1 to gray area 1.
- **B** Detach HEAD template. Insert tabs 2–5 on BODY into slots on bottom of HEAD and glue to gray areas 2–5.
- **C** Detach LEFT ARM template. Insert tab 6 into slot on left side of HEAD and glue to gray area 6.
- **D** Detach RIGHT ARM template. Insert tab 7 into slot on right side of HEAD and glue to gray area 7.
- **E** Glue tabs 8–18 on HEAD to gray areas 8–18.
- **F** Detach LEFT WING TOP template. Glue tab 19 to gray area 19 on HEAD.
- **G** Detach RIGHT WING TOP template. Glue tab 20 to gray area 20 on HEAD.
- **H** Detach LEFT WING BOTTOM template. Glue tab 21 to gray area 21 on HEAD.
- **I** Detach RIGHT WING BOTTOM template. Glue tab 22 to gray area 22 on HEAD.
- **J** Detach HEADLAMP template. Glue tabs 23–30 to gray areas 23–30.
- **K** Glue HEADLAMP to HEAD at gray areas 31–33.
- **L** Add glow-in-the-dark stickers.

There's nothing more fun than flying freely in the night sky. Just ask Lighting Bee2! This sky-patrol droid loves buzzing just below the Earth's atmosphere. Lighting Bee2 is part of the Global Night Patrol Force, a collection of hundreds of droids who protect our starry skies against enemies from above and below. It's an important assignment, and Lighting Bee2 was built specifically for the task. Its larger set of wings absorbs energy from starlight and gets this bot airborne. The smaller pair purifies the air below and scans for enemy combatants. Stargazers take note: Lighting Bee2 is often confused with a shooting star.

GLITCH HARDWIRE

MODEL NAME: GH20
DESCRIPTION: 20 feet tall; slight coat of rust
FUNCTION: decommissioned subaquatic research android
ABILITIES: can plunge up to 950 feet underwater

DIFFICULTY: Intermediate

Assembly Instructions

Discovered by J. Edwards

(see template, page 173)

A Detach BODY and RIGHT ARM templates. Insert RIGHT ARM into slot on right side of BODY and glue tab 1 to gray area 1.

B Detach LEFT ARM template. Insert LEFT ARM into slot on left side of BODY and glue tab 2 to gray area 2.

C Glue tabs 3–10 on BODY to gray areas 3–10.

D Detach WAIST template. Glue tabs 11–14 to gray areas 11–14.

E Detach LEFT LEG template. Glue tab 15 to gray area 15. Insert tabs 16 and 17 into slots on left of WAIST and glue to gray areas 16 and 17.

F Detach RIGHT LEG template. Glue tab 18 to gray area 18. Insert tabs 19 and 20 into slots on right of WAIST and glue to gray areas 19 and 20.

G Detach LEFT FOOT template. Glue tab 21 to gray area 21.

H Glue LEFT LEG to LEFT FOOT at gray area 22.

I Detach RIGHT FOOT template. Glue tab 23 to gray area 23.

J Glue RIGHT LEG to RIGHT FOOT at gray area 24.

K Detach HEAD template. Glue tabs 25–28 to gray areas 25–28.

L Insert tabs 29 and 30 on HEAD into slots on top of BODY. Glue tabs 29 and 30 to gray areas 29 and 30.

M Place BODY on top of WAIST.

N Add glow-in-the-dark stickers.

Before being decommissioned by the navy, Glitch was a top-of-the-line, state-of-the-art deep-sea underwater research android. Glitch was able to explore and map the ocean floor at depths no human or manned vessel could withstand. One day, while mapping a pirate shipwreck, Glitch slipped and fell 20,000 leagues under the sea into a deep-sea abyss. The enormous amount of pressure combined with what scientists believe to be damage from a giant squid caused the droid to malfunction. It took a team several months to recover and return Glitch to the surface. Nowadays, Glitch is enjoying its retirement, but this old sea droid still yearns for its days of unearthing the mysteries of the deep.

NICKNAME: LEONARDO
DESCRIPTION: 6 feet tall; aquarium cockpit; cross-terrain feet; anti-barnacle and rust-resistant shell
FUNCTION: amphibious walker
ABILITIES: walking on both land and sea; ocean cave rappeling; jump-roping; doing the underwater moonwalk
Hi!
LROLBOT

DIFFICULTY: Intermediate

Assembly Instructions

DISCOVERED BY CASTLEFORTE

(SEE TEMPLATE, PAGE 175)

A Detach BODY and RIGHT ARM templates. Insert tab 1 on RIGHT ARM into slot on right side of BODY and glue to gray area 1.

B Detach LEFT ARM template. Insert tab 2 on LEFT ARM into slot on left side of BODY and glue to gray area 2.

C Detach ANTENNA template. Glue tab 3 to BODY at gray area 3.

D Glue tabs 4–17 on BODY to gray areas 4–17. (*Note:* Fold down back window for easy access to glue tabs 9–12, then fold window up and glue tabs 13–17.)

E Detach RIGHT LEG template. Glue tabs 18–26 to gray areas 18–26.

F Detach two KNEE JOINT templates and glue to RIGHT LEG at gray areas 27 and 28.

G Detach RIGHT FOOT template. Glue tabs 29–37 to gray areas 29–37.

H Add glue to bottom of RIGHT LEG and fully insert into RIGHT FOOT. Press to secure. Insert RIGHT LEG into BODY.

I Detach LEFT LEG template. Glue tabs 38–46 to gray areas 38–46.

J Detach two KNEE JOINT templates and glue to LEFT LEG at gray areas 47 and 48.

K Detach LEFT FOOT template. Glue tabs 49–57 to gray areas 49–57.

L Add glue to bottom of LEFT LEG and fully insert into LEFT FOOT. Press to secure. Insert LEFT LEG into BODY.

M Detach SONAR RADAR template. Insert into slot on top of HEAD.

N Add glow-in-the-dark stickers.

Trot Bot was designed by Octavius Squidonious. Octavius is from the all-liquid planet Liquidus. He traveled to Earth with the rest of his people, the Liquidites (affectionately known as Drips), when their planet was destroyed. The Drips have lived at the bottom of Earth's ocean ever since. Octavius is not like the other Drips. He is much happier on dry land. Unfortunately, Drips can't breathe out of water. That's why he built his amphibious Trot Bot, Leonardo. Named after the brilliant inventor Leonardo da Vinci, Trot Bot is Octavius's best buddy. They travel everywhere together. With its state-of-the-art aquarium cockpit, Leonardo allows Octavius to explore the exciting dry surface of Earth.

LIGHTINGFLY

MODEL NAME: LIGHTING FLIES PE2S
DESCRIPTION: 10 feet tall; glowing armor; eight legs; one eye
FUNCTION: search and rescue
ABILITIES: flying through the dust- and sand-choked desert air; building sand castles

DIFFICULTY: Easy

Assembly Instructions

DISCOVERED BY GUILLAUME PAIN, AKA TOUGUI

(SEE TEMPLATE, PAGE 177)

A Detach BODY 1 template. Glue tabs 1–9 to gray areas 1–9.

B Detach HEAD template. Glue tabs 10–13 to gray areas 10–13.

C Glue tabs 14–15 on HEAD to gray areas 14–15 on BODY.

D Detach BODY 2 template. Glue tabs 16–30 to gray areas 16–30.

E Detach eight LEGS templates. Insert tabs 31 into each slot on BODY 2.

F Glue BODY 2 to BODY 1 at gray area 32.

G Detach RIGHT WING template. Insert tab 33 into slot on right side of BODY 1.

H Detach LEFT WING template. Insert tab 34 into slot on left side of BODY 1.

I Add glow-in-the-dark stickers.

With a combined surface area of more than 9 million kilometers, the Sahara desert spans ten countries and is the largest desert in the world. It's also no place to get lost. Lighting Flies are a series of search-and-rescue robots programmed to find people lost in the Sahara and other deserts around the world. They are deployed and stationed at various outposts throughout arid landscapes and make 24/7 patrols of the area. Lightning-fast and built to withstand the strongest headwinds, the bots have wings that make a specific buzzing and flapping noise that can be easily identified by those in need of rescue. Most important, their glowing armor makes them visible at night and during sandstorms.

MODEL NAME: CH1PP3R 1324

DESCRIPTION: 7 feet tall; lime green; smokestack; gets extremely hot (do not touch!)

FUNCTION: anything, as long as it doesn't require any movement

ABILITIES: everything . . . but moving; can also shoot major side-eye

Assembly Instructions

CREATED BY SJORS TRIMBACH

(SEE TEMPLATE, PAGE 179)

A Detach FOOT template. Glue tabs 1–7 to gray areas 1–7.

B Detach LEG template. Glue tabs 8–14 to gray areas 8–14. Glue tab 15 on LEG to gray area 15 on FOOT.

C Detach SPRING 1 and SPRING 2 templates. Glue tab 16 on SPRING 1 to gray area 16 on SPRING 2 to create an L shape. To create spring, fold one strip over the other until you can fold no more.

D Glue tab 17 on SPRING 2 to gray area 17 on SPRING 1.

E Glue SPRING to LEG at gray area 18.

F Detach EXHAUST template. Glue tabs 19–22 to gray areas 19–22.

G Detach BODY template. Glue tabs 23–26 on EXHAUST to gray areas 23–26 on BODY.

H Glue tabs 27–30 on BODY to gray areas 27–30.

I Glue tab 31 on SPRING to gray area 31 on BODY.

J Add glow-in-the-dark stickers.

Ch1pp3Rs can't move around by themselves. They need to be maneuvered by other robots or by human beings, but once on location they get the job done. What job, you ask? Any job! Ch1ppr3Rs have one of the smartest artificial intelligence systems on Earth. The secret is what lies inside of them. Hundreds of highly advanced, integrated circuit chips run through these robots and help them calculate any request in fewer than three nanoseconds. You might say it's a brain on legs—if it had legs. So maybe don't say that. During the daytime these chips do their work unseen, but when darkness falls, you can see them all at work as they shine through the Ch1pp3R.

RED TOP 800

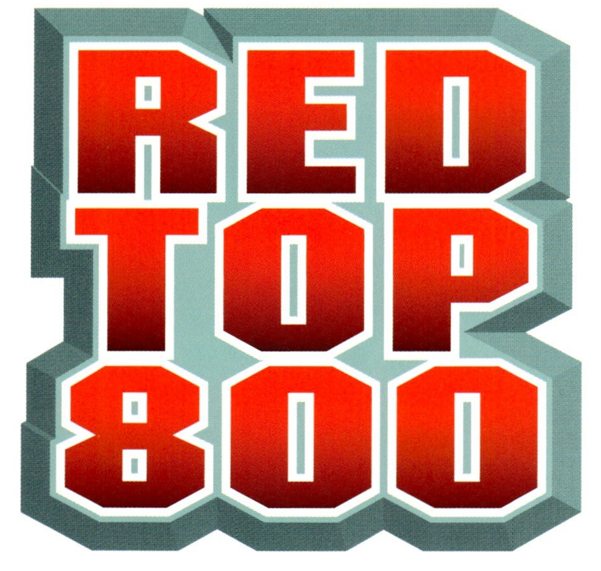

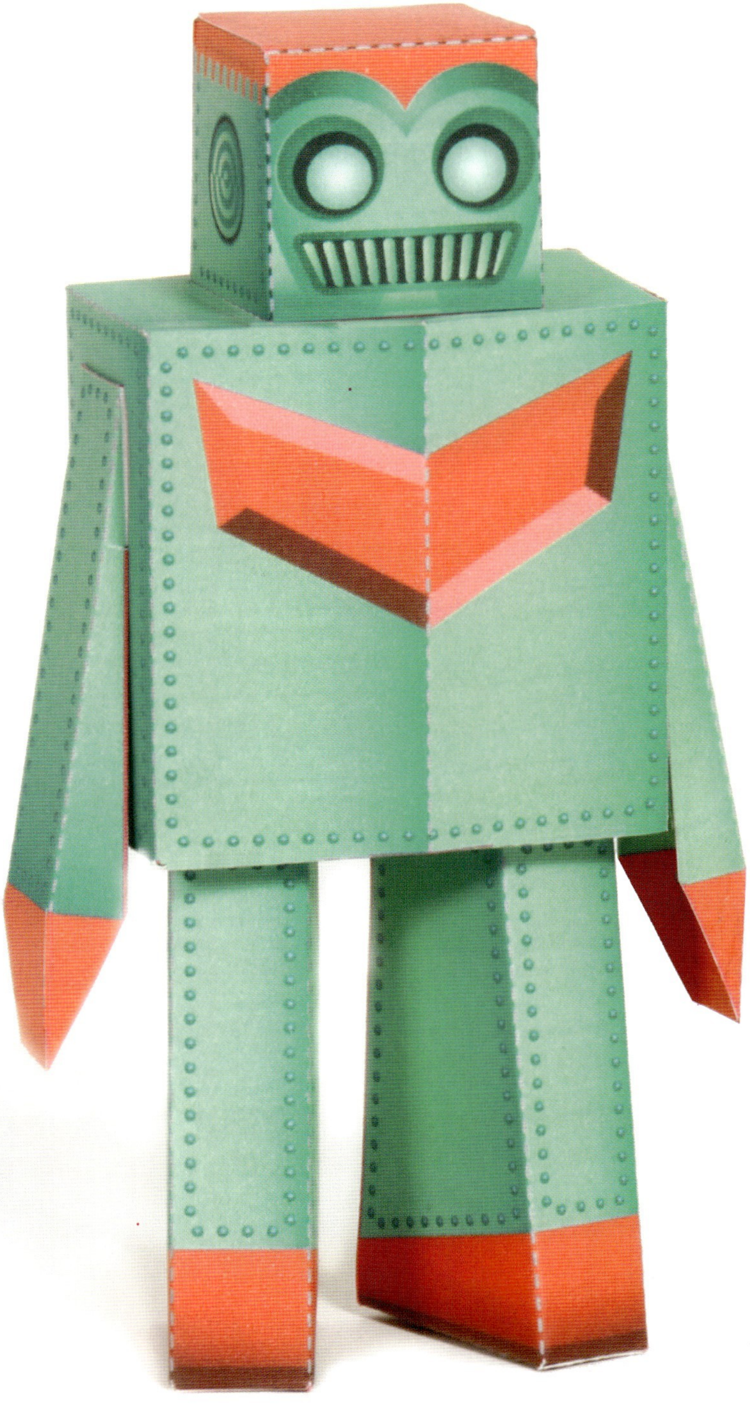

MODEL NAME: RT8
DESCRIPTION: 40 feet tall; 50 percent titanium, 20 percent aluminum, 29 percent iron, 1 percent chewing gum
FUNCTION: disaster relief; debris removal (formerly)
ABILITIES: rescue; demolition and construction

DIFFICULTY: Easy

Assembly Instructions

DISCOVERED BY CHRISTOPHER BONNETTE, AKA MACULA

(SEE TEMPLATE, PAGE 181)

A Detach BODY template. Glue tabs 1–11 to gray areas 1–11.

B Detach HEAD template. Glue tabs 12–15 to gray areas 12–15.

C Insert remaining tabs on HEAD into slots on top of BODY.

D Detach LEFT ARM template. Glue tabs 16–17 to gray areas 16–17. Insert tabs into slots on left side of BODY.

E Detach RIGHT ARM template. Glue tabs 18–19 to gray areas 18–19. Insert tabs into slots on right side of BODY.

F Detach LEFT LEG template. Glue tabs 20–23 to gray areas 20–23. Insert remaining tabs into slots on bottom left of BODY.

G Detach RIGHT LEG template. Glue tabs 24–27 to gray areas 24–27. Insert remaining tabs into slots on bottom right of BODY.

H Add glow-in-the-dark stickers.

Red Top 800 was invented to clear and remove heavy debris from construction sites at recently demolished buildings. First designed in 1965, this old tin can of a robot is still in use today. However, as the times changed, so did Red Top's job. RT8 was soon recruited to assist rescue and rebuilding after disasters such as earthquakes, hurricanes, and tsunamis. Red Top 800 has personally saved more than 800,000 lives and aided in the speedy rebuilding of communities all over the world.

MODEL NAME: SQ-EEZ

DESCRIPTION: 3 feet tall; retractable arms; massively strong claw hands

FUNCTION: rock crushing

ABILITIES: can turn rough rocks into clean-cut gems; microscopic vision; champion arm wrestler

DIFFICULTY: Easy

Assembly Instructions

Discovered by Christopher Bonnette, aka Macula

(see template, page 183)

A Detach UPPER BODY template. Glue tabs 1–9 to gray areas 1–9.

B Detach HEAD template. Glue tabs 10–20 to gray areas 10–20.

C Glue HEAD to UPPER BODY at gray areas 21 and 22.

D Detach RIGHT ARM and LEFT ARM templates. Glue to UPPER BODY at gray areas 23 and 24.

E Detach CORE BODY template. Glue tabs 25 and 26 to gray areas 25 and 26. Add glue to square, open end and insert into slot on bottom of UPPER BODY. Press to secure.

F Detach LEFT LEGS A and B, RIGHT LEGS A and B, and LEG PANEL templates. Glue tabs 27–52 to gray areas 27–52.

G Glue LEGS to CORE BODY at gray areas 53 and 54. Make sure legs match up evenly so bot can stand level on the ground.

H Add glow-in-the-dark stickers.

Squeeze-O-Tron A GoGo is a robot that was first designed to locate, dig, and grind rocks in search of rare minerals, valuable ore, and precious gems. Built by two geologists and friends Toshi and Jim, this robot started as just a fun side project. Jim studied general quarry rocks. Toshi loved the shiny brilliance of precious stones. They collaborated and created the Squeeze-O-Tron A GoGo (model name SQ-EEZ) to go with them on their geological digs. Toshi and Jim soon discovered that SQ-EEZ was a very valuable asset. With its massively strong grip, it can turn coal into diamonds. Toshi and Jim are now billionaires. Talk about a diamond in the rough!

MODEL NAME: XIX

DESCRIPTION: 9 feet tall; starry eyes; disco ball head

PURPOSE: dance floor motivator; professional ballet dancer (formerly); Hype Bot

ABILITIES: ballet; hip-hop; modern dance; jazz; disco; break dancing; swing; tap; krumping; rumba; samba; salsa; merengue; Chicago stepping; the Cabbage Patch; popping and locking

DIFFICULTY: Easy

Assembly Instructions

Discovered by Nick Knite

(see template, page 185)

- **A** Detach BODY template. Glue tabs 1–7 to gray areas 1–7.
- **B** Detach DISCO LIGHT template. Glue tabs 8–15 to gray areas 8–15.
- **C** Detach RIGHT FOOT template. Glue tabs 16–26 to gray areas 16–26.
- **D** Glue RIGHT FOOT to BODY at gray area 27.
- **E** Detach LEFT FOOT template. Glue tabs 28–38 to gray areas 28–38.
- **F** Glue LEFT FOOT to BODY at gray area 39.
- **G** Place electric tea light inside BODY. Insert tabs 40 and 41 on DISCO LIGHT into slots on BODY.
- **H** Add glow-in-the-dark stickers.

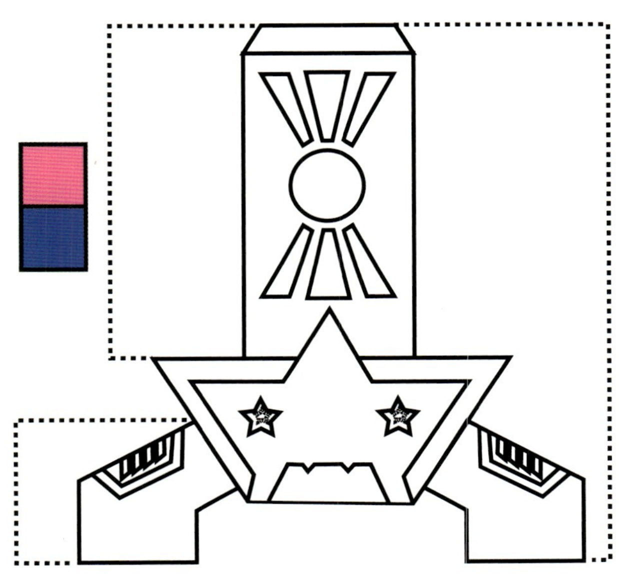

Spinach is a mover and a shaker, and she'll get you moving and shaking, too! All Bot Catering Services hired this former professional ballet bot because of her tremendous dancing skills and her ability to get everybody on the dance floor. She also functions as a disco ball, thanks to her glow-in-the-dark head. Whether she's doing the tango, samba, or foxtrot, one thing is for sure: Spinach will always be the last one to leave the party. Just try to keep up as her fancy feet move to the sweet beat!

CT Scout Elf

Technology has made life a little difficult for Santa. With 24/7 live video home surveillance, stealthy gift-giving is nearly impossible. To help with this dilemma, crafty elves devised the CT Scout Elf. The Scout Elf looks like just another ornament, but it packs a lot of features into its little body. It provides eyes-on-the-ground surveillance for Santa to determine naughty-or-niceness levels, layout specs for his arrival, and video-jamming technology that provides Ol' Saint Nick with an envelope of stealth to deliver his gifts and evade detection.

DIFFICULTY: Advanced

Assembly Instructions

DISCOVERED BY SCOTT SCHALLER

(SEE TEMPLATE, PAGE 187)

A Detach LOWER HAT template. Glue tabs 1–5 to gray areas 1–5.

B Detach HEAD template. Glue tabs 6–11 to gray areas 6–11.

C Insert tabs 12 and 13 on LOWER HAT into slots on HEAD and glue tabs 12–14 to gray areas 12–14.

D Glue tabs 15–19 on HEAD to gray areas 15–19.

E Detach UPPER HAT template. Glue tab 20 on LOWER HAT to gray area 20. Insert tabs 21 and 22 on LOWER HAT into slots on UPPER HAT and glue tabs 20–22 to gray areas 20–22.

F Detach the HANGER template. Apply glue to gray area 23 and fold in half. Insert tabs 24 and 25 into slot on UPPER HAT and glue to areas 24 and 25.

G Glue tabs 26–33 on UPPER HAT to gray areas 26–33. Don't worry if the tips don't meet perfectly. The HAT BALL will cover any misalignments.

H Detach HAT BALL template. Glue tabs 34–40 to gray areas 34–40. Glue to tip of UPPER HAT.

I Detach TORSO template. Glue tabs 41–53 to gray areas 41–53.

J Detach LOWER TORSO template. Insert tabs 54 and 55 on TORSO into slots on LOWER TORSO and glue tabs 54–56 to gray areas 54–56.

K Glue tabs 57–67 on LOWER TORSO to gray areas 57–67.

L Detach LEFT LEG template. Glue tab 68 to gray area 68 and fold leg in half. Apply glue to gray area 69 and fold again to create knee. Apply glue to gray area 70 and fold over to create ankle.

M Detach RIGHT LEG template. Glue tab 71 to gray area 71 and fold leg in half. Apply glue to gray area 72 and fold again to create knee. Apply glue to gray area 73 and fold over to create ankle.

N Glue LEFT LEG to LOWER TORSO at gray area 74 and glue RIGHT LEG to LOWER TORSO at gray area 75.

O Detach LEFT ARM and RIGHT ARM templates. Glue LEFT ARM to TORSO at gray area 76. Glue RIGHT ARM to TORSO at gray area 77.

P Detach GIFT BOX template. Glue tabs 78–84 to gray areas 78–84.

Q Glue GIFT BOX to LEFT ARM and RIGHT ARM at gray areas 85 and 86.

R Glue HEAD to TORSO at gray area 87.

S Attach CT Scout Elf to a tree light or an ornament hanger and place on your Christmas tree, stocking, or shelf.

ABOUT THE ARTISTS

Castleforte
B.A.A.R.T., page 13; Traxx, page 45; HUGZ, page 29; KeiKoko, page 41; Moon Walker, page 51; Trot Bot, page 79; Yujein, page 57

BASED IN: Los Angeles, CA, USA

WHAT I DO: Artist, designer, illustrator, toy maker, motion graphics animator, and creative entrepreneur

ABOUT ME: aka NiceBunny. California native. Creator of nicepapertoys.com. I have a smile for everyone. I live in the now. I love toys and characters, the movies, all kinds of music, the universe entire, nice people, organic food, Dr. Seuss, my lovely wife, Linda, and my amazing dog, Soul.

WHAT I LIKE ABOUT PAPERTOYS: They are amazing, fun, challenging, original, creative, collaborative, accessible, affordable, and unstoppable.

castleforte.com
nicebunny.com
nicepapertoys.com

Faisal Azad, aka Salazad
Lighting Bee2, page 75; Hydro Bulb, page 53; Blitztrail, page 15; SPARXY, page 63

BASED IN: Bandung, Indonesia

WHAT I DO: Graphic designer and explorer of the papertoy world

ABOUT ME: I always like to incorporate the art and traditional culture of Indonesia in every job that I do. I especially love playing with colors.

WHAT I LIKE ABOUT PAPERTOYS: In addition to being inexpensive and easy to make, a papertoy is not just a toy; it allows you to interact with many people and exercise your design skills.

salazad.com

Abi Braceros, aka Abz
Big Fun, page 17; Caid, page 25; Frosty Frost, page 5

BASED IN: Kahului, HI, USA

WHAT I DO: Graphic designer/illustrator

ABOUT ME: Drawing, designing, making stuff—that about sums it up. I'm inspired by music, movies, cartoons—anything and everything.

WHAT I LIKE ABOUT PAPERTOYS: I like the challenge a papertoy presents. The process of building it out into a 3-D form, dismantling it, and figuring out how to put it together again in an efficient way. The fun of designing (skinning) that 3-D form. More than that, what I absolutely love about papertoys is that they are available to everyone (with access to a computer and internet connection), anytime, and anywhere. It sparks curiosity and inspires creativity.

oh-sheet.com

Christopher Bonnette, aka Macula
Disinfectoid, page 33; Red Top 800, page 85; Squeeze-O-Tron A GoGo, page 87

BASED IN: Los Angeles, CA, USA

WHAT I DO: Art director and graphic designer

ABOUT ME: My illustrations are whimsical, cute, and a bit creepy. Nothing makes me happier than to imagine a character, an icon, or a whole universe and see it evolve from concept to finished product—especially if monsters, aliens, or robots are involved.

WHAT I LIKE ABOUT PAPERTOYS: Papertoys are fun to build and can be shared all around the world. You have to invest some time into building each one, making it a more prized possession. It is very rewarding to see people building one of your creations and being so proud they made it themselves.

macula.tv

J. Edwards
Mega Byte, page 21; Glitch Hardwire, page 77; IQ 4.0, page 65

BASED IN: San Diego, CA, USA

WHAT WE DO: Find inspiration, take that inspiration, and make it tangible.

ABOUT US: We're a father/daughter team that believes a child's imagination is one of the most important untapped natural resources. Make toys, not war.

WHAT I LIKE ABOUT PAPERTOYS: If at first you don't succeed, fold and fold again.

instagram.com/toygami

Jon Greenwell, aka Jonny Chiba
Lampy, page 3; Glow-Go, page 7; Mecha Nom Nom, page 31

BASED IN: Liverpool, UK

WHAT I DO: Computer game artist

ABOUT ME: My interest in art was fired by the graffiti explosion of the 1980s, although I am currently retired from the scene.

WHAT I LIKE ABOUT PAPERTOYS: I like the way papertoys are available to everyone to build and customize.

jonnychiba.blogspot.com

Matthijs Kamstra, aka [mck]
Drillrr, page 9; TaTiki, page 43; Evv, page 47

BASED IN: Amsterdam, The Netherlands

WHAT I DO: Creative developer

ABOUT ME: Designing papertoys is a balancing act for me—in the daytime I'm a creative developer at an agency that develops creative digital products, but in the nighttime I turn into an urban papertoy hero.

WHAT I LIKE ABOUT PAPERTOYS: I spend lots of time making paper do stuff it's not supposed to do; that's why I use more and more curved and round shapes in my work. I prefer to make robots. When I was a kid I loved them, and now that I'm older I want to build them myself.

matthijskamstra.nl/blog

Nick Knite
Garlic, page 19; Broccoli, page 59; Spinach, page 89

BASED IN: Essen, Germany

WHAT I DO: Designer and paper engineer; I also DJ and make music.

ABOUT ME: I used to have jug ears. I want to own a wombat someday. I am a quick learner, but I forget almost as quickly. I have a really good ear for music. Surfing is my favorite sport.

WHAT I LIKE ABOUT PAPERTOYS: With papertoys, we are one step ahead of technology: We can beam three-dimensional stuff to places all over the world . . . 2-D paper templates become 3-D toys!

nickknite.com

Dolly Oblong
Daisujin 9000, page 1; ED-03, page 37; Dairobo G, page 61

BASED IN: The Netherlands

WHAT I DO: Self-taught plush maker and papertoy designer

ABOUT ME: I've always been into creating cute characters with a twist, and I first started designing papertoys as a fun way to promote my hand-knit plush. After my initial design—bunnies wearing stripy trunks—I caught the papertoy bug, and I haven't stopped designing them since.

WHAT I LIKE ABOUT PAPERTOYS: Anyone with basic materials like a printer, scissors, and some glue can start his or her own toy collection.

dollyoblong.com

Guillaume Pain, aka Tougui
Bionic Yeti, page 23; Lighting Fly, page 89; Lighting Walker, page 67

BASED IN: Annecy, France

WHAT I DO: I spend my time creating things with all kind of mediums, but first of all with paper!

ABOUT ME: I'm an artist, freelance illustrator, and papertoy maker.

WHAT I LIKE ABOUT PAPERTOYS: The freedom of creation, no rules, just my imagination

tougui.fr

Filippo Perin, aka PHIL
Ardore, page 39; Folgore, page 71

BASED IN: Conegliano, a town near Venice, Italy

WHAT I DO: In life I deal with promotion and trade, but my real passion is papertoys.

ABOUT ME: I live in hope of being able to get my art all over the world, so I'm working hard on my toys and my style to reach the highest peaks. I continually find inspiration for my toys, trying to incorporate my life experiences into them.

WHAT I LIKE ABOUT PAPERTOYS: You can make lots of friends, as has happened to me over the years.

behance.net/philtoys

LouLou & Tummie
ERR-07, page 35; Spence-o-nator, page 55

BASED IN: Tilburg, The Netherlands

WHAT WE DO: Illustrators trying to make a living out of creating robots and cute stuff.

ABOUT US: We have a little white dog covered in spots with big ears and no tail named Bowser. He sleeps a lot, drools even more, and snores loudly. He doesn't listen to us, but we love him anyway—and he is much more interesting than we are.

WHAT WE LIKE ABOUT PAPERTOYS: It's a fun and cheap way of building your own toys. Bringing something to life from just a flat piece of paper is quite magical!

loulouandtummie.com

Bryan Rollins
S.S. Tubmarine, page 11; WavForm, page 27

BASED IN: Memphis, TN, USA

WHAT I DO: Attended Memphis College of Art with a concentration in graphic design

ABOUT ME: I grew up wanting to be an animator and learned to draw by copying *The Flintstones*, Looney Tunes, the characters of *Dragon Ball Z*, and *Sonic the Hedgehog*.

WHAT I LIKE ABOUT PAPERTOYS: Paper has been one of my favorite mediums since I discovered origami at the age of eight, and I'm still having fun mixing it up with my design and illustration.

bryanrollins.com

Scott Schaller
S.A.B.I.R., page 49; Dr. Maxwell Hubert-Babcock, page 73; O.S.C.A.R., page 69; CT Scout Elf, page 91

BASED IN: Lompoc, CA, USA

WHAT I DO: High school graphic design and innovation/design thinking teacher

ABOUT ME: I have been teaching design to teens for twenty-two years.

WHAT I LIKE ABOUT PAPERTOYS: They are a visually exciting, dimensional, tactile form of art. I have found them to be a perfect bridge between my students and teaching design. And who, growing up, hasn't wanted to become a toy maker? We all harbor a secret Santa in our souls. Papertoy designers get to tap into that desire.

chsgraphicslab.com

Sjors Trimbach
Ch1pp3R, page 83

BASED IN: Enschede, The Netherlands

WHAT I DO: I pick my nose when no one is watching.

ABOUT ME: I am an illustrator. I read comic books and I collect Hot Wheels cars. Being the father of a young boy is the best excuse to buy more of both.

WHAT I LIKE ABOUT PAPERTOYS: Papertoys are the easiest way to make your vision into a real object. An idea in the morning is an object in the evening. And if you mess up, you just build a new one.

sjorstrimbach.com

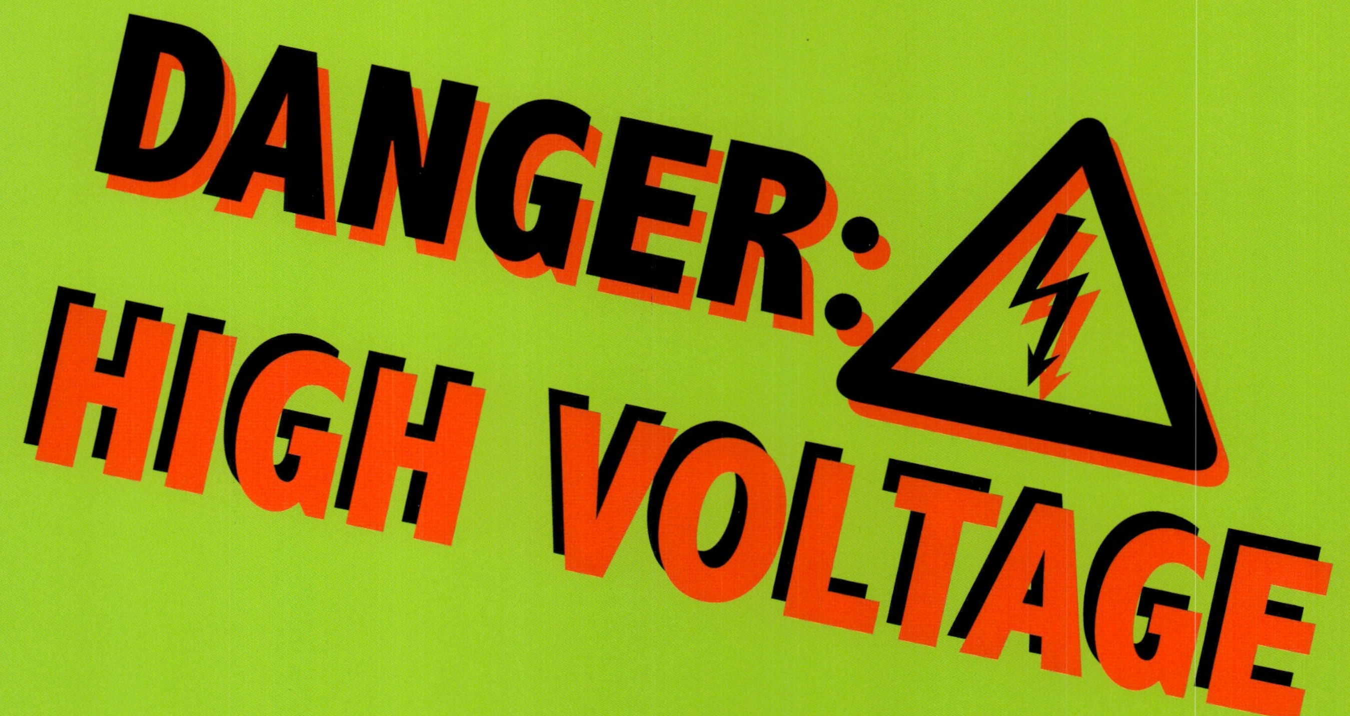

GLOWBOT TEMPLATES AHEAD

01001111 01100010 01100101 01111001 01011111 0111100
01101111 01110101 01110010 01011111 01010010 0110111
01100010 01101111 01110100 01011111 01001111 0111011
01100101 01110010 01101100 01101111 01110010 0110010
01110011 00100000 01001111 01100010 01100101 0111100
01011111 01111001 01101111 01110101 01110010 0101111
01010010 01101111 01100010 01101111 01110100 0101111
01001111 01110110 01100101 01110010 01101100 0110111
01110010 01100100 01110011 00100000 01001111 0110001
01100101 01111001 01011111 01111001 01101111 0111010
01110010 01011111 01010010 01101111 01100010 0110111
01110100 01011111 01001111 01110110 01100101 0111001
01101100 01101111 01110010 01100100 01110011 0010000
01001111 01100010 01100101 01111001 01011111 0111100
01101111 01110101 01110010 01011111 01010010 0110111
01100010 01101111 01110100 01011111 01001111 0111011
01100101 01110010 01101100 01101111 01110010 0110010
01110011 00100000 01001111 01100010 01100101 0111100
01011111 01111001 01101111 01110101 01110010 0101111
01010010 01101111 01100010 01101111 01110100 0101111
01001111 01110110 01100101 01110010 01101100 0110111
01110010 01100100 01110011 00100000 01001111 0110001
01100101 01111001 01011111 01111001 01101111 0111010
01110010 01011111 01010010 01101111 01100010 0110111
01110100 01011111 01001111 01110110 01100101 0111001
01101100 01101111 01110010 01100100 01110011 0010000
01001111 01100010 01100101 01111001 01011111 0111100
01101111 01110101 01110010 01011111 01010010 0110111
01100010 01101111 01110100 01011111 01001111 0111011
01100101 01110010 01101100 01101111 01110010 0110010
01110011 00100000 01001111 01100010 01100101 0111100
01011111 01111001 01101111 01110101 01110010 0101111
01010010 01101111 01100010 01101111 01110100 0101111
01001111 01110110 01100101 01110010 01101100 0110111
01110010 01100100 01110011 00100000 01001111 0110001

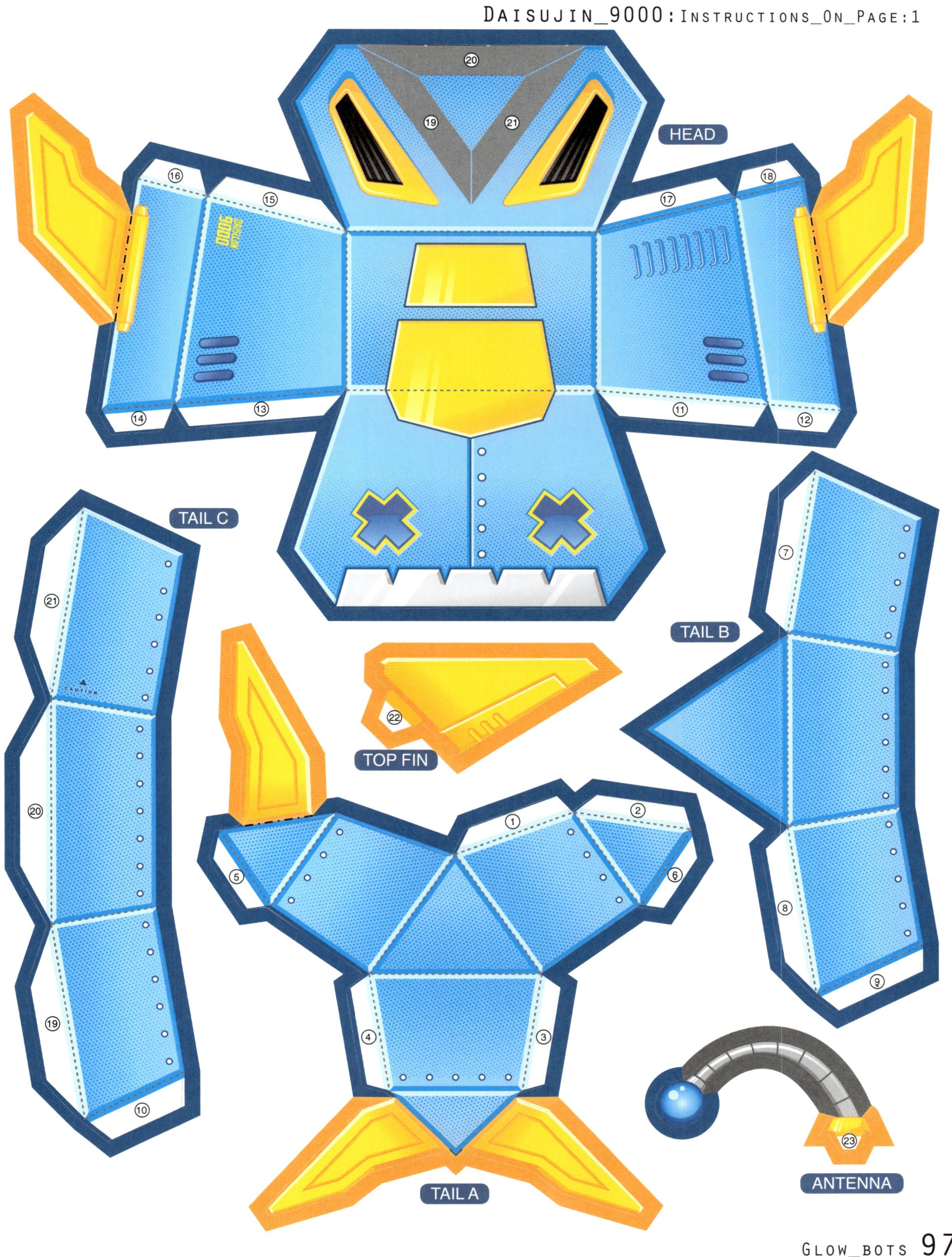
HEAD
TAIL C
TAIL B
TOP FIN
TAIL A
ANTENNA
DAISUJIN 9000
CAUTION
1
2
3
4
5
6
7
8
9
10
11
12
13
14
15
16
17
18
19
20
21
22
23

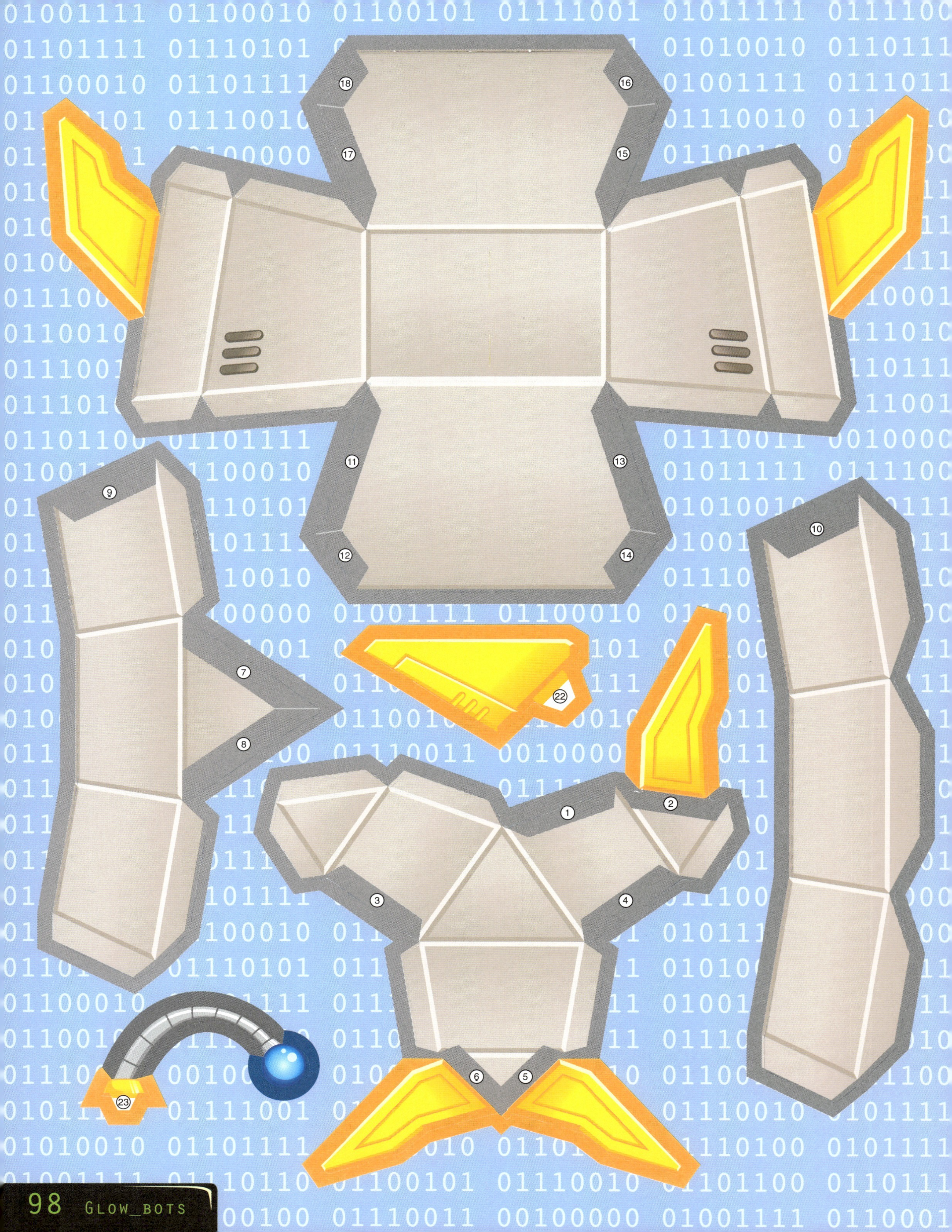

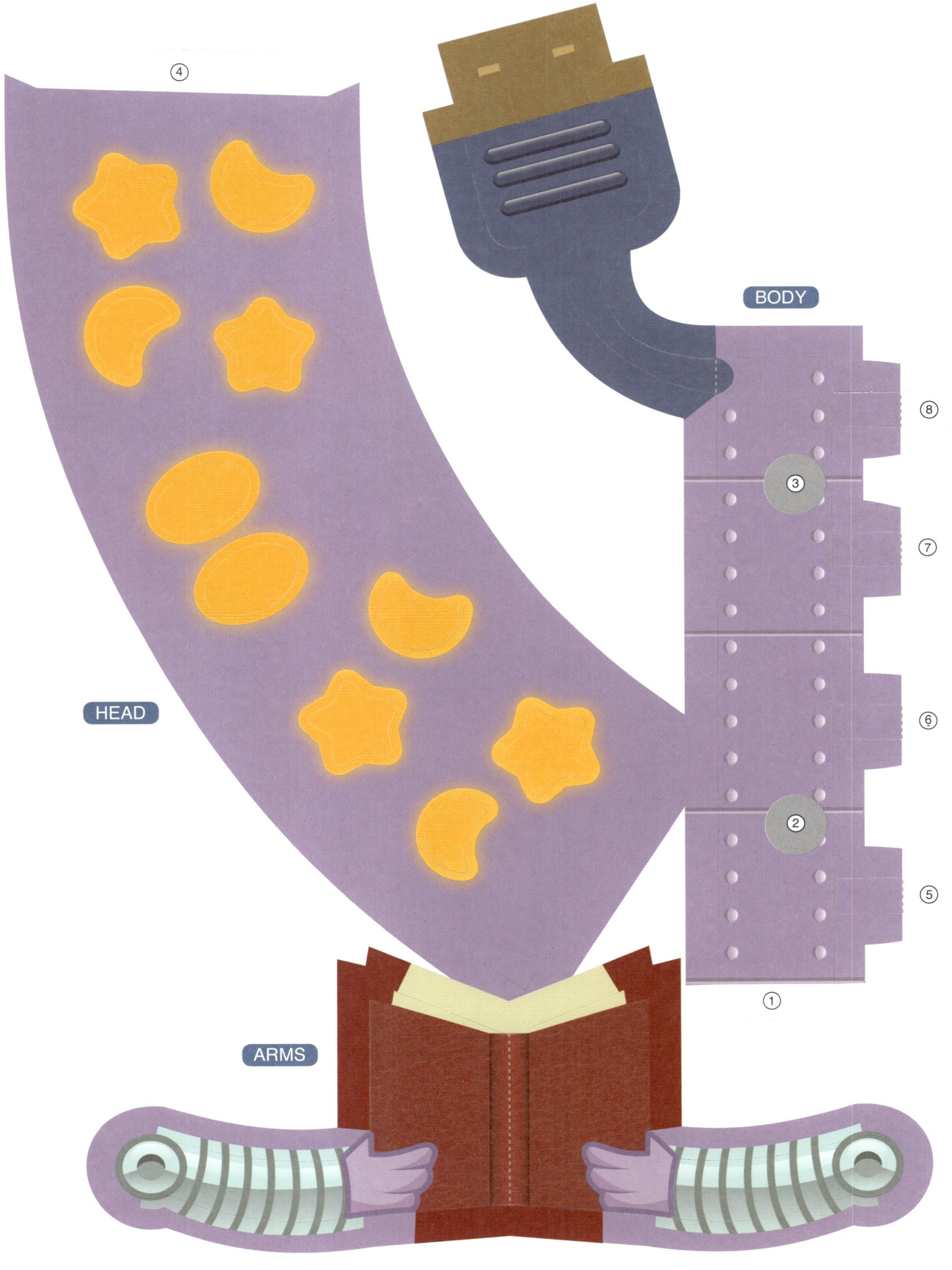
④
BODY
⑧
③
⑦
⑥
HEAD
②
⑤
①
ARMS

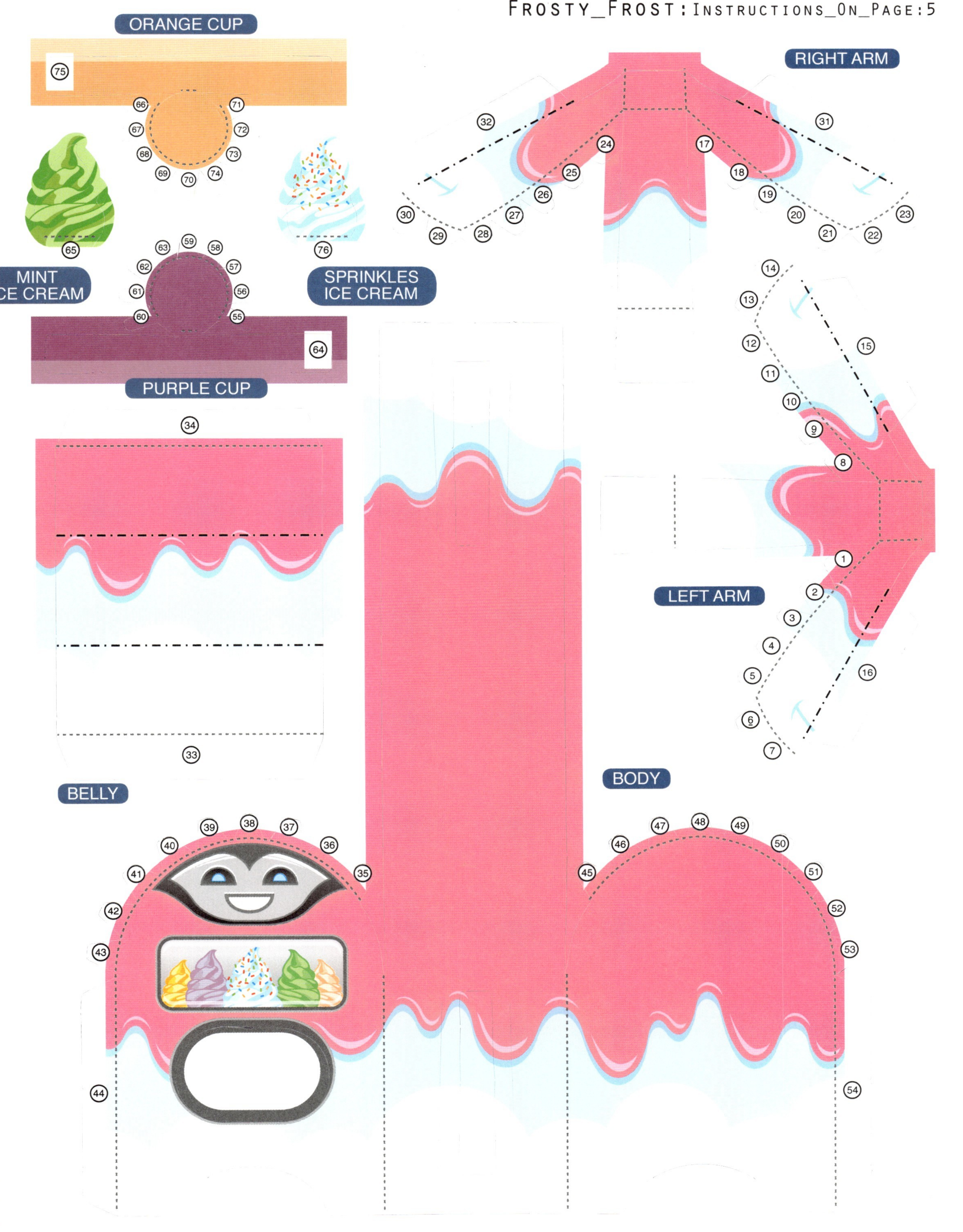
ORANGE CUP
75
66
67
68
69
70
74
73
72
71
MINT ICE CREAM
65
SPRINKLES ICE CREAM
76
63
59
58
62
57
61
56
60
55
64
PURPLE CUP
RIGHT ARM
32
24
17
31
25
18
26
19
30
27
20
23
29
28
21
22
14
13
15
12
11
10
9
8
1
LEFT ARM
2
3
4
5
16
6
7
34
33
BELLY
BODY
39
38
37
40
36
41
35
42
43
44
45
46
47
48
49
50
51
52
53
54

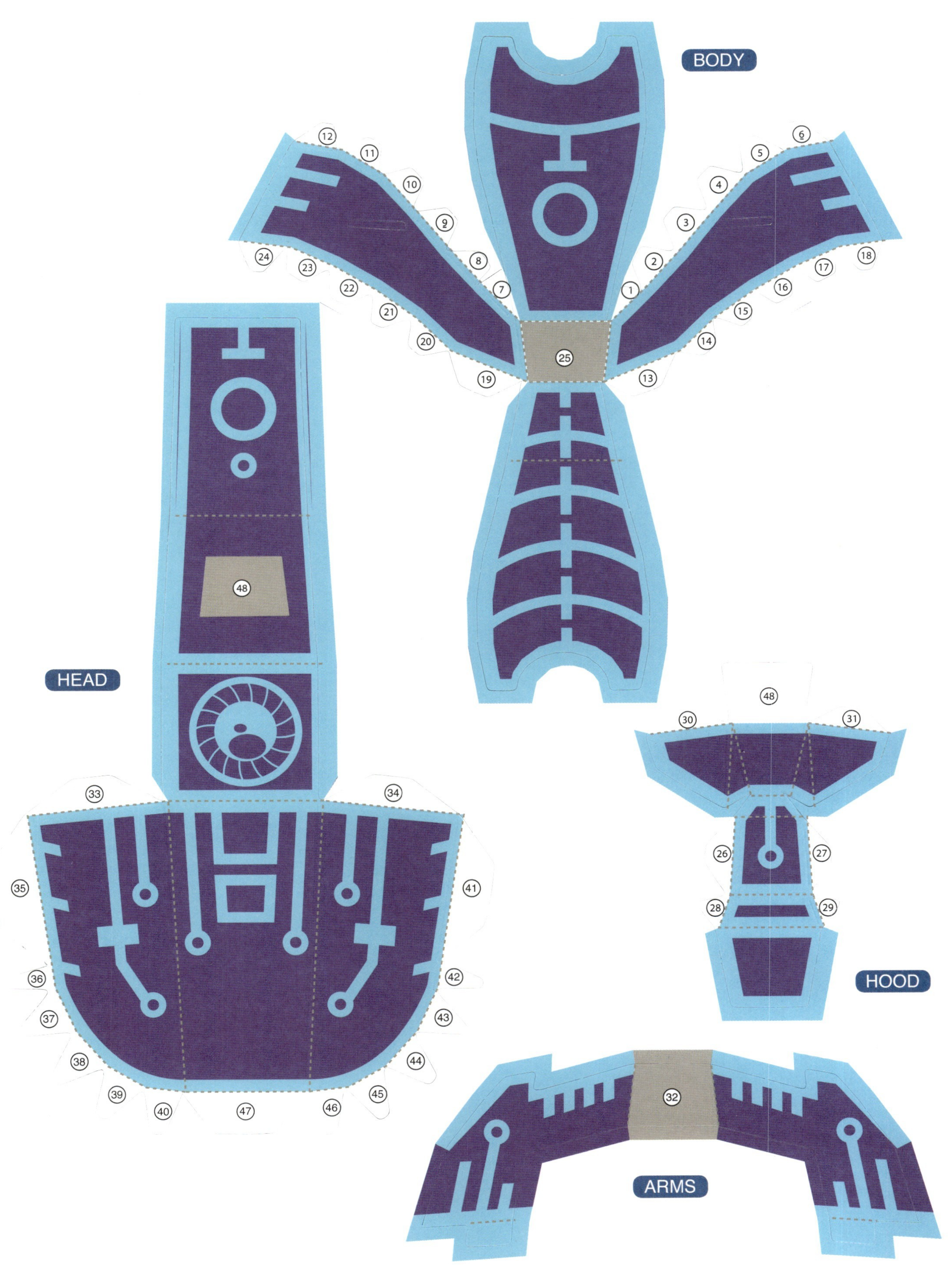

BODY
HEAD
HOOD
ARMS

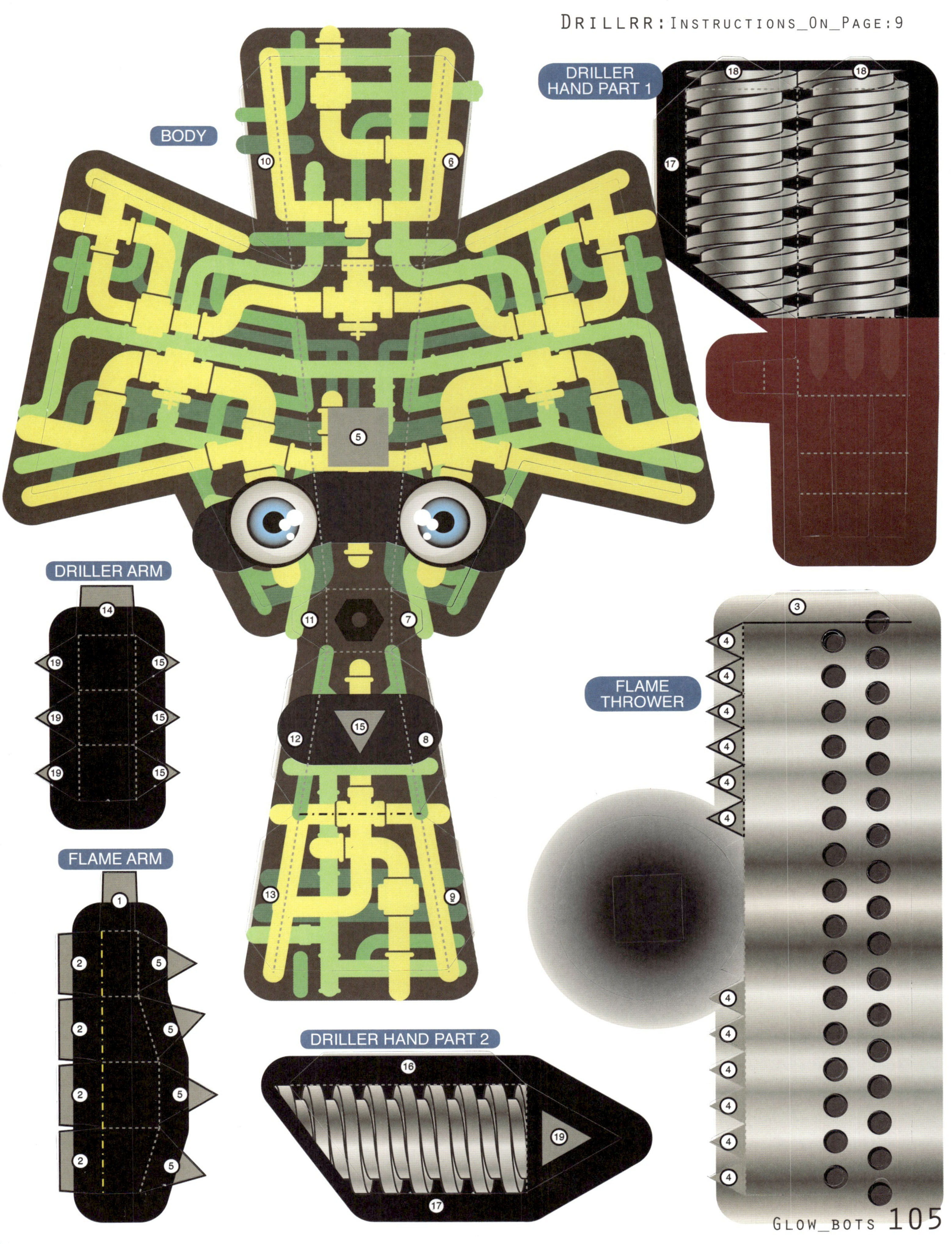

DRILLER HAND PART 1
18
18
17
BODY
10
6
5
11
7
15
12
8
13
9
DRILLER ARM
14
19
15
19
15
19
15
FLAME ARM
1
2
5
2
5
2
5
2
5
DRILLER HAND PART 2
16
19
17
FLAME THROWER
3
4
4
4
4
4
4
4
4
4
4
4
4

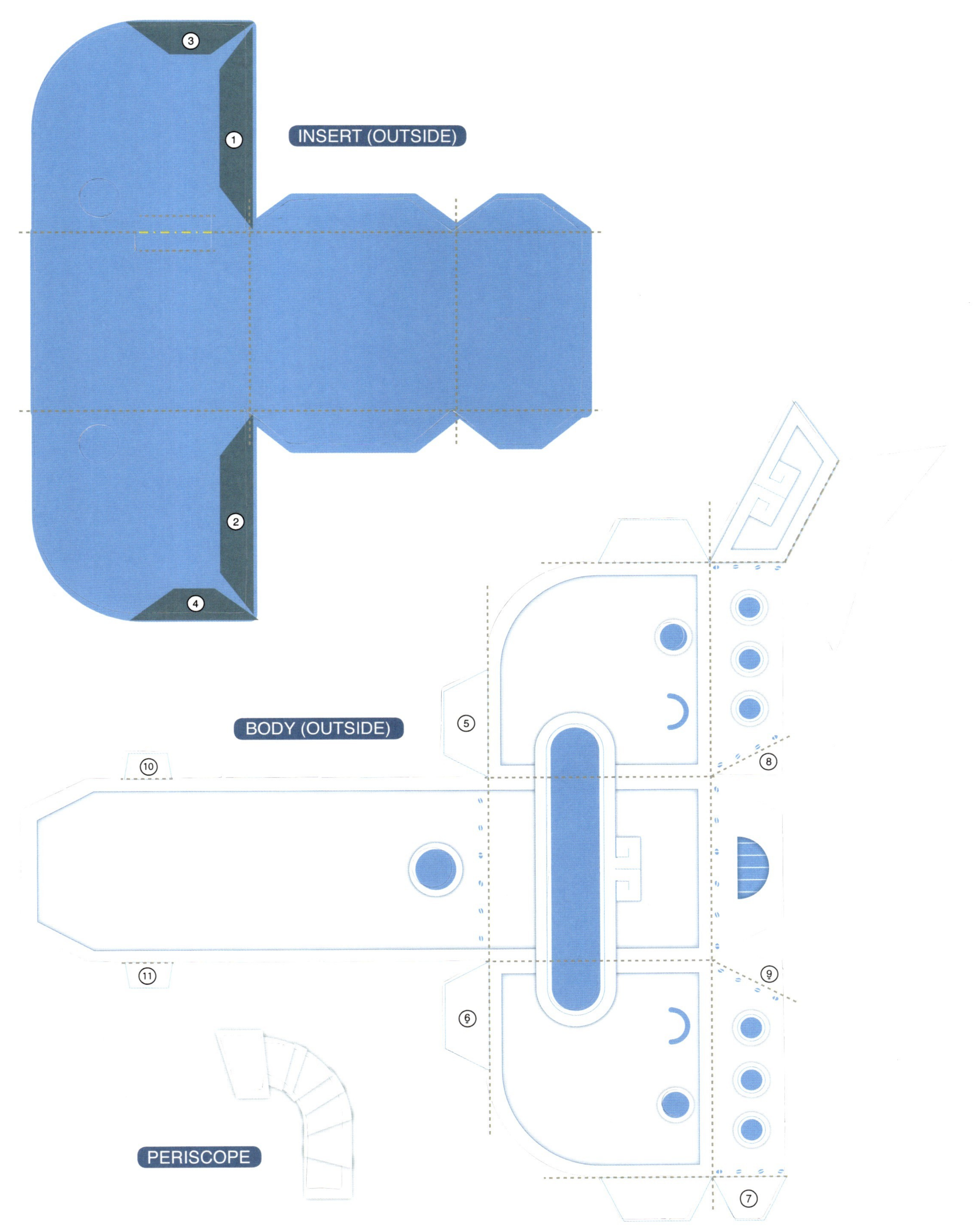
INSERT (OUTSIDE)
3
1
2
4
BODY (OUTSIDE)
5
6
7
8
9
10
11
PERISCOPE

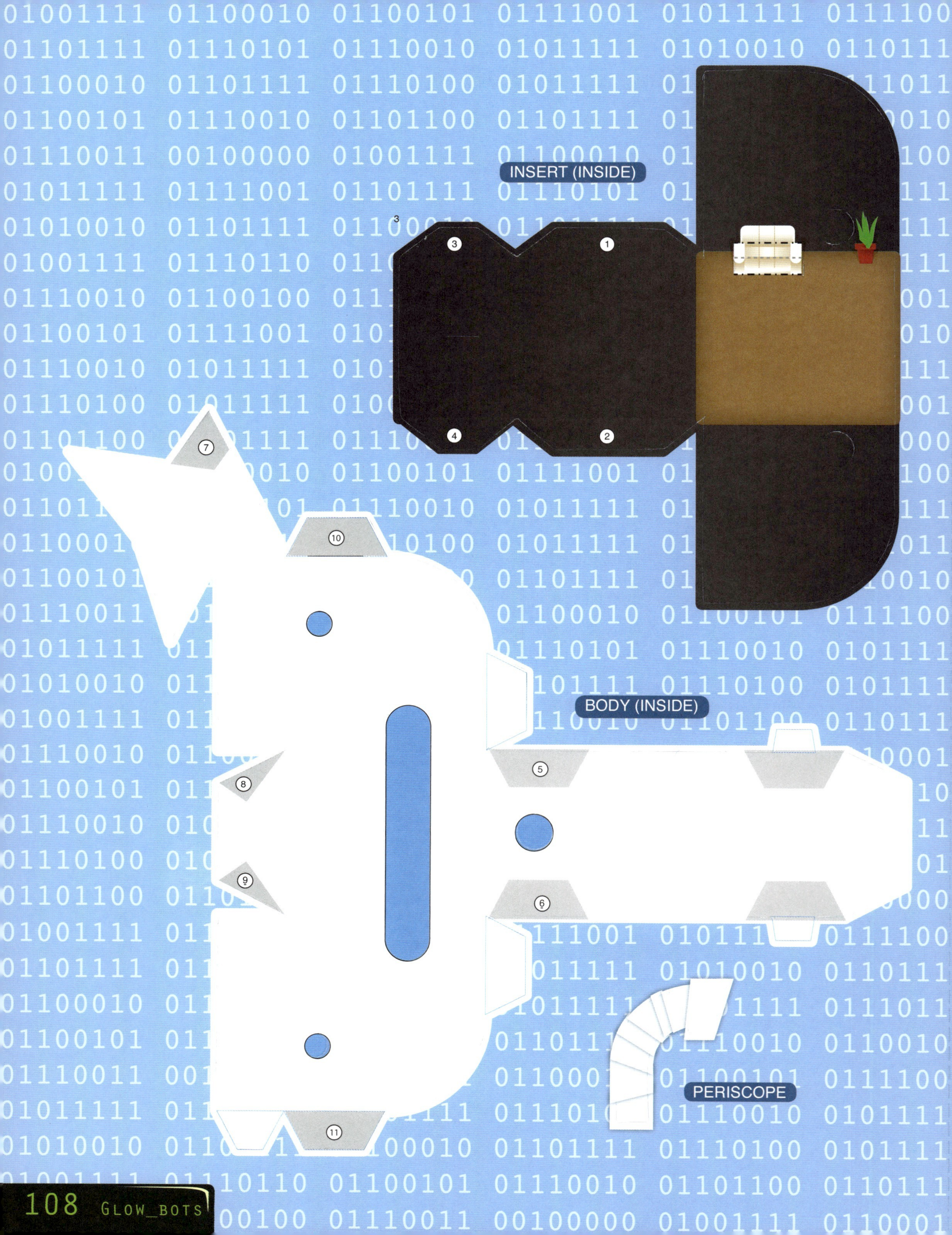
INSERT (INSIDE)
BODY (INSIDE)
PERISCOPE

RIGHT ARM
BODY
SPACE ROCKS
SPACE ROCKS
LEFT ARM
BRAIN
VSVN
BAART
1
2
4
5
6
7
8
9
10
11
12

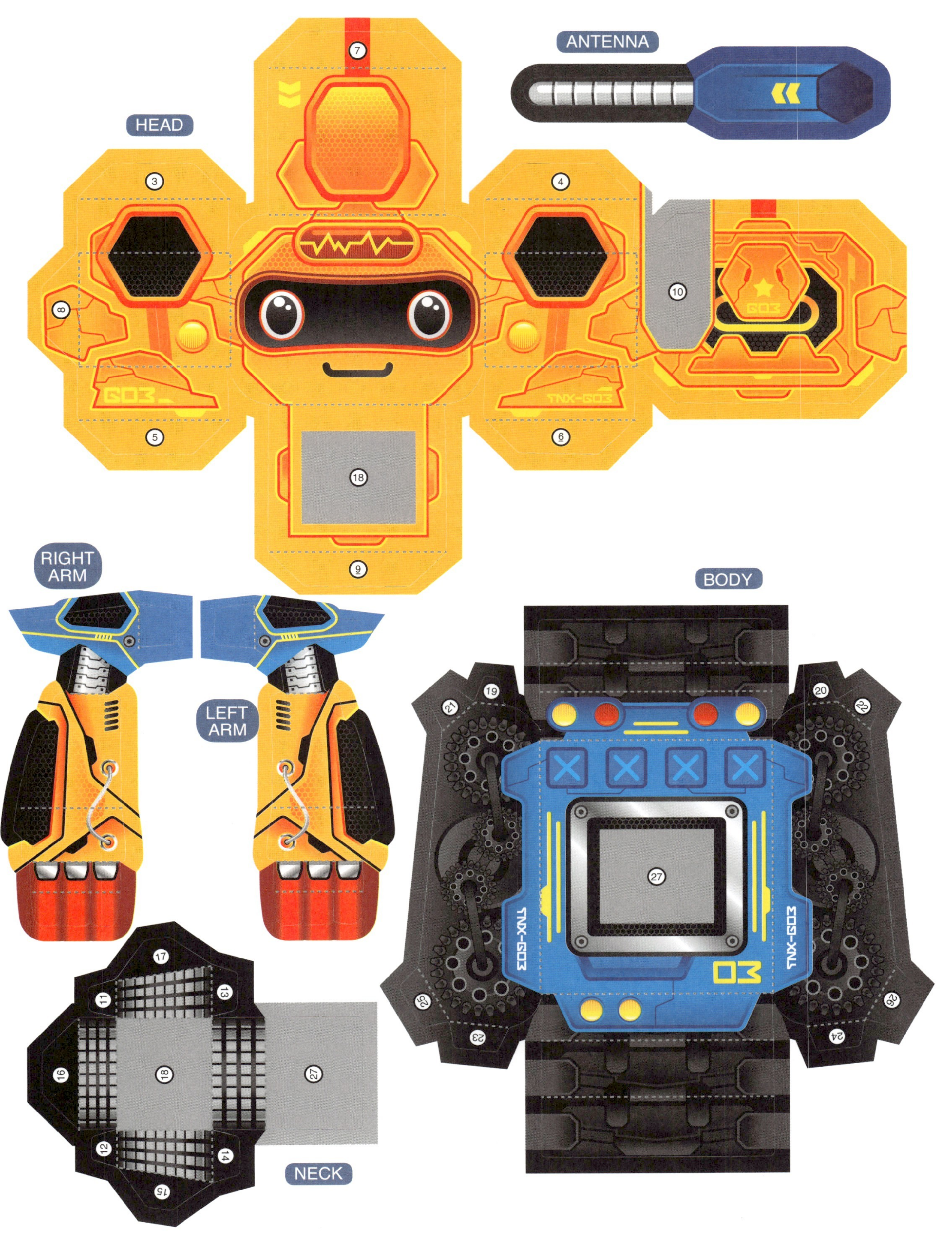

ANTENNA
HEAD
RIGHT ARM
LEFT ARM
BODY
NECK
TNX-G03
03

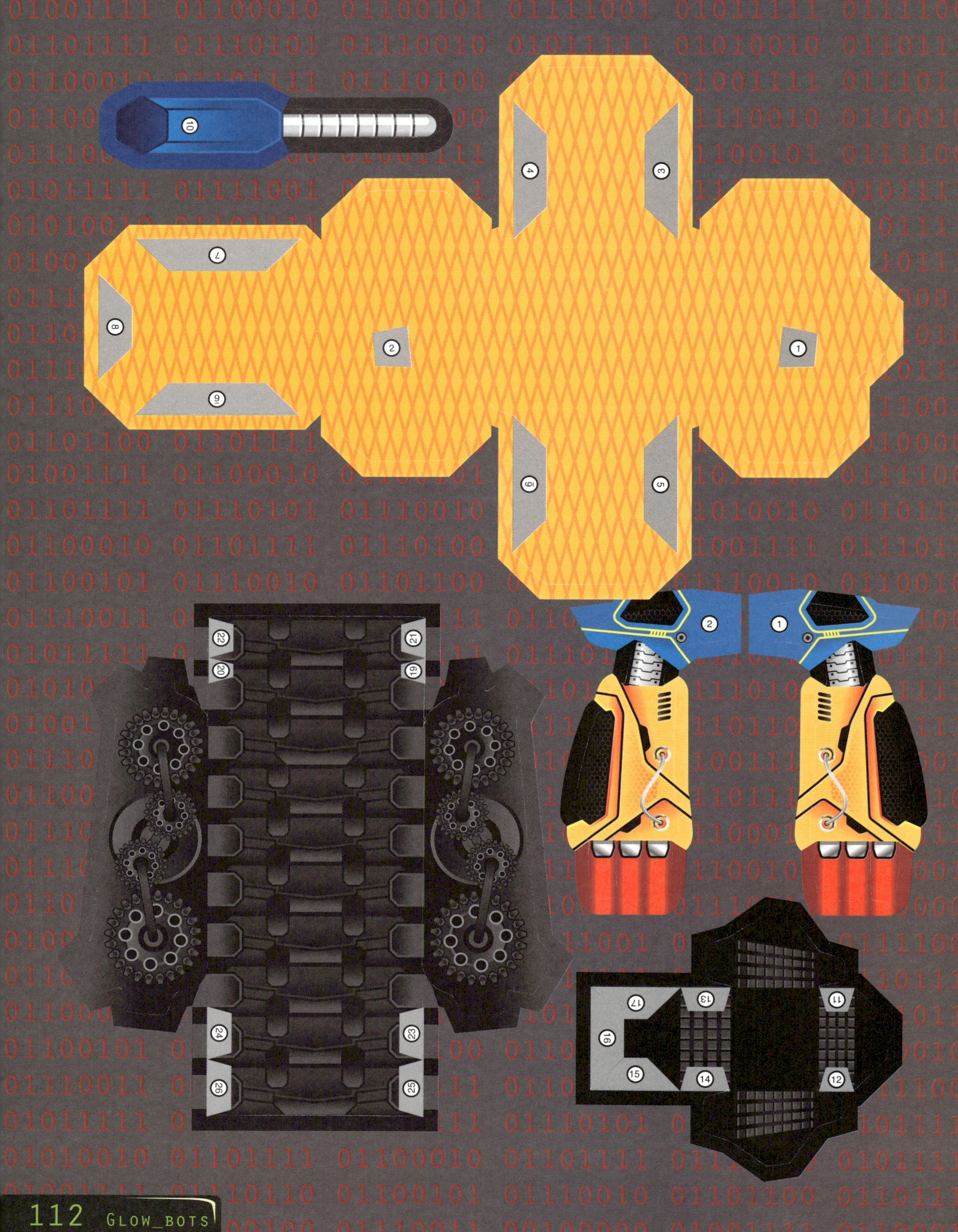

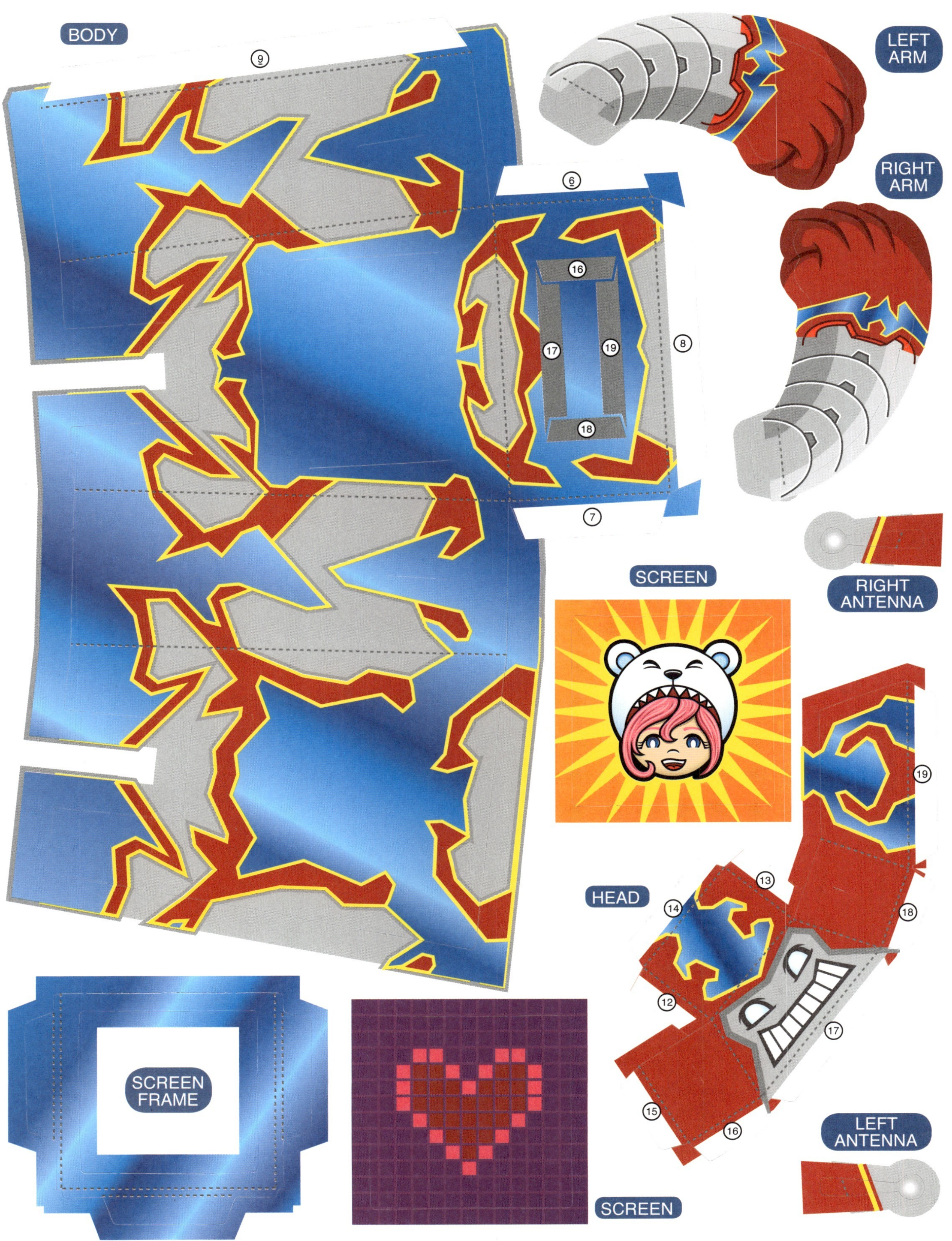

BODY
9
6
16
17
19
18
8
7
LEFT ARM
RIGHT ARM
RIGHT ANTENNA
SCREEN
HEAD
13
14
18
19
12
17
15
16
LEFT ANTENNA
SCREEN FRAME
SCREEN

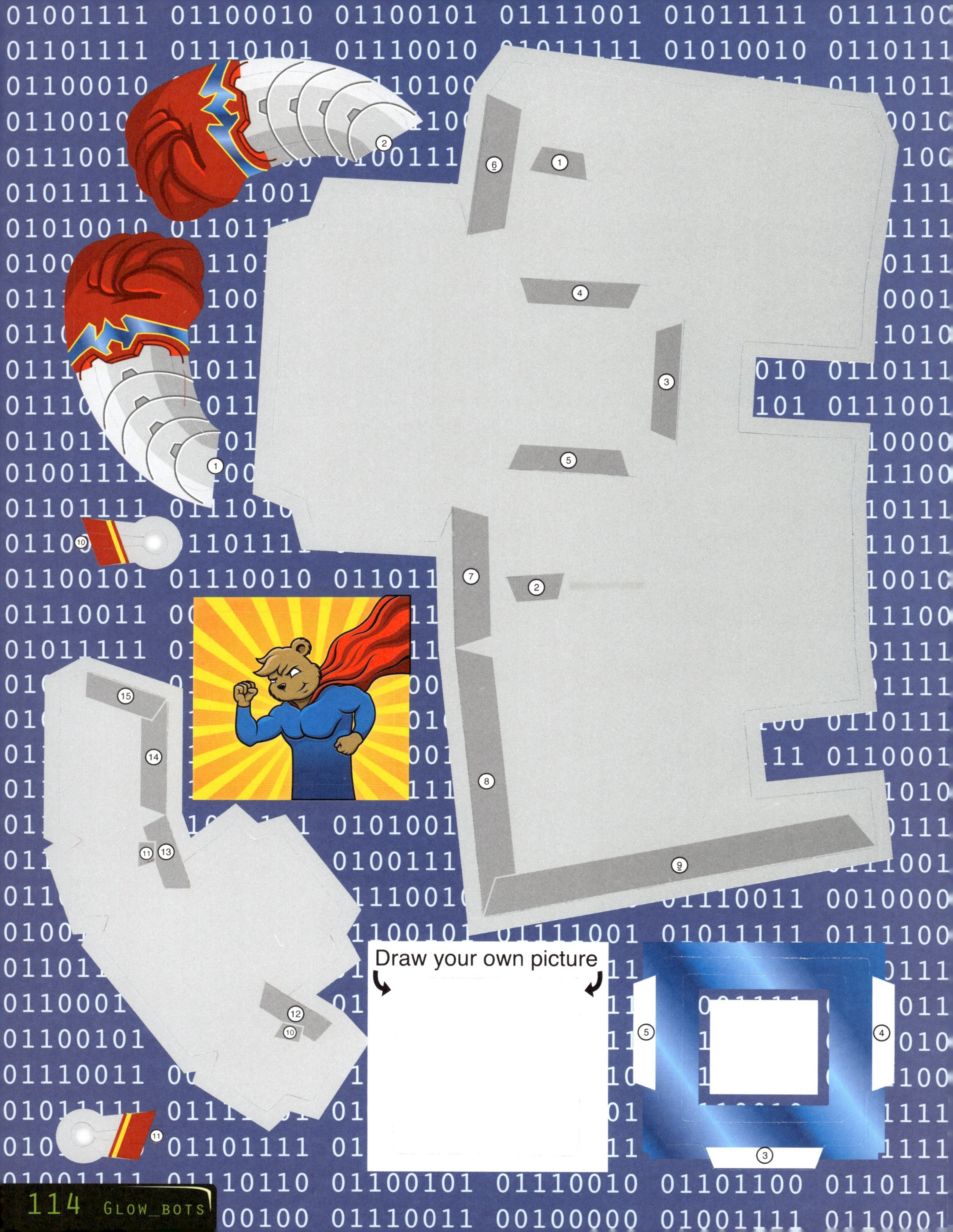
Draw your own picture

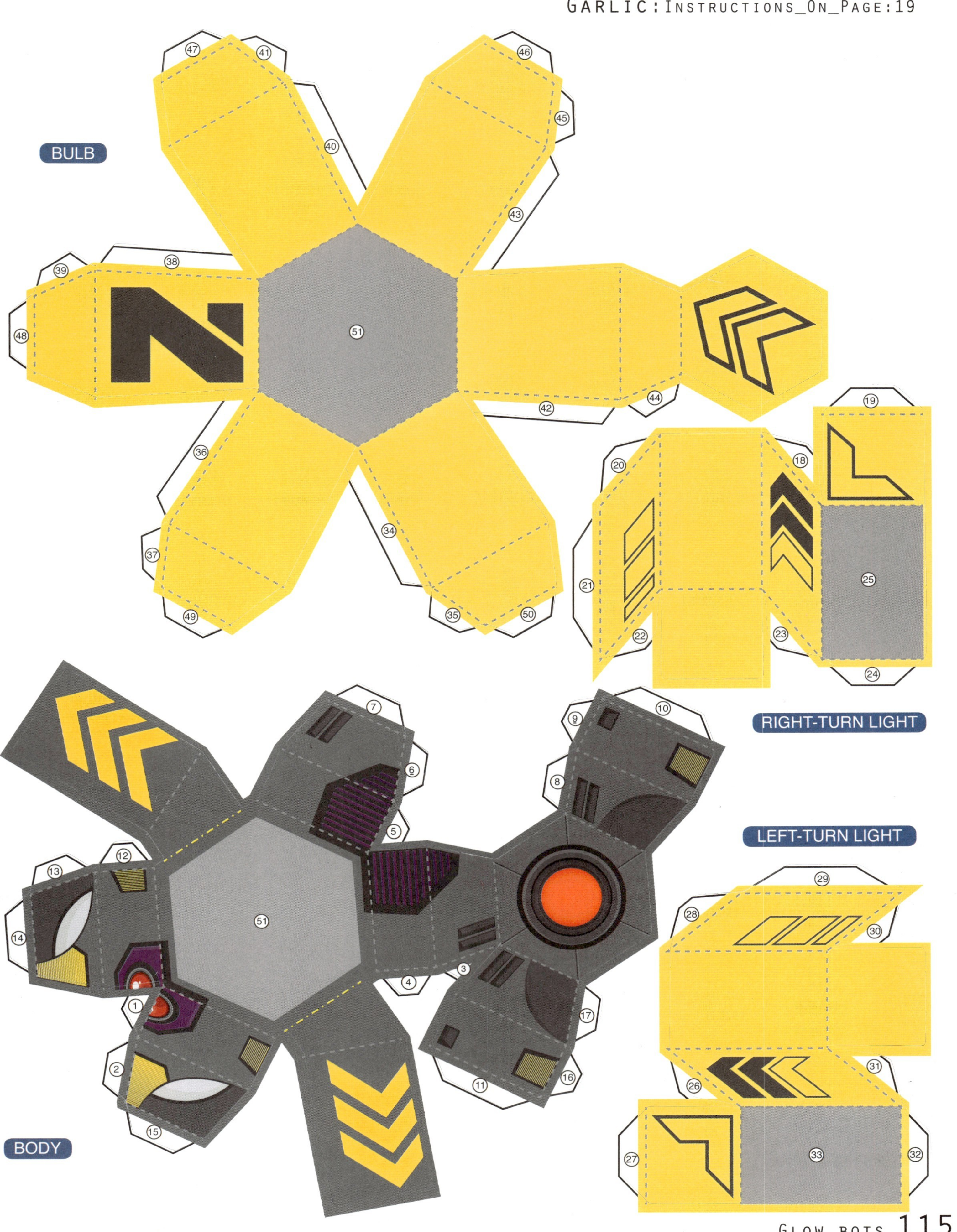
BULB
RIGHT-TURN LIGHT
LEFT-TURN LIGHT
BODY

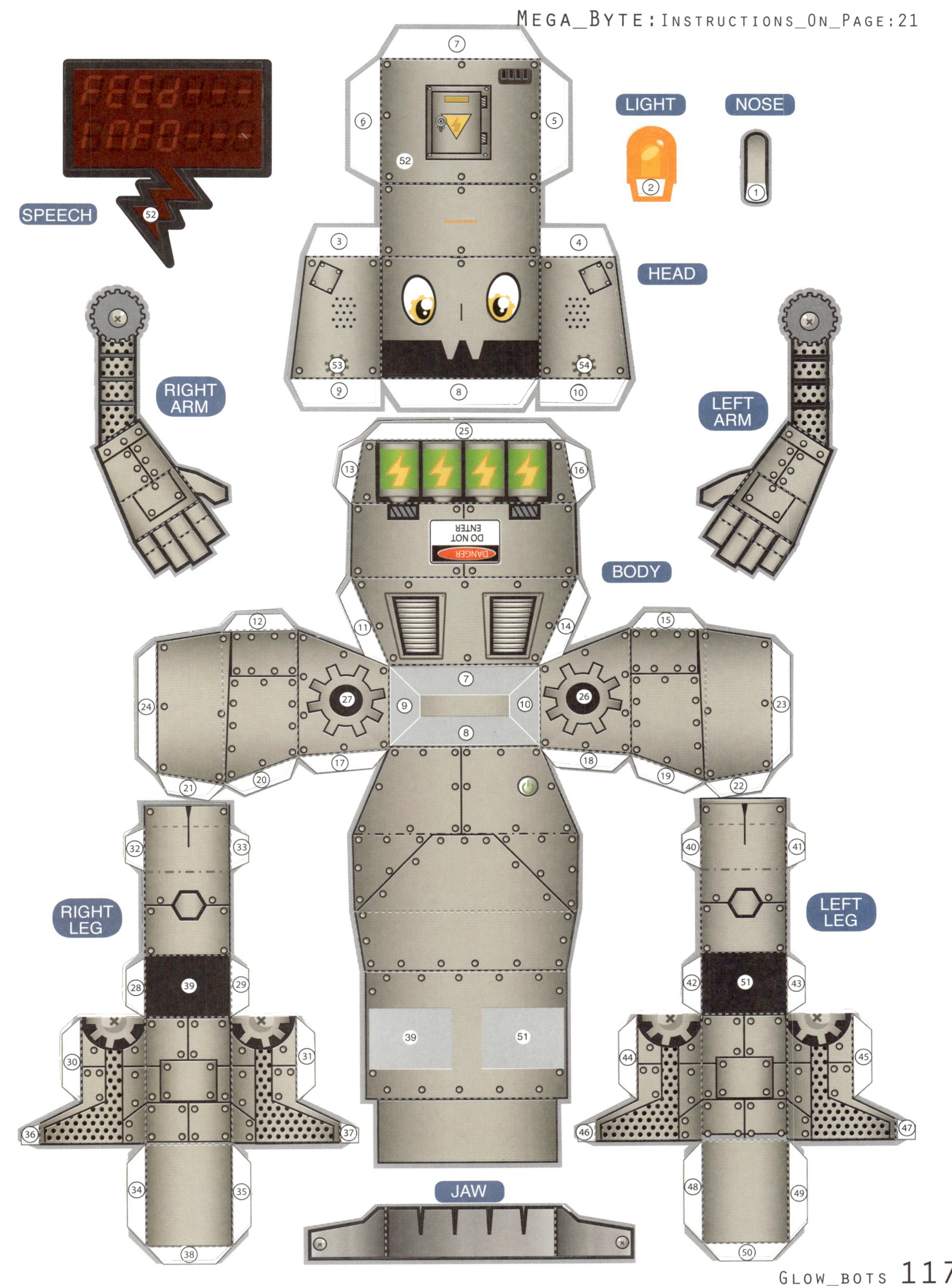
SPEECH
LIGHT
NOSE
HEAD
RIGHT ARM
LEFT ARM
BODY
DANGER
DO NOT ENTER
RIGHT LEG
LEFT LEG
JAW

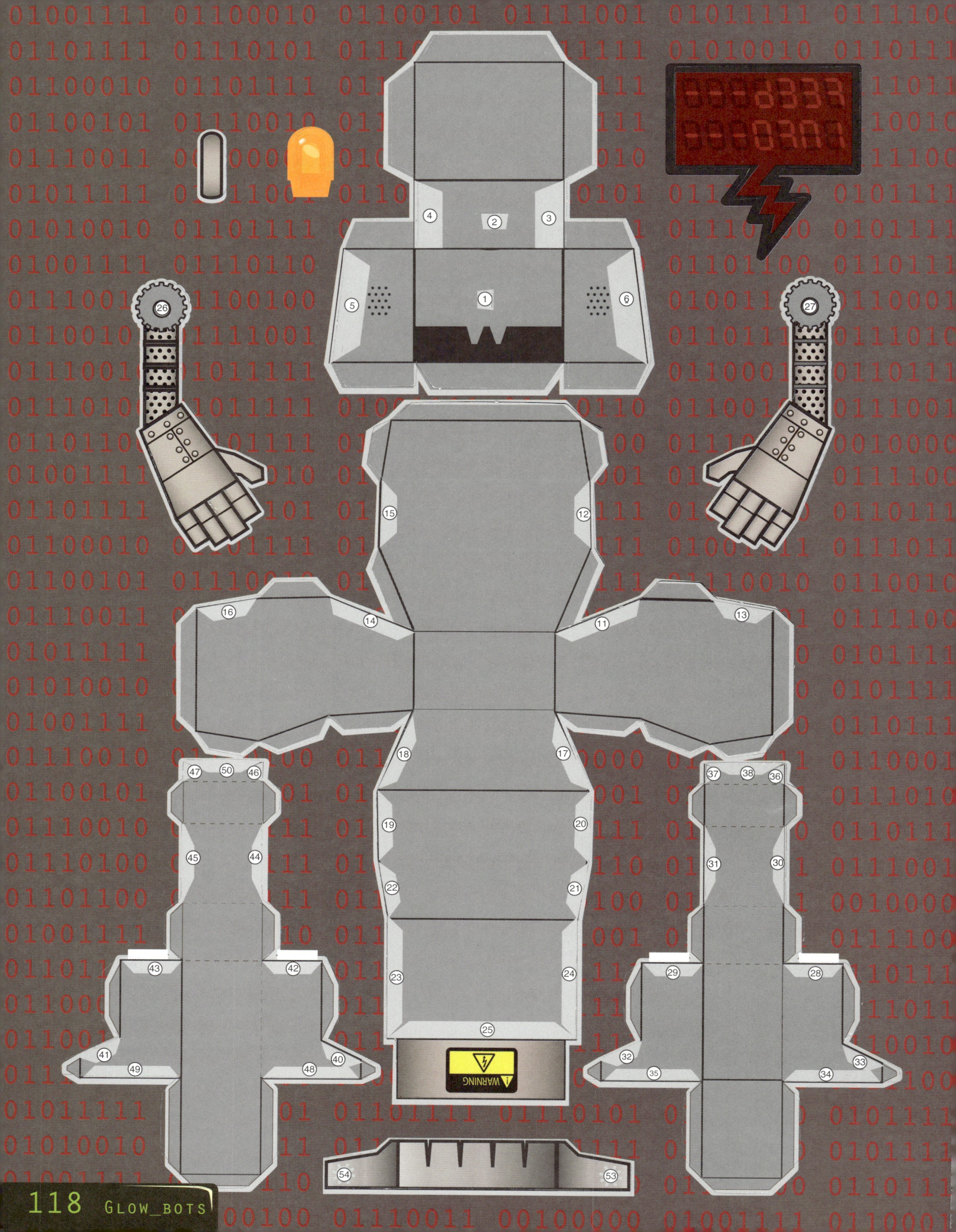

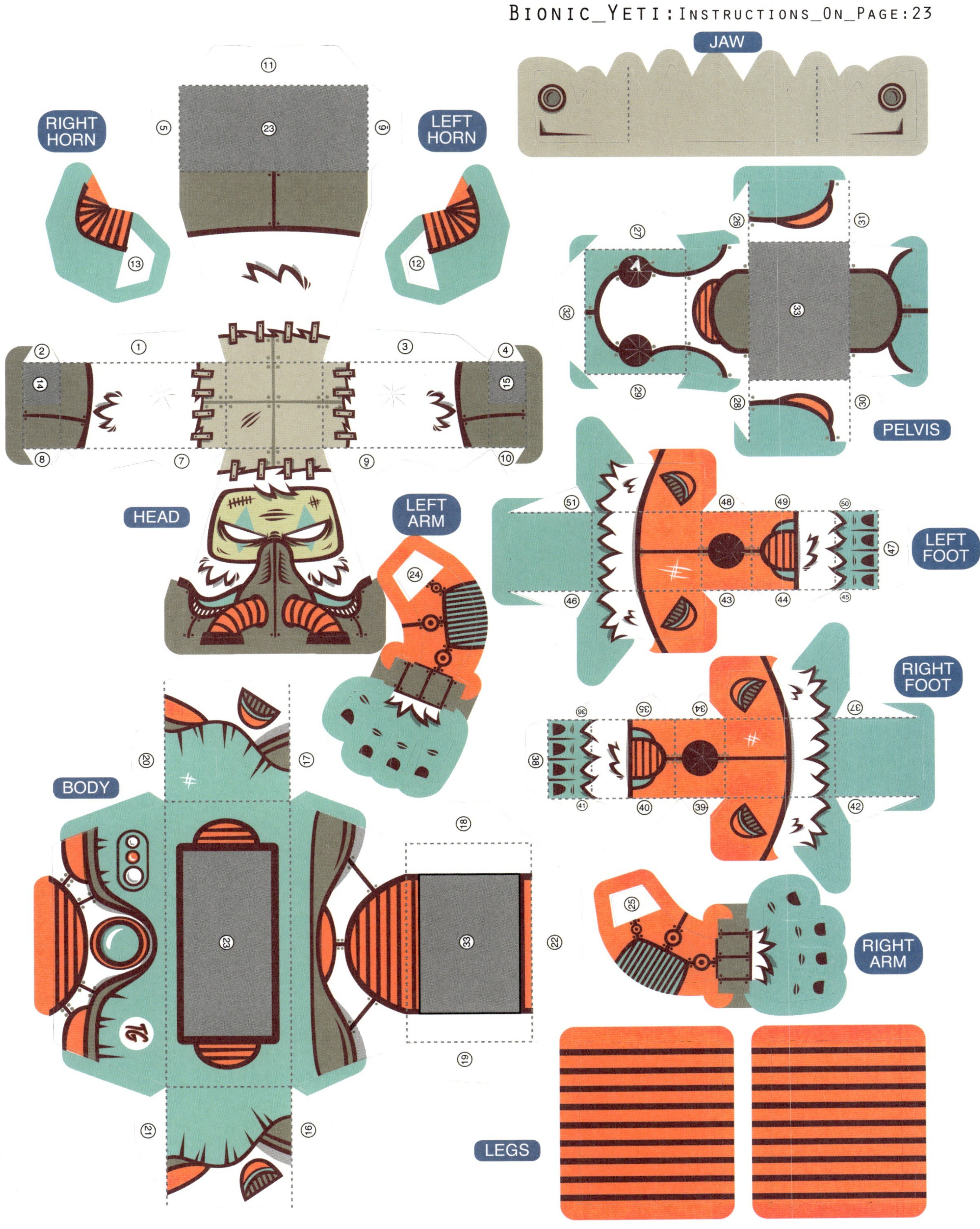
JAW
RIGHT HORN
LEFT HORN
PELVIS
HEAD
LEFT ARM
LEFT FOOT
RIGHT FOOT
BODY
RIGHT ARM
LEGS

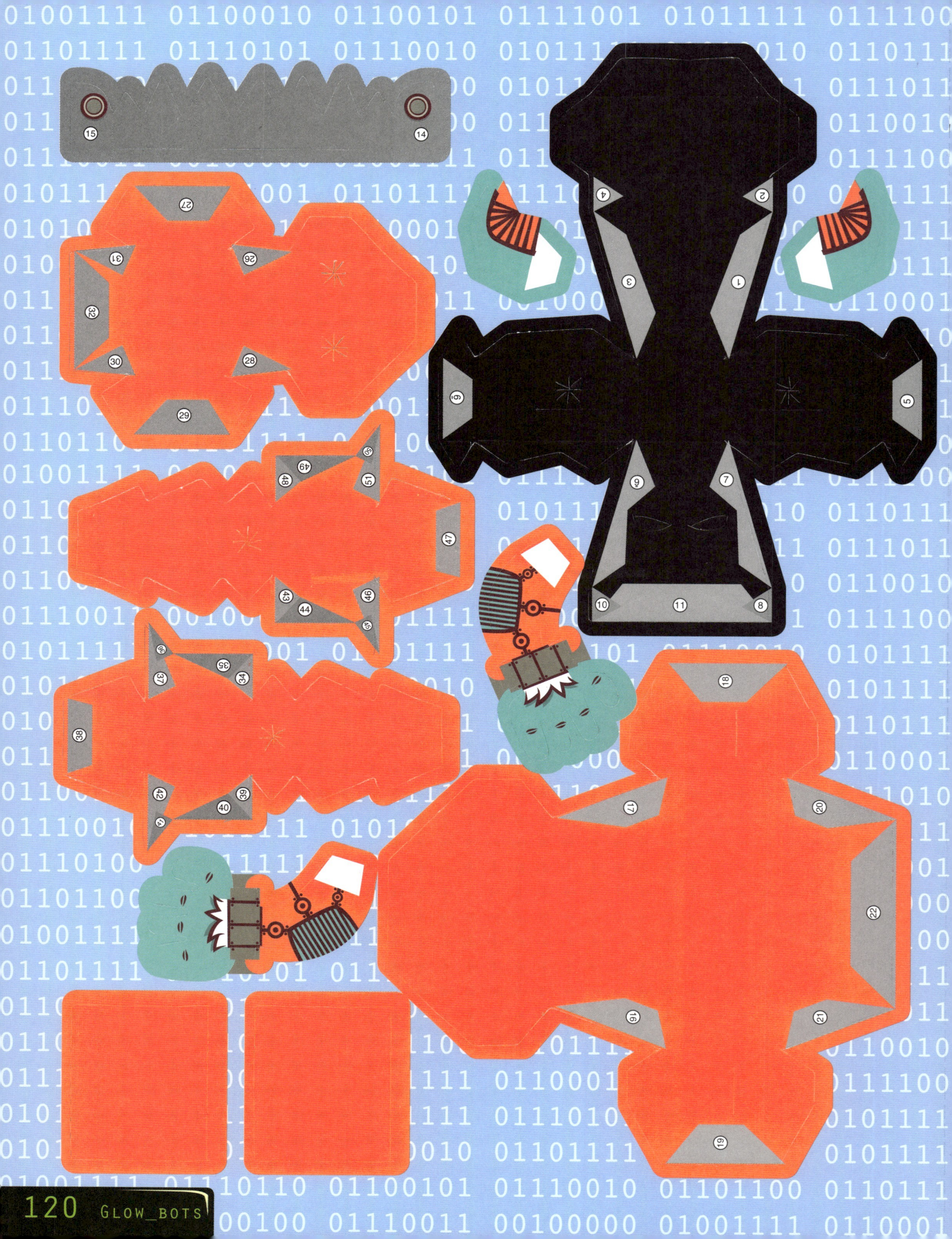

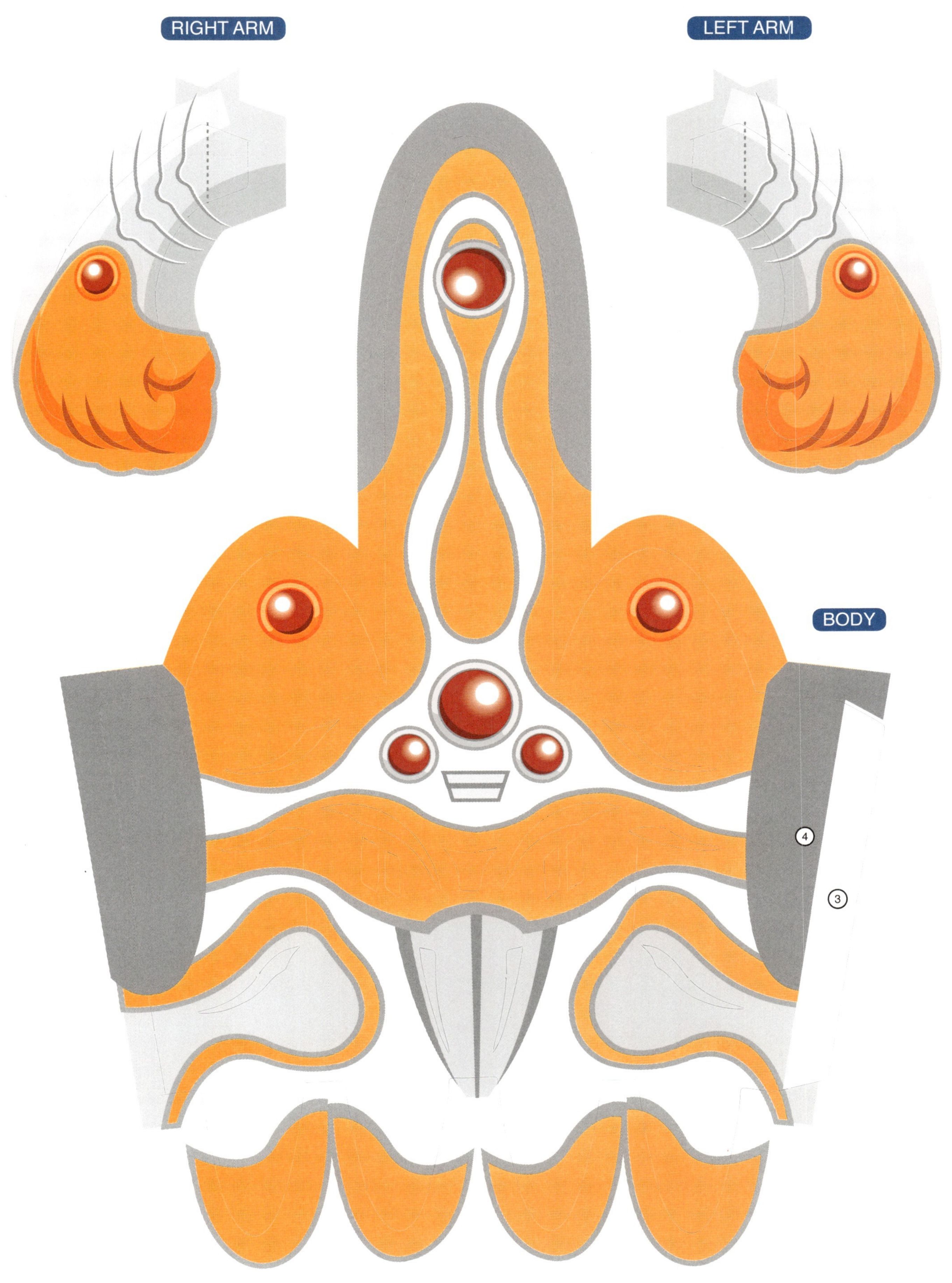
RIGHT ARM
LEFT ARM
BODY
4
3

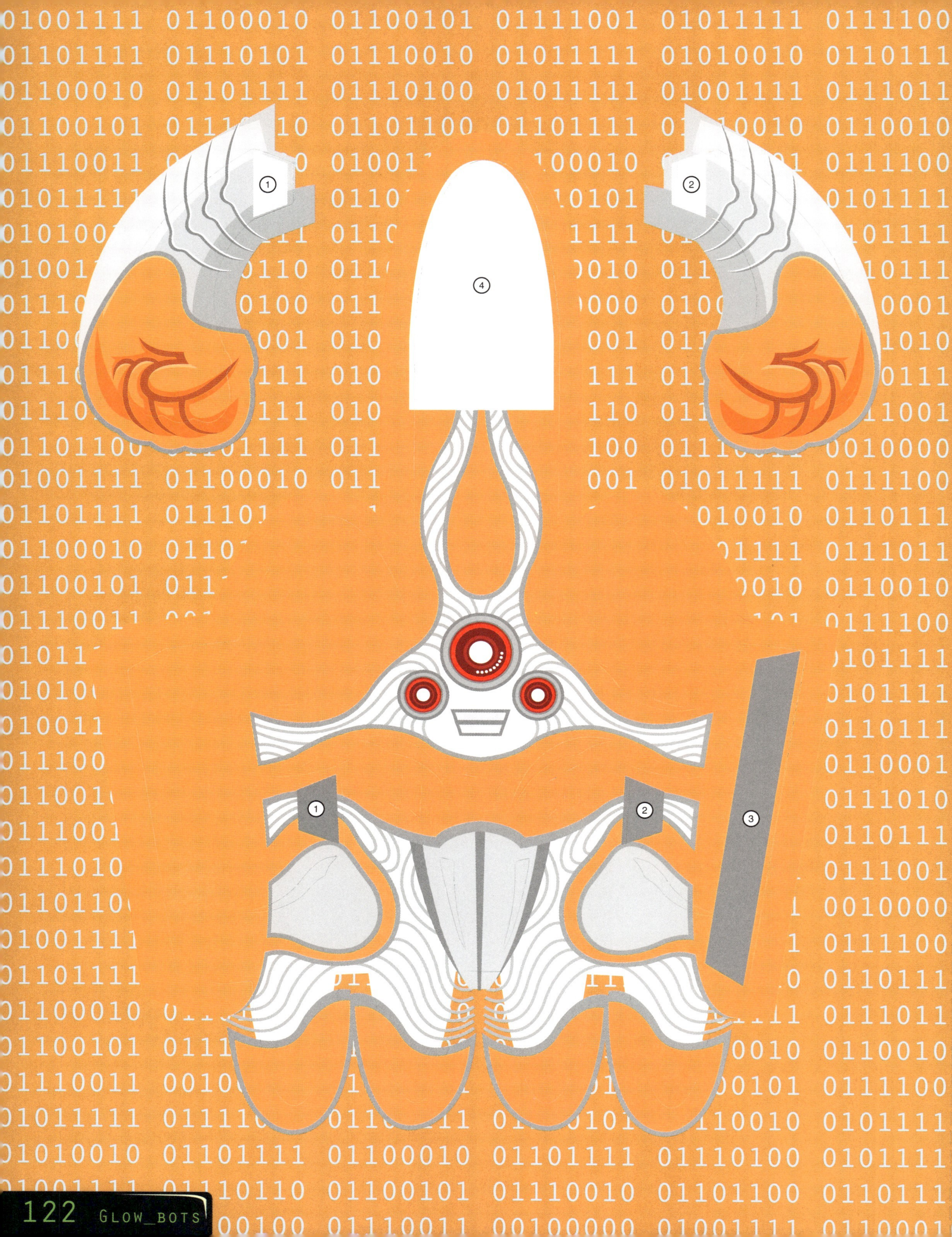

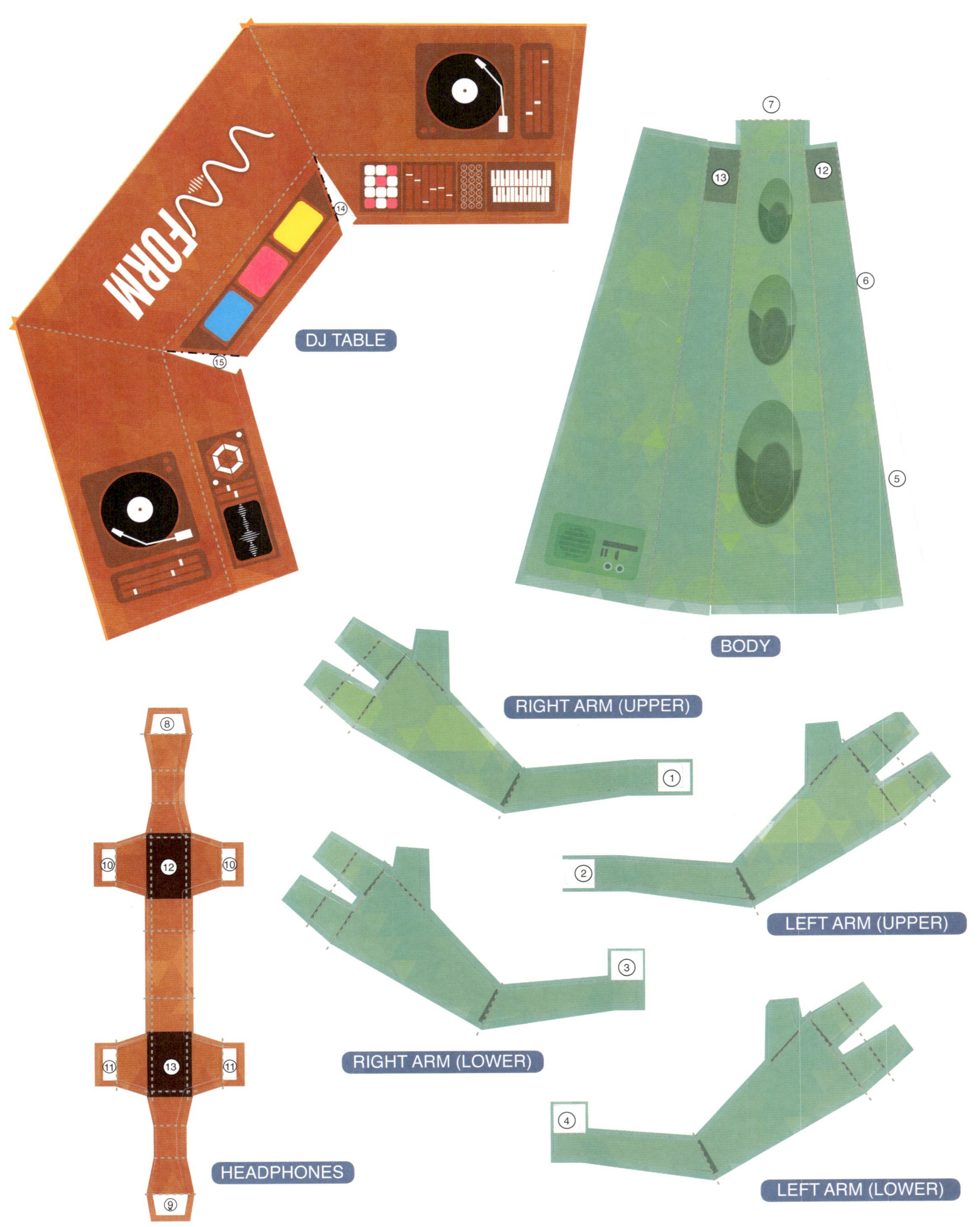

DJ TABLE
WAVFORM
BODY
RIGHT ARM (UPPER)
LEFT ARM (UPPER)
RIGHT ARM (LOWER)
LEFT ARM (LOWER)
HEADPHONES

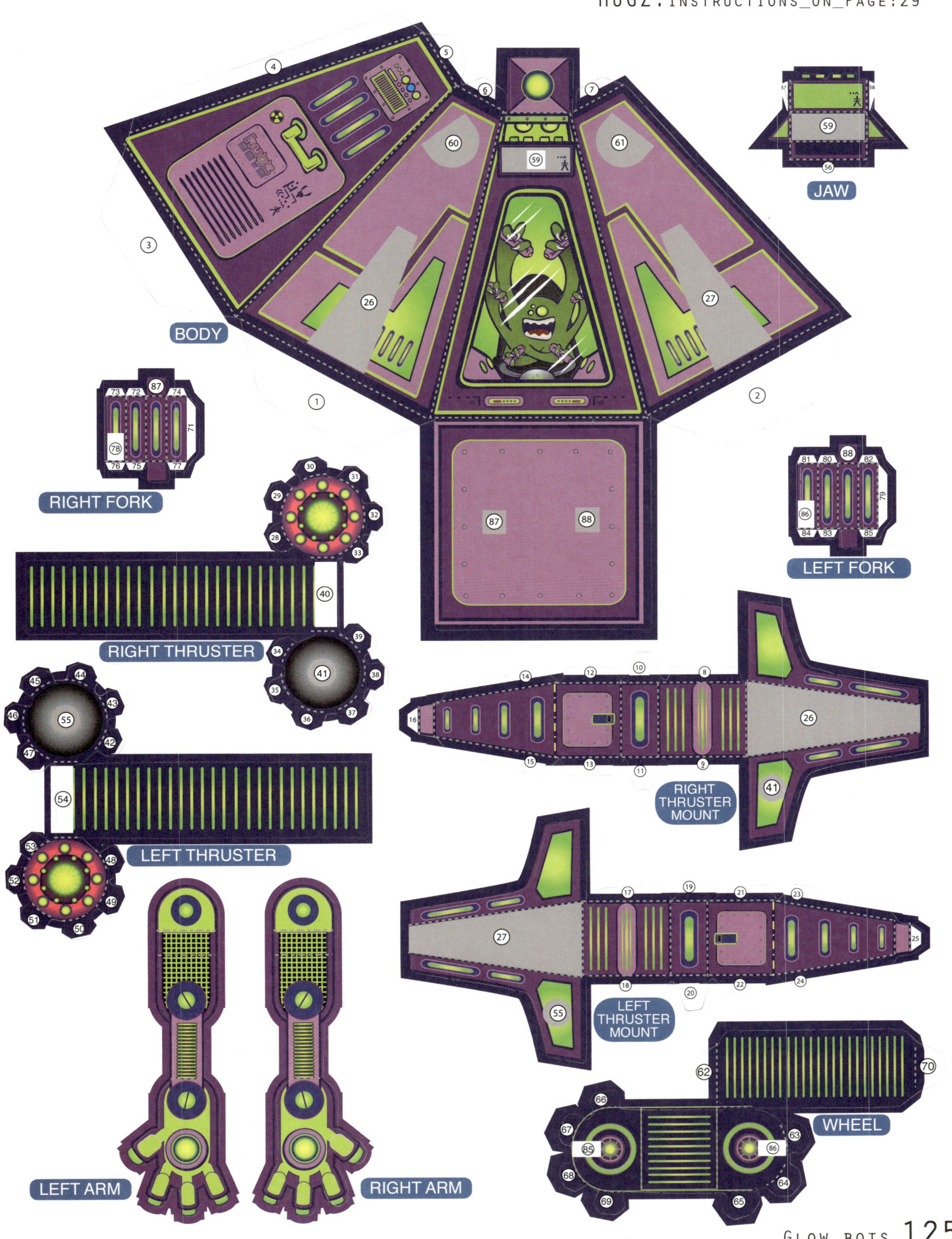
BODY
JAW
RIGHT FORK
LEFT FORK
RIGHT THRUSTER
LEFT THRUSTER
RIGHT THRUSTER MOUNT
LEFT THRUSTER MOUNT
WHEEL
LEFT ARM
RIGHT ARM

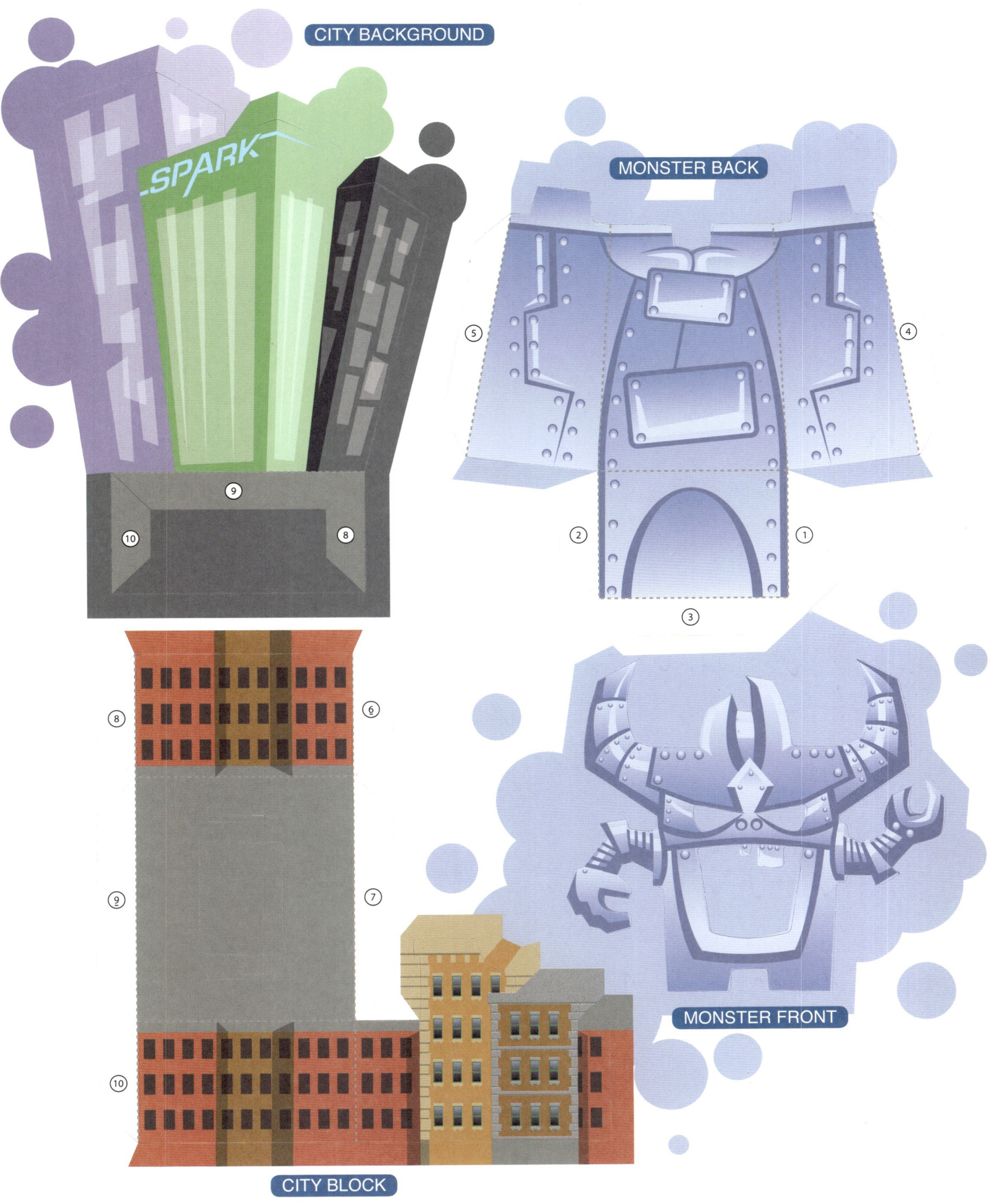
CITY BACKGROUND
SPARK
9
10
8
MONSTER BACK
5
4
2
1
3
8
6
9
7
10
MONSTER FRONT
CITY BLOCK

1
2
3
4
5
6
7

BODY
45
25
26
27
17
24
23
32
37
22
18
21
19
20
RED PYRAMID
5
4
1
3
2
LOWER BODY
6
41
42
7
16
40
43
8
15
9
14
10
13
39
44
11
12
38
HEAD
45
28
33
29
32
30
31
36
35
37
34
RIGHT ARM
LEFT ARM

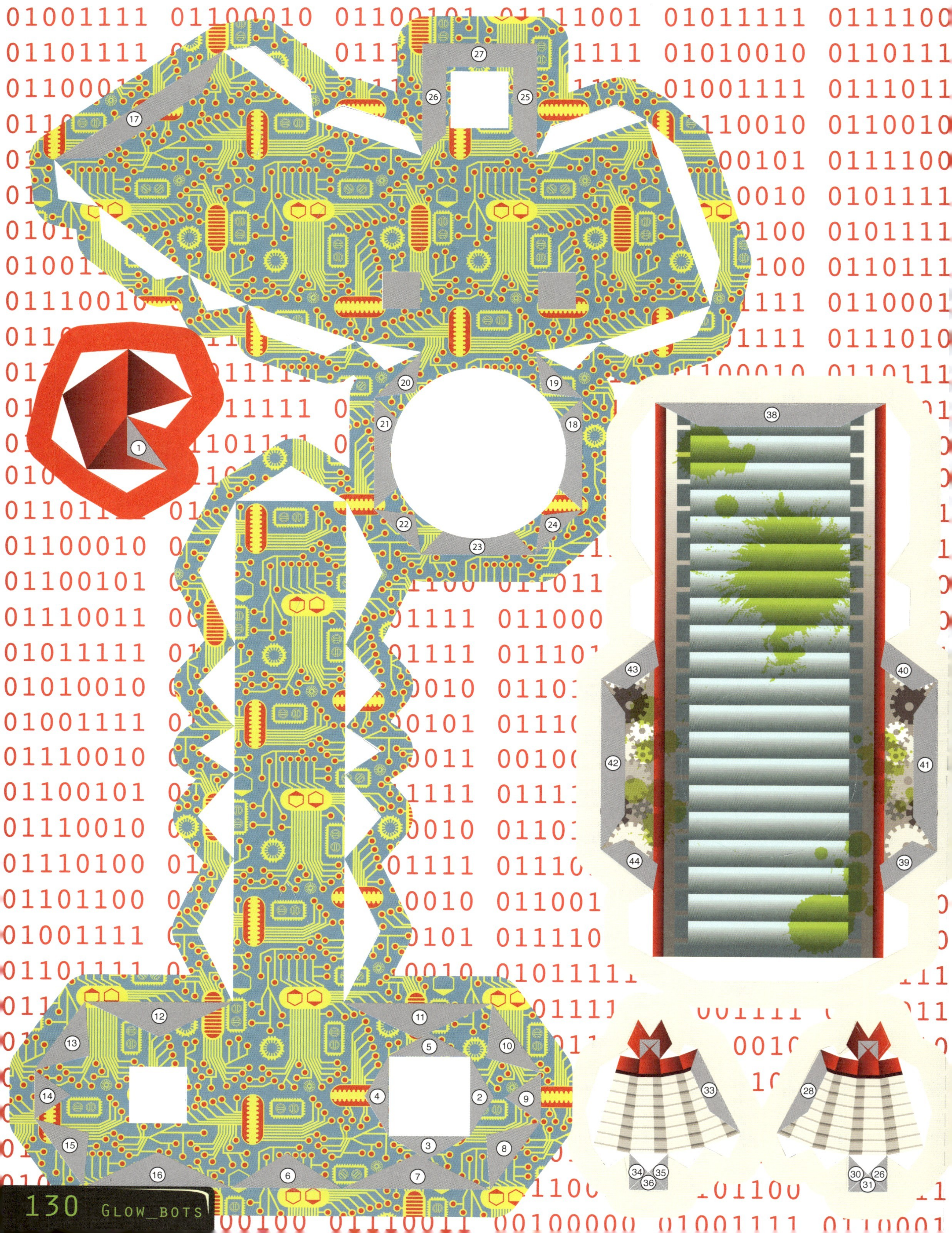

CAP EDGE
ARM A
FOOT A
BODY
CAP TOP
FOOT B
CAP BOTTOM
ARM B
ERR 07

JOINT B

BOTTOM

BRAINS

JOINT A

LEGS

HELMET

JOINT B BOTTOM

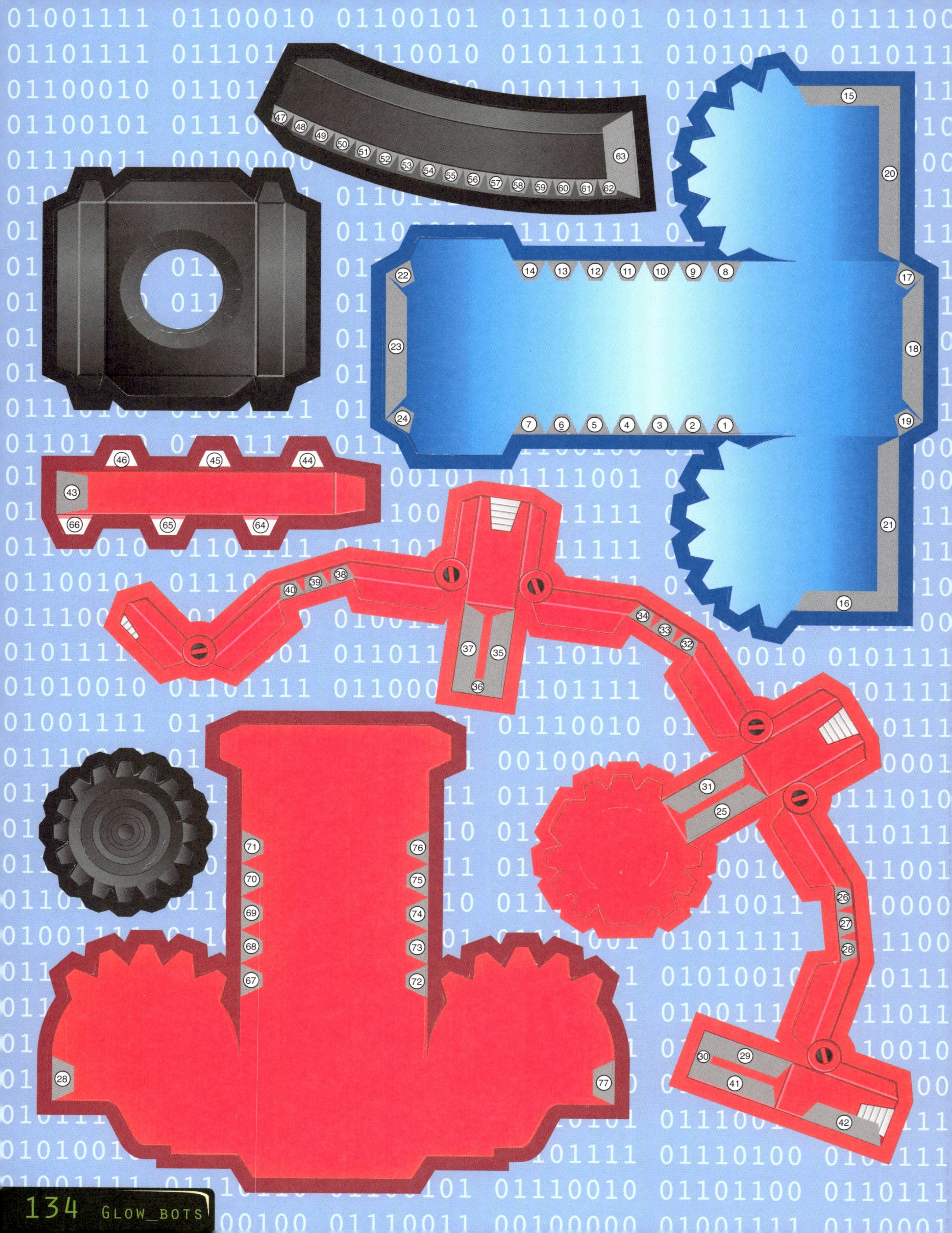

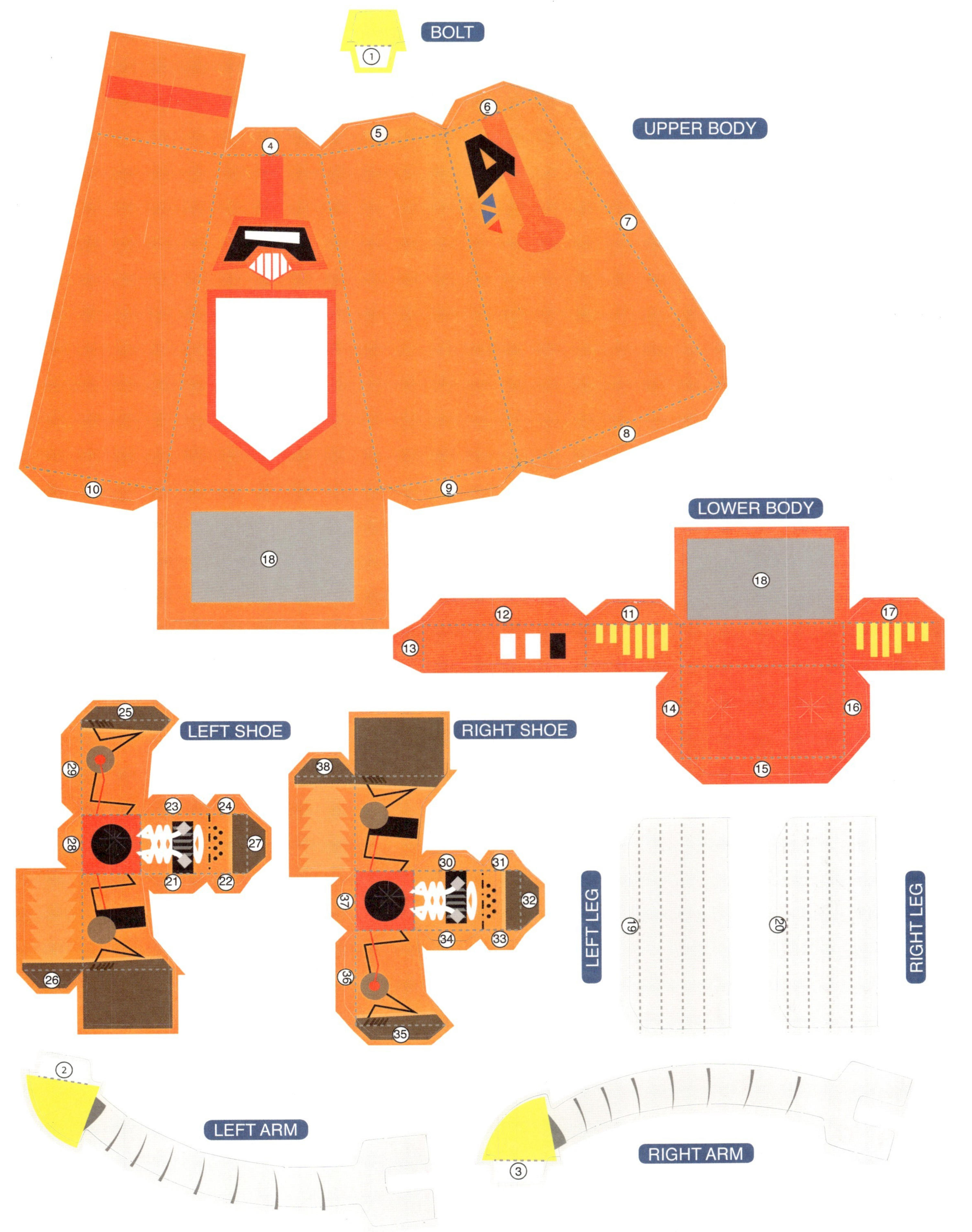
BOLT
UPPER BODY
LOWER BODY
LEFT SHOE
RIGHT SHOE
LEFT LEG
RIGHT LEG
LEFT ARM
RIGHT ARM

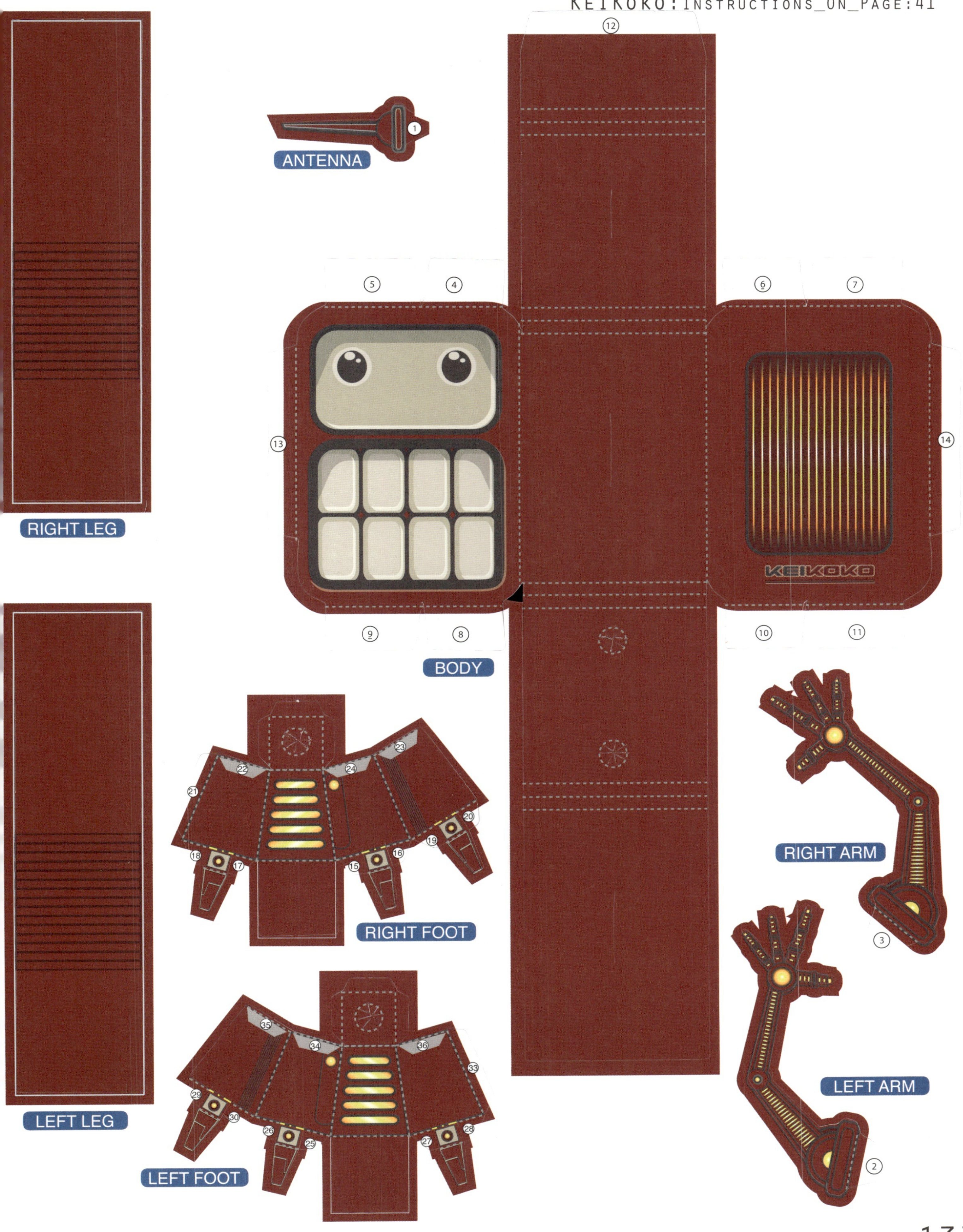

ANTENNA
RIGHT LEG
LEFT LEG
BODY
KEIKOKO
RIGHT FOOT
LEFT FOOT
RIGHT ARM
LEFT ARM
1
2
3
4
5
6
7
8
9
10
11
12
13
14

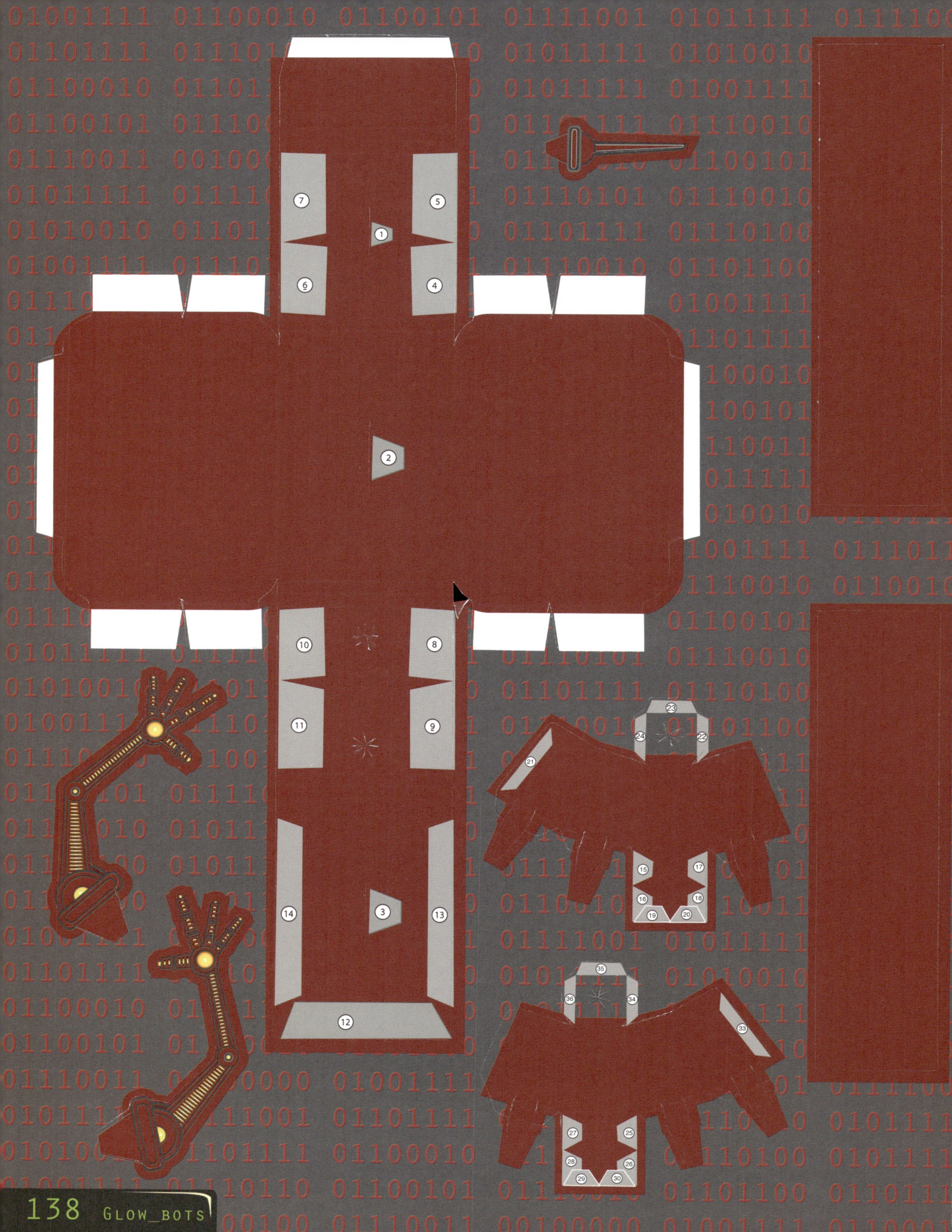

HIPS
ARM A
ARM B
LEG A
BOARDS
BODY
LEG B
LEG C

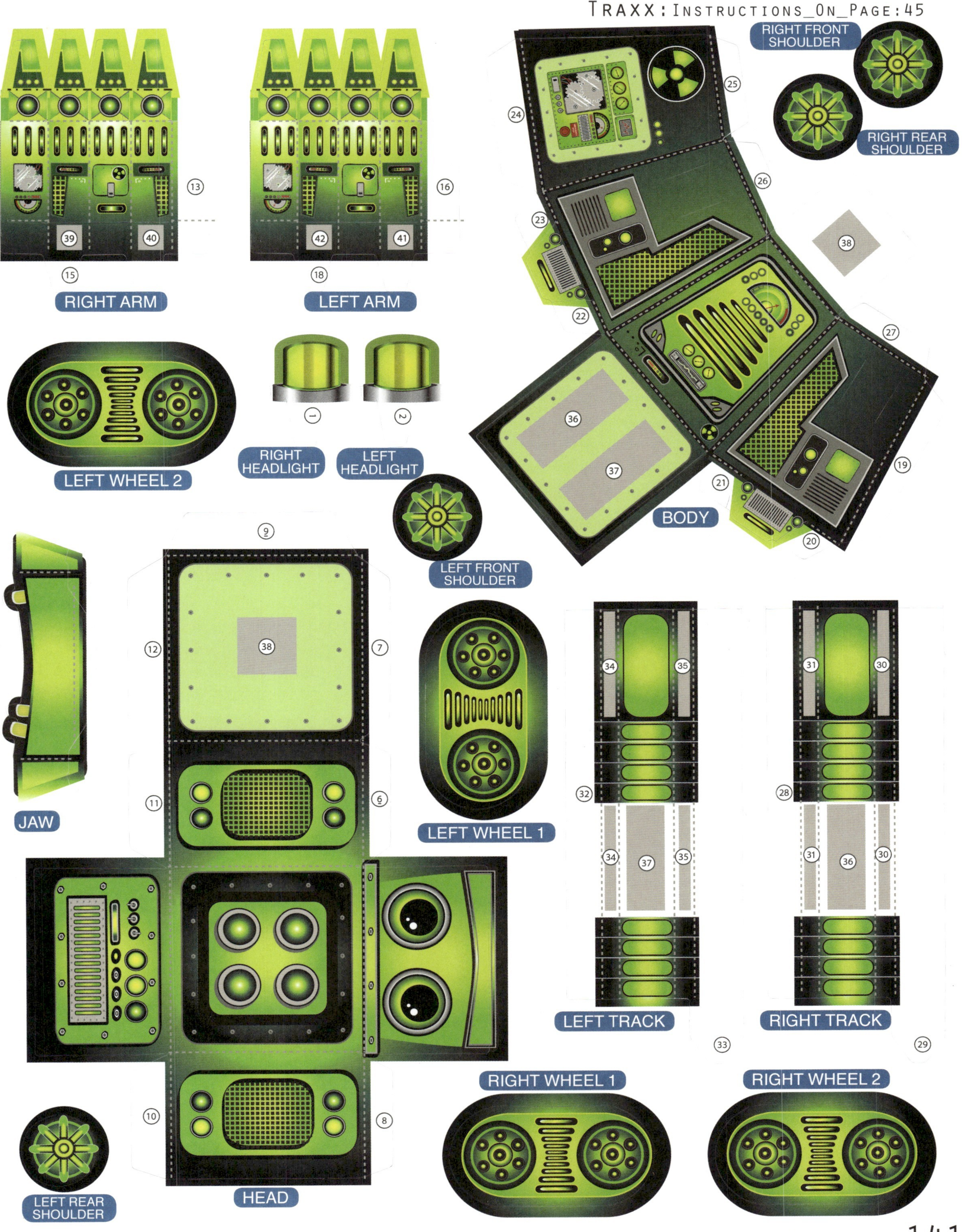
RIGHT ARM
LEFT ARM
RIGHT FRONT SHOULDER
RIGHT REAR SHOULDER
BODY
LEFT WHEEL 2
RIGHT HEADLIGHT
LEFT HEADLIGHT
LEFT FRONT SHOULDER
JAW
LEFT WHEEL 1
LEFT TRACK
RIGHT TRACK
HEAD
LEFT REAR SHOULDER
RIGHT WHEEL 1
RIGHT WHEEL 2

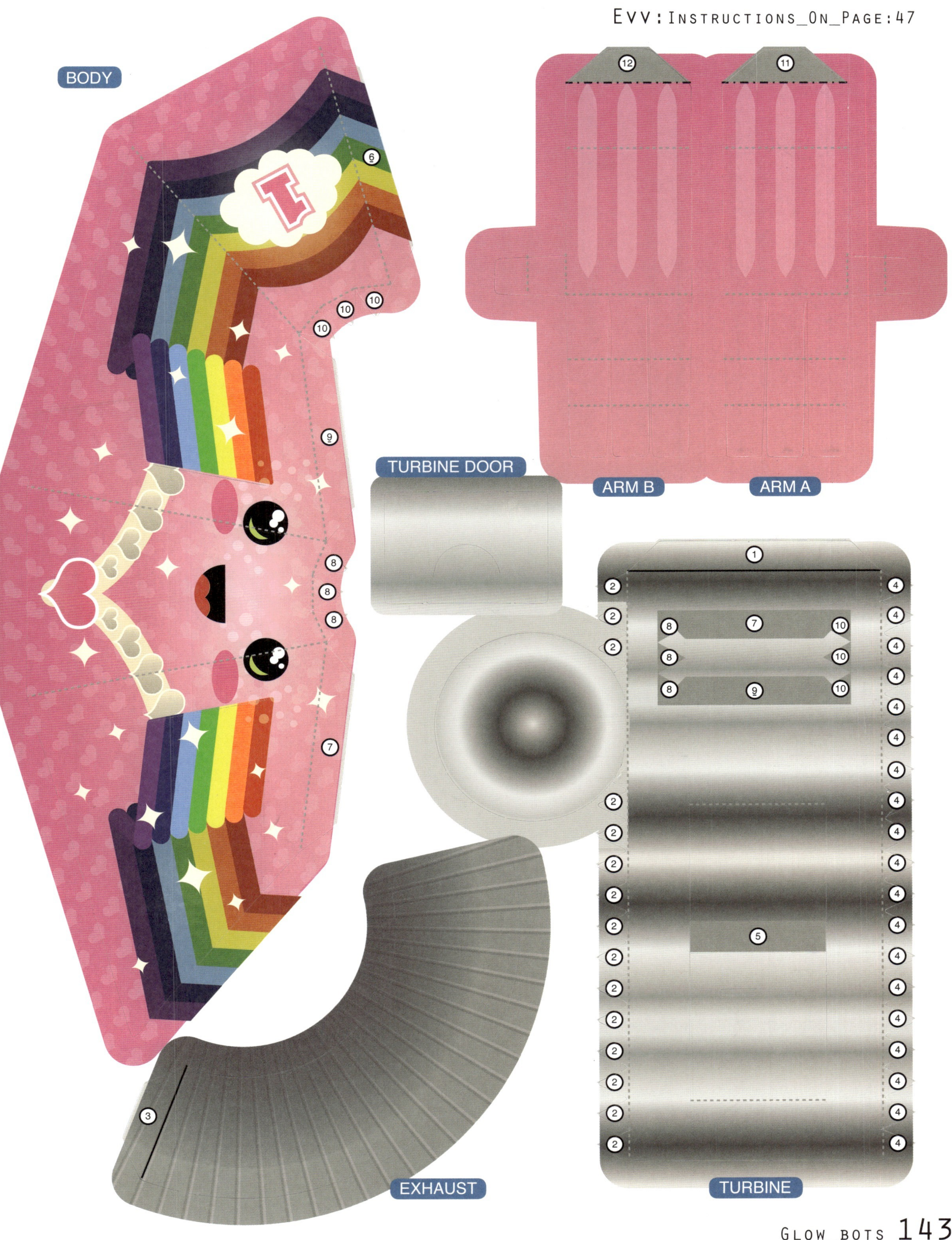
BODY
ARM B
ARM A
TURBINE DOOR
TURBINE
EXHAUST

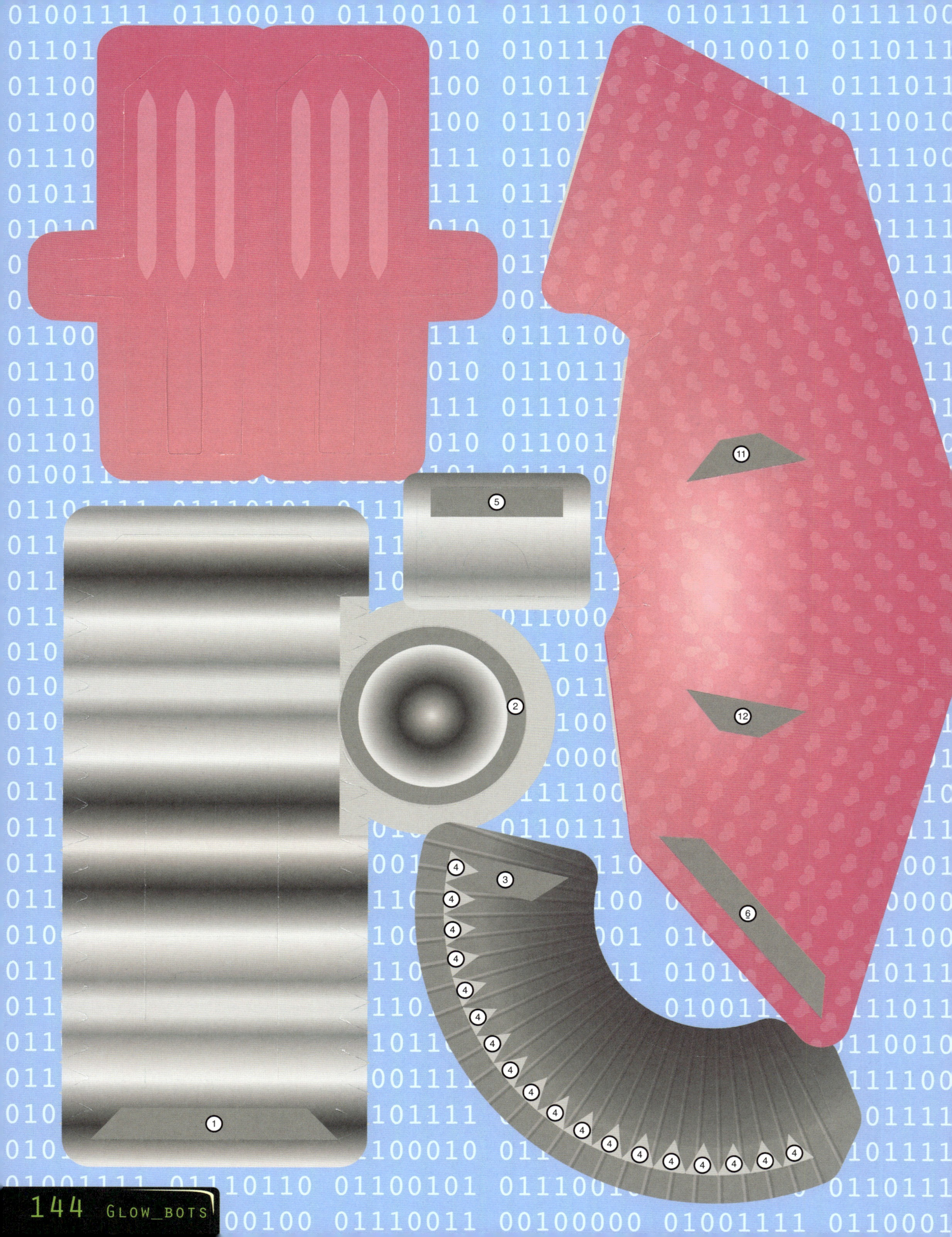

1
2
3
4
5
6
11
12

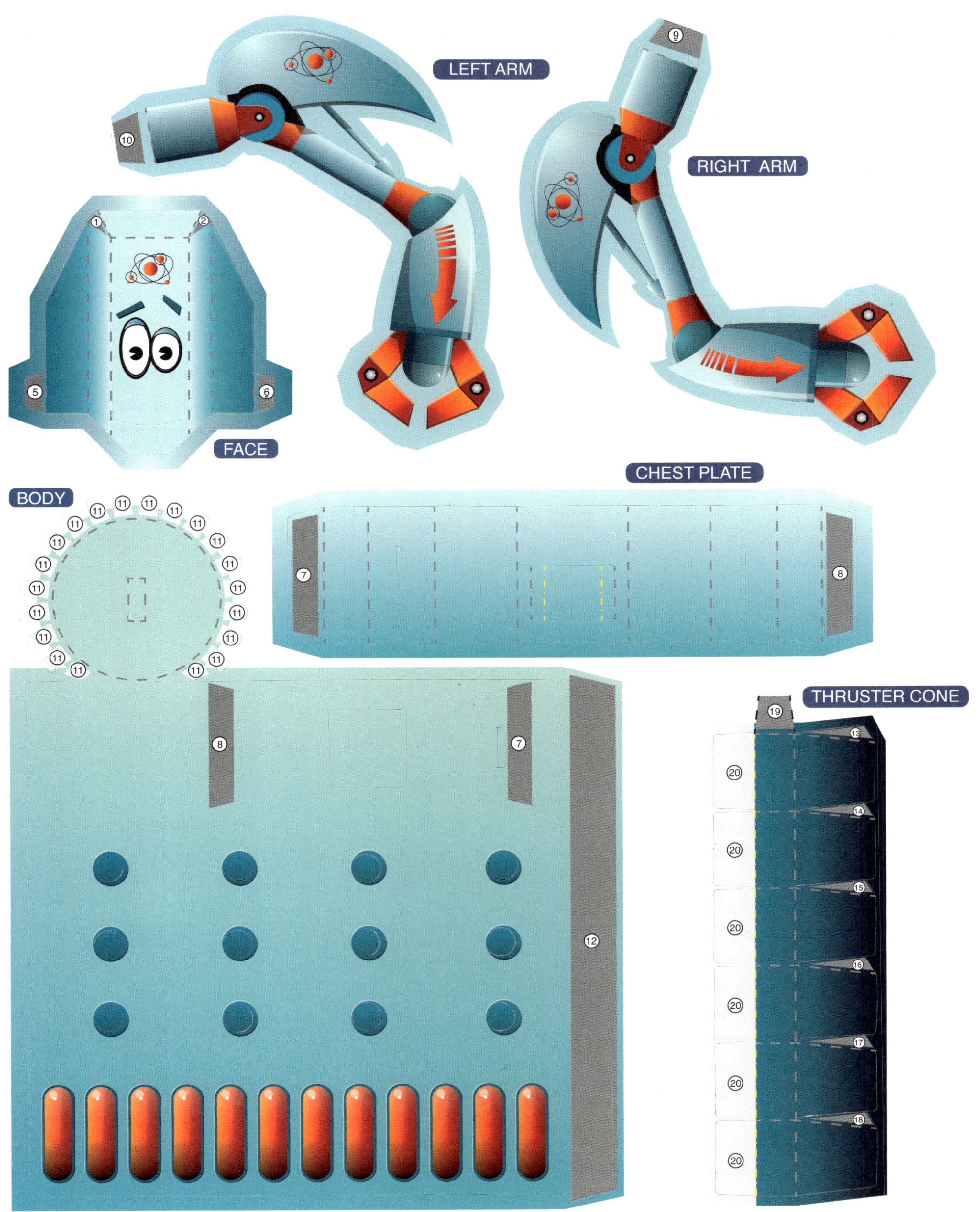

LEFT ARM
RIGHT ARM
FACE
CHEST PLATE
BODY
THRUSTER CONE

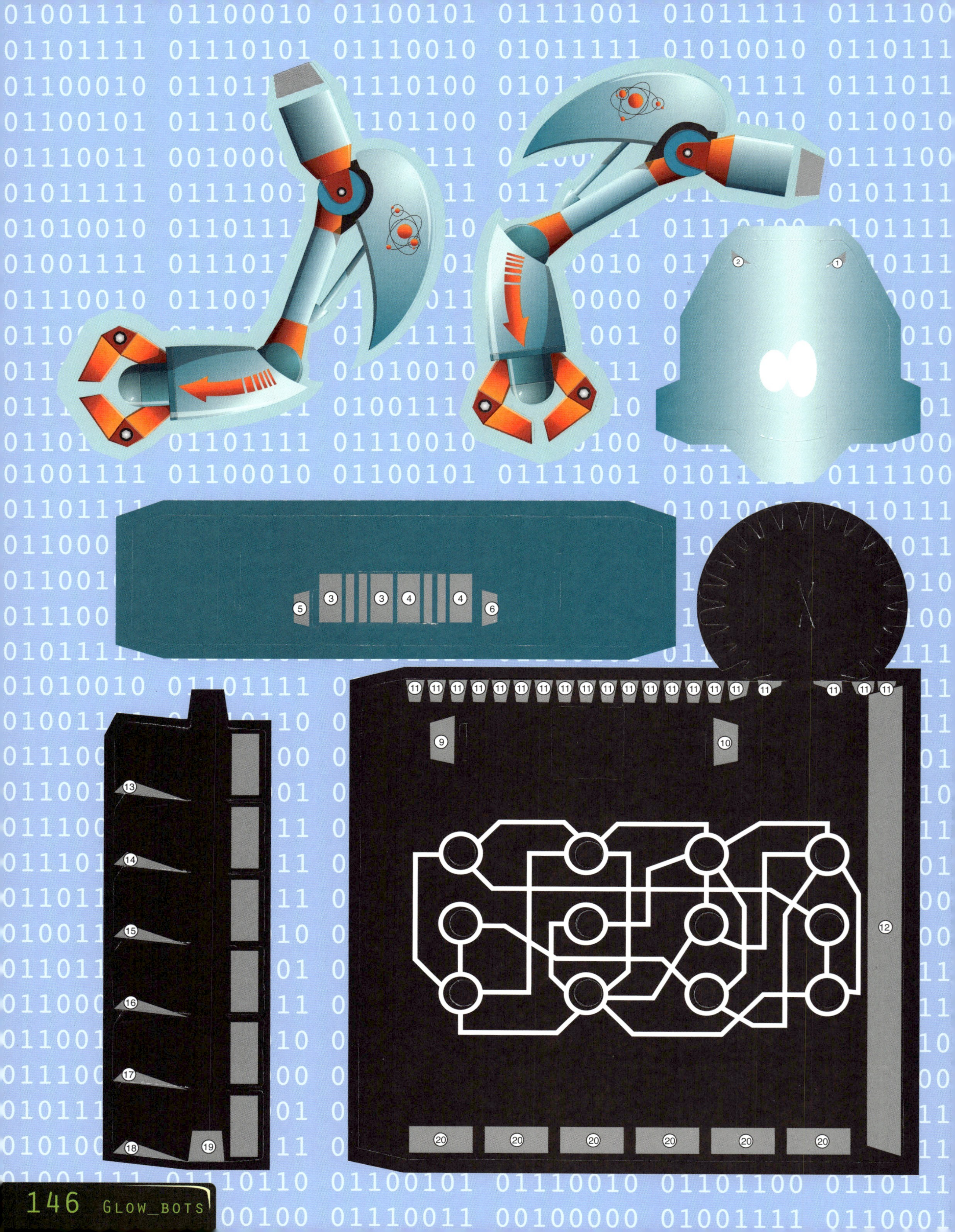

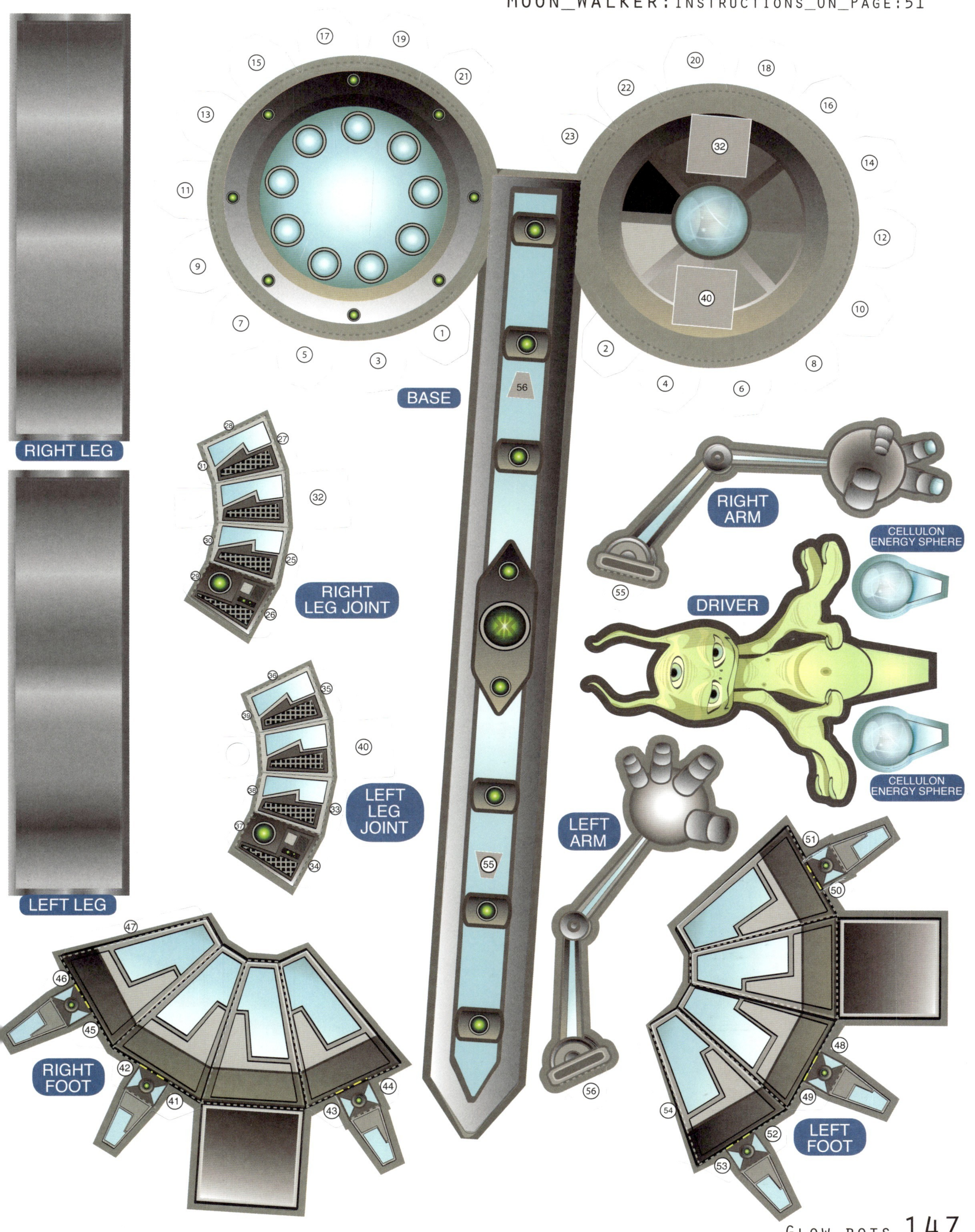

RIGHT LEG
LEFT LEG
BASE
RIGHT LEG JOINT
LEFT LEG JOINT
RIGHT ARM
LEFT ARM
DRIVER
CELLULON ENERGY SPHERE
CELLULON ENERGY SPHERE
RIGHT FOOT
LEFT FOOT

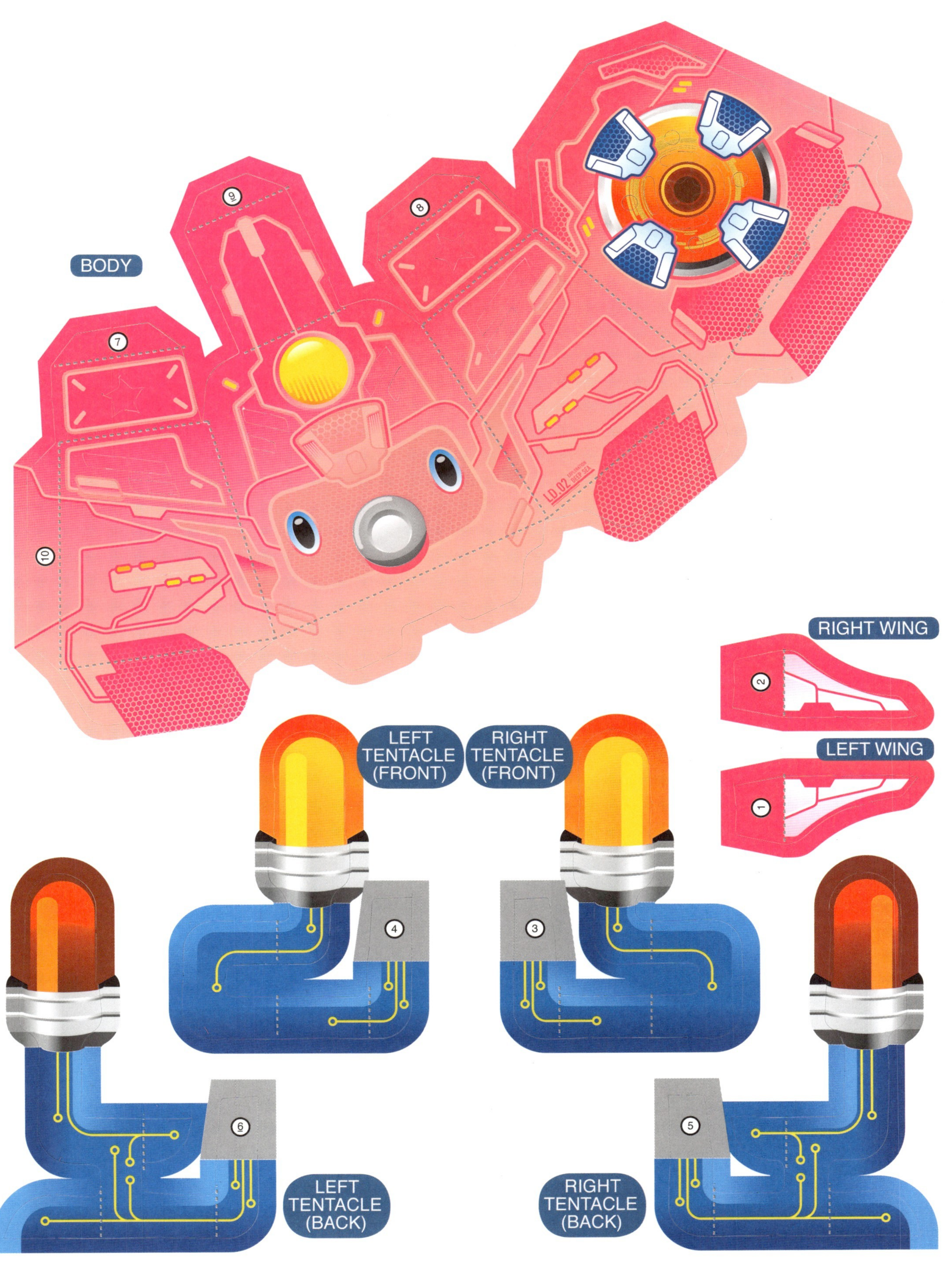
BODY
7
8
9
10
LD.02
RIGHT WING
2
LEFT WING
1
LEFT TENTACLE (FRONT)
RIGHT TENTACLE (FRONT)
4
3
6
5
LEFT TENTACLE (BACK)
RIGHT TENTACLE (BACK)

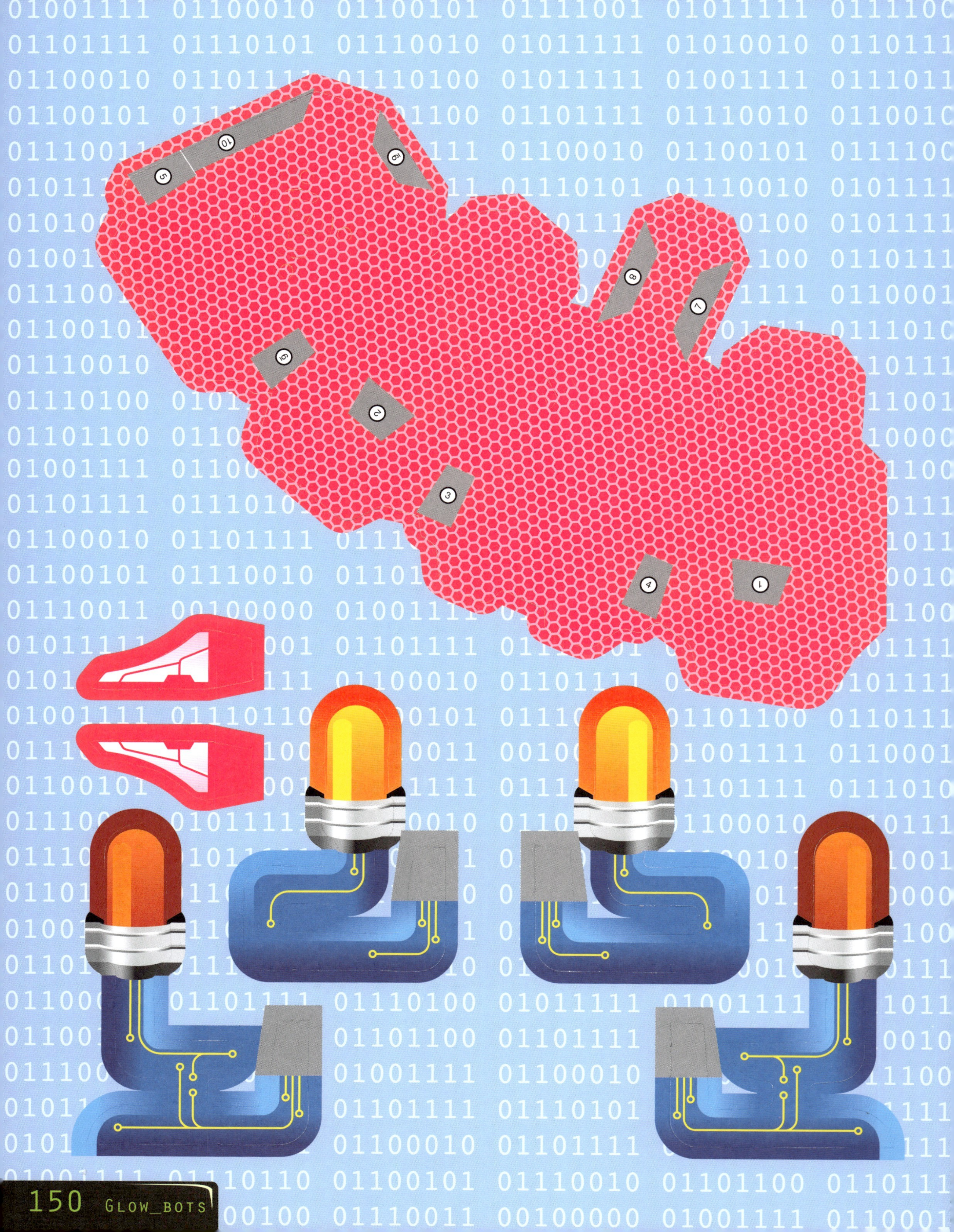

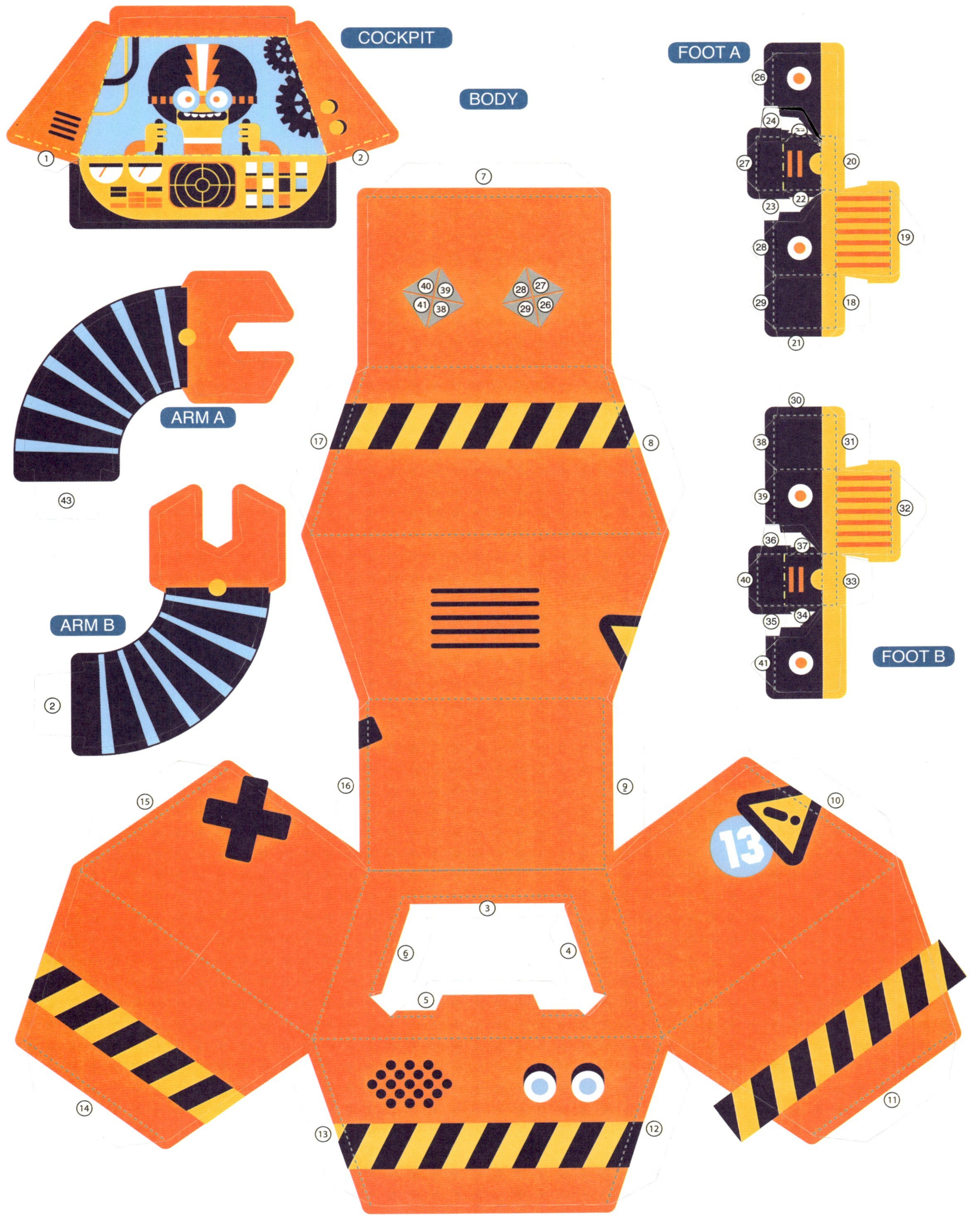
COCKPIT
BODY
FOOT A
ARM A
ARM B
FOOT B

RIGHT LEG
LEFT LEG
BODY
yujein
LEFT ARM
RIGHT FOOT
LEFT FOOT
RIGHT ARM
RIGHT ANTENNA
LEFT ANTENNA

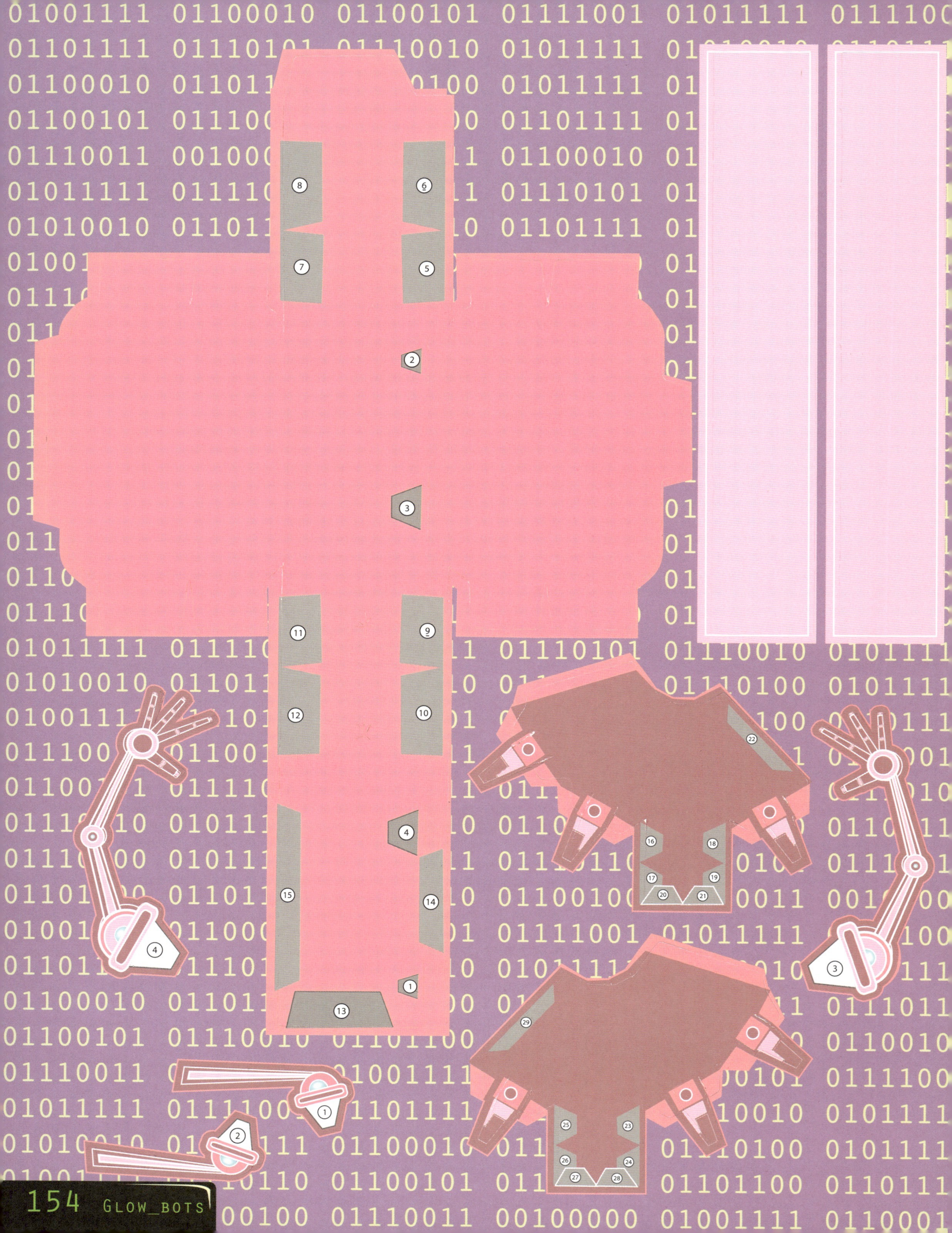

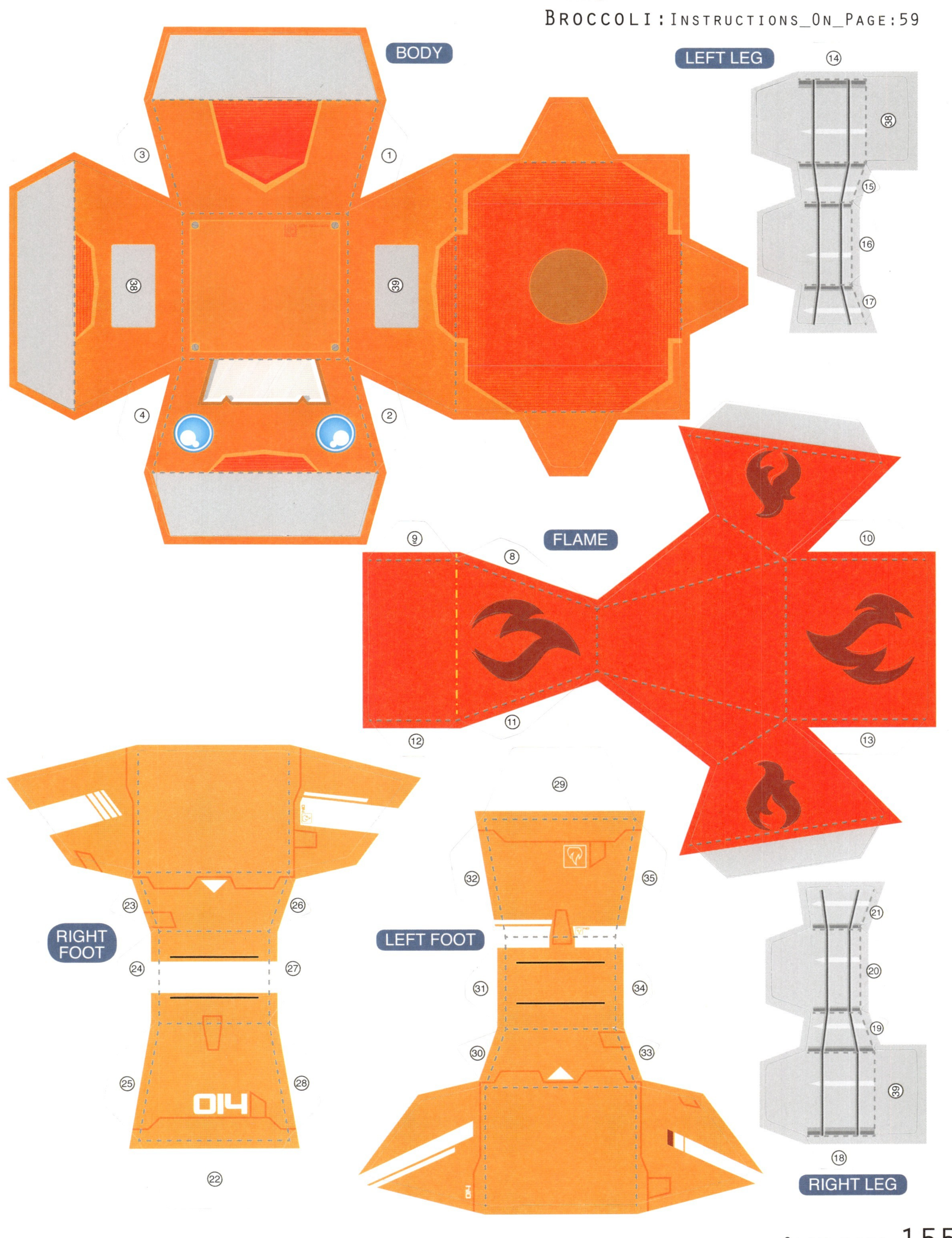

BODY
LEFT LEG
FLAME
RIGHT FOOT
LEFT FOOT
RIGHT LEG
014

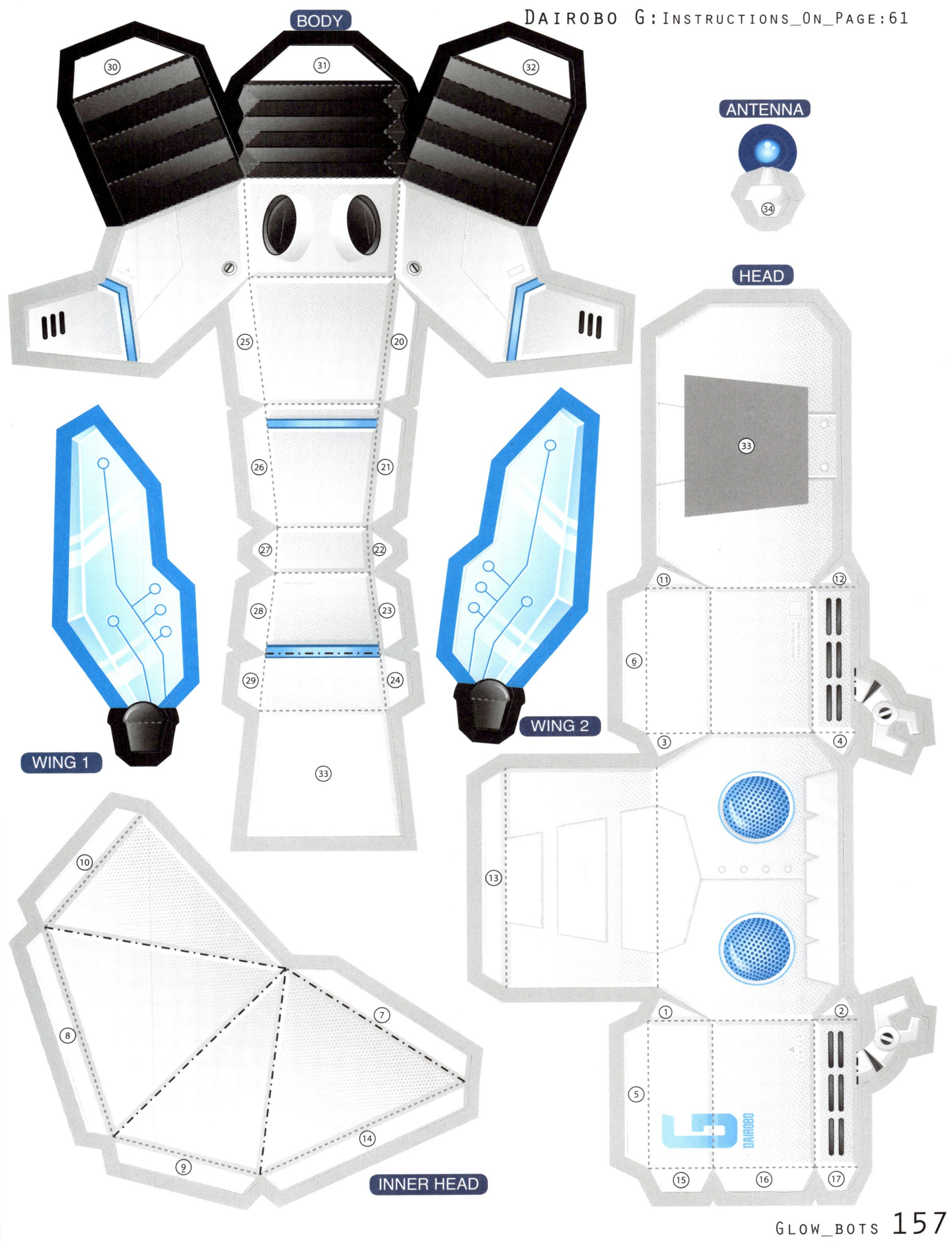
BODY
ANTENNA
HEAD
WING 1
WING 2
INNER HEAD
DAIROBO

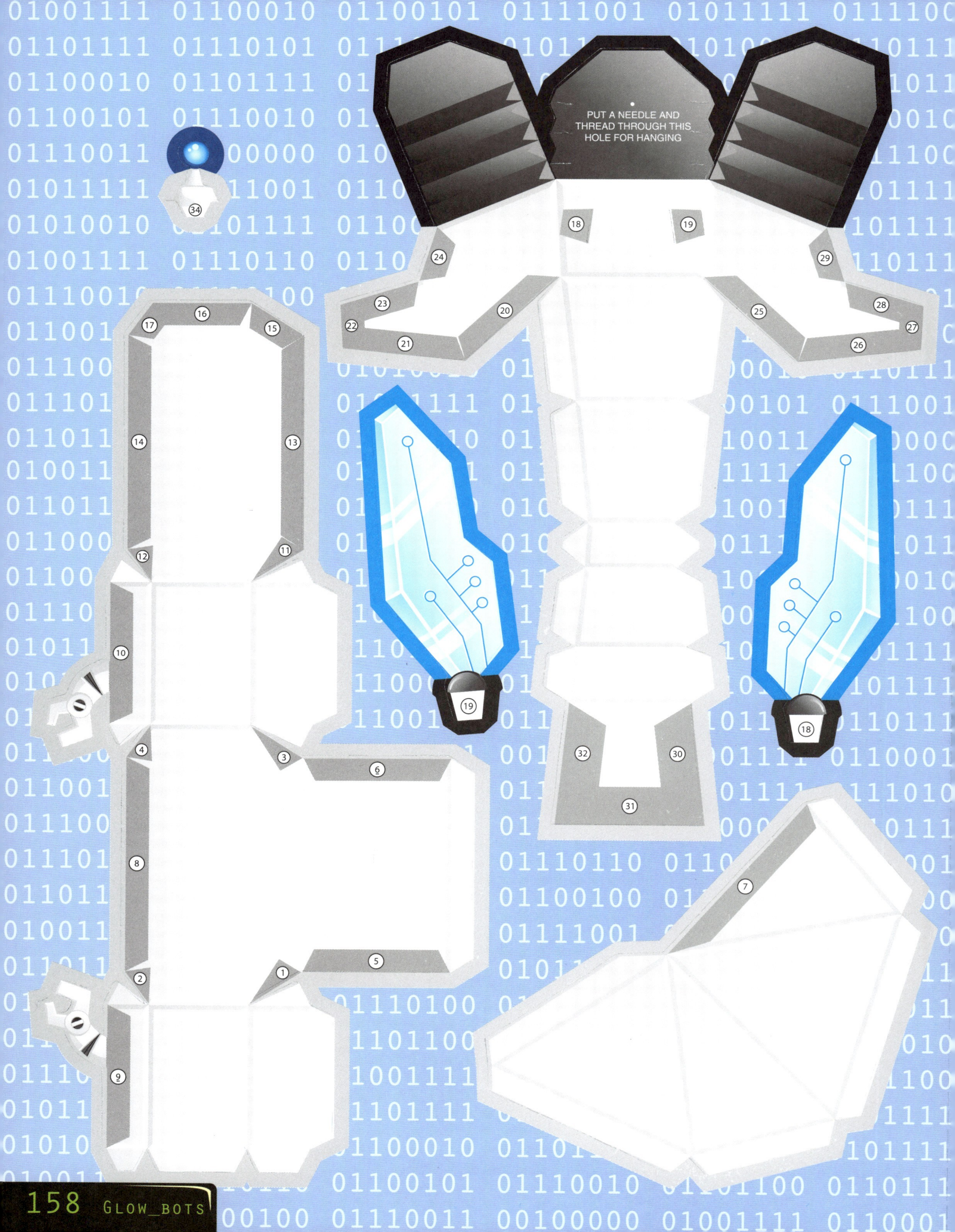
PUT A NEEDLE AND
THREAD THROUGH THIS
HOLE FOR HANGING

VISOR
11
12
13
HEAD
14
15
18
19
SPARX
26
27
20
21
22
23
16
17
25
24
LEFT ARM
2
1
RIGHT ARM
RIGHT WING
LEFT WING
BODY
9
10
5
6
25
7
3
4
8

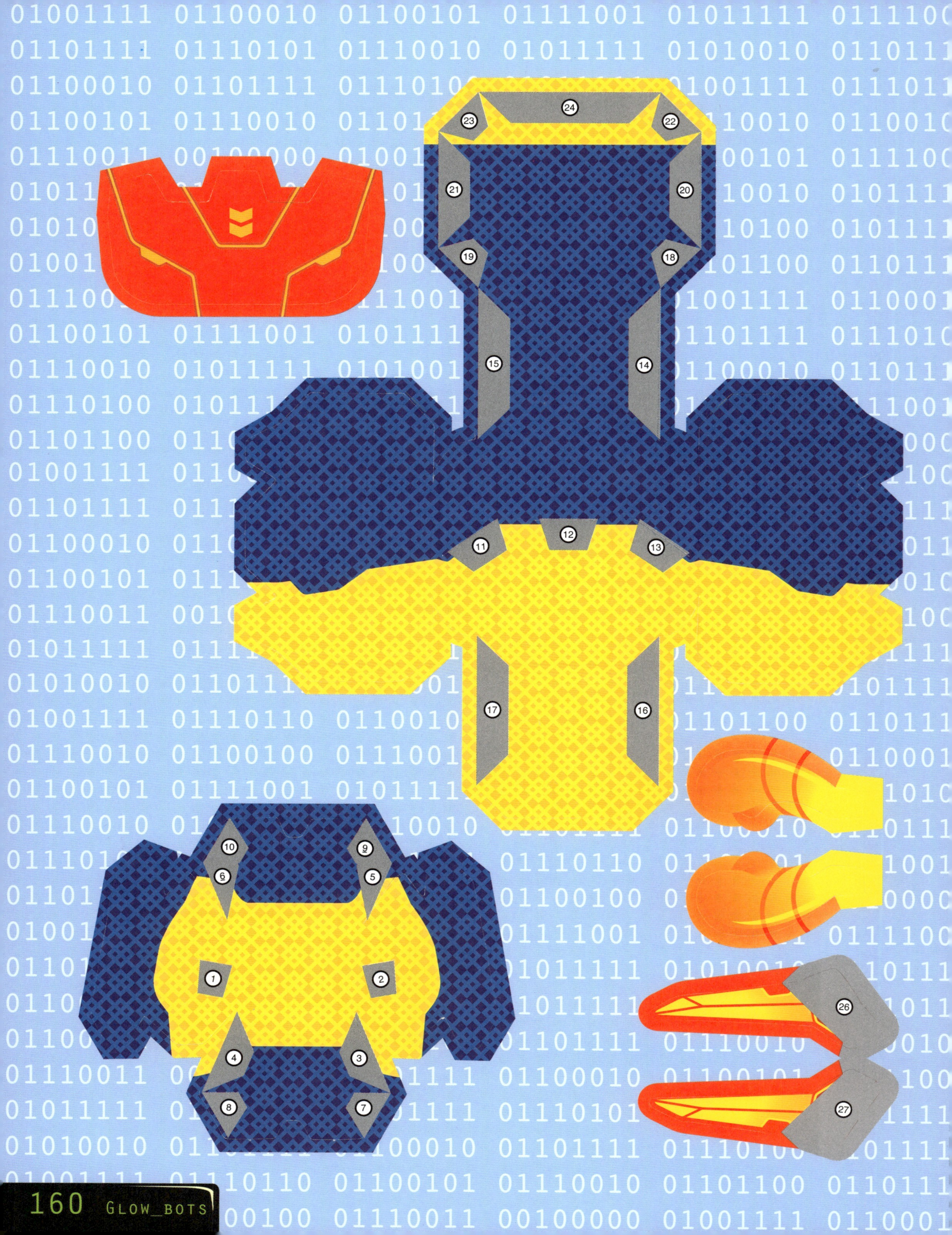

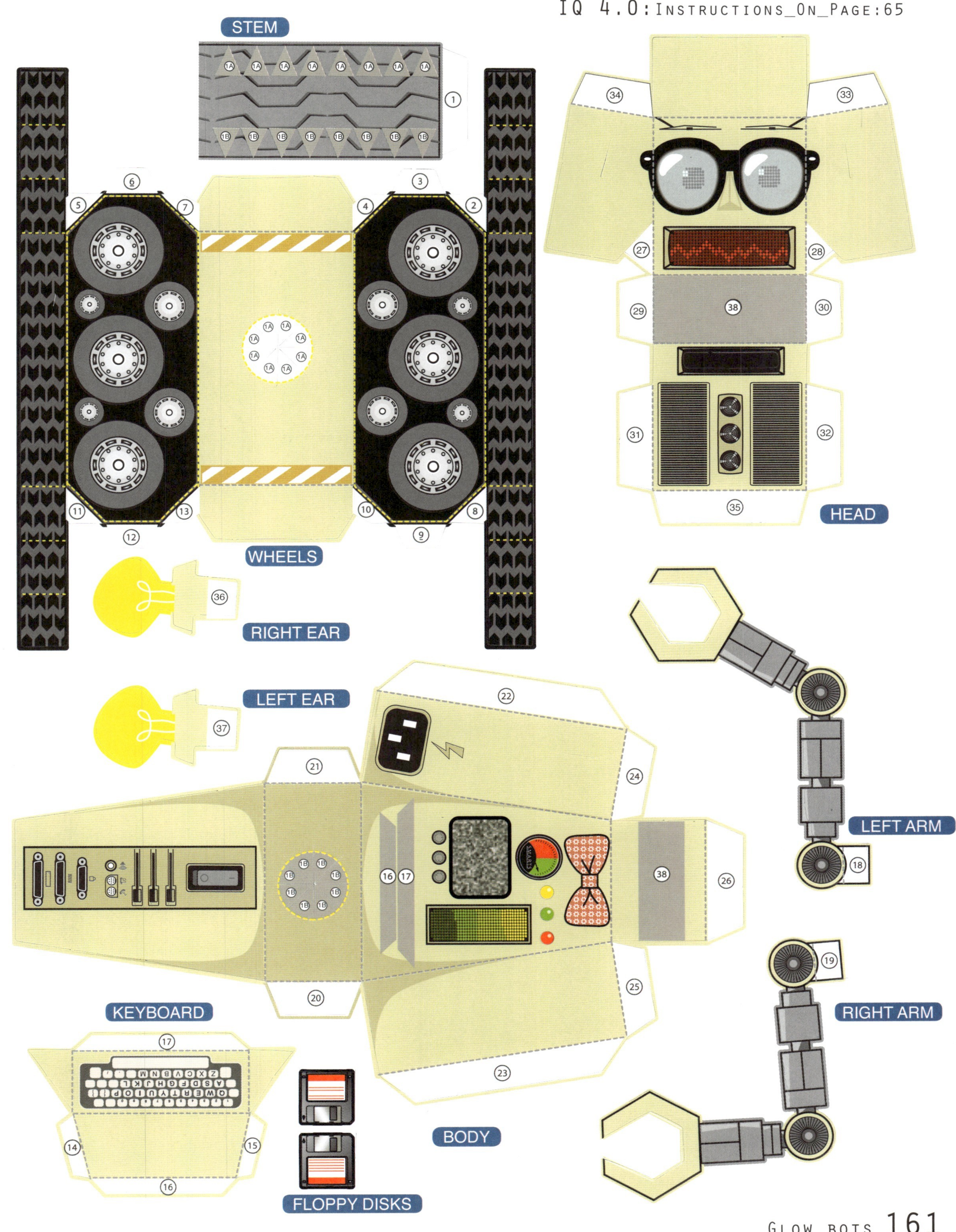
STEM
WHEELS
RIGHT EAR
LEFT EAR
HEAD
LEFT ARM
RIGHT ARM
KEYBOARD
BODY
FLOPPY DISKS

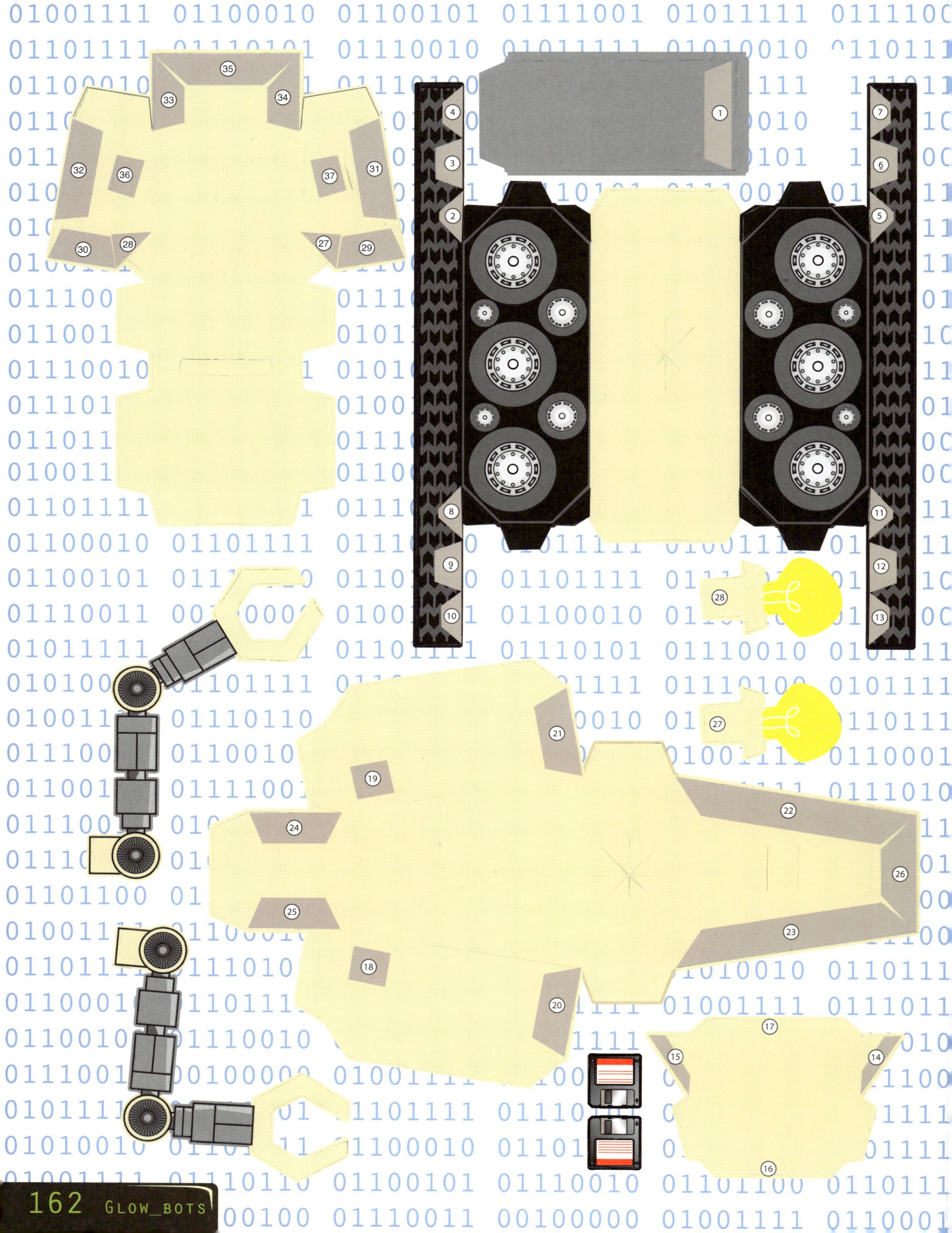

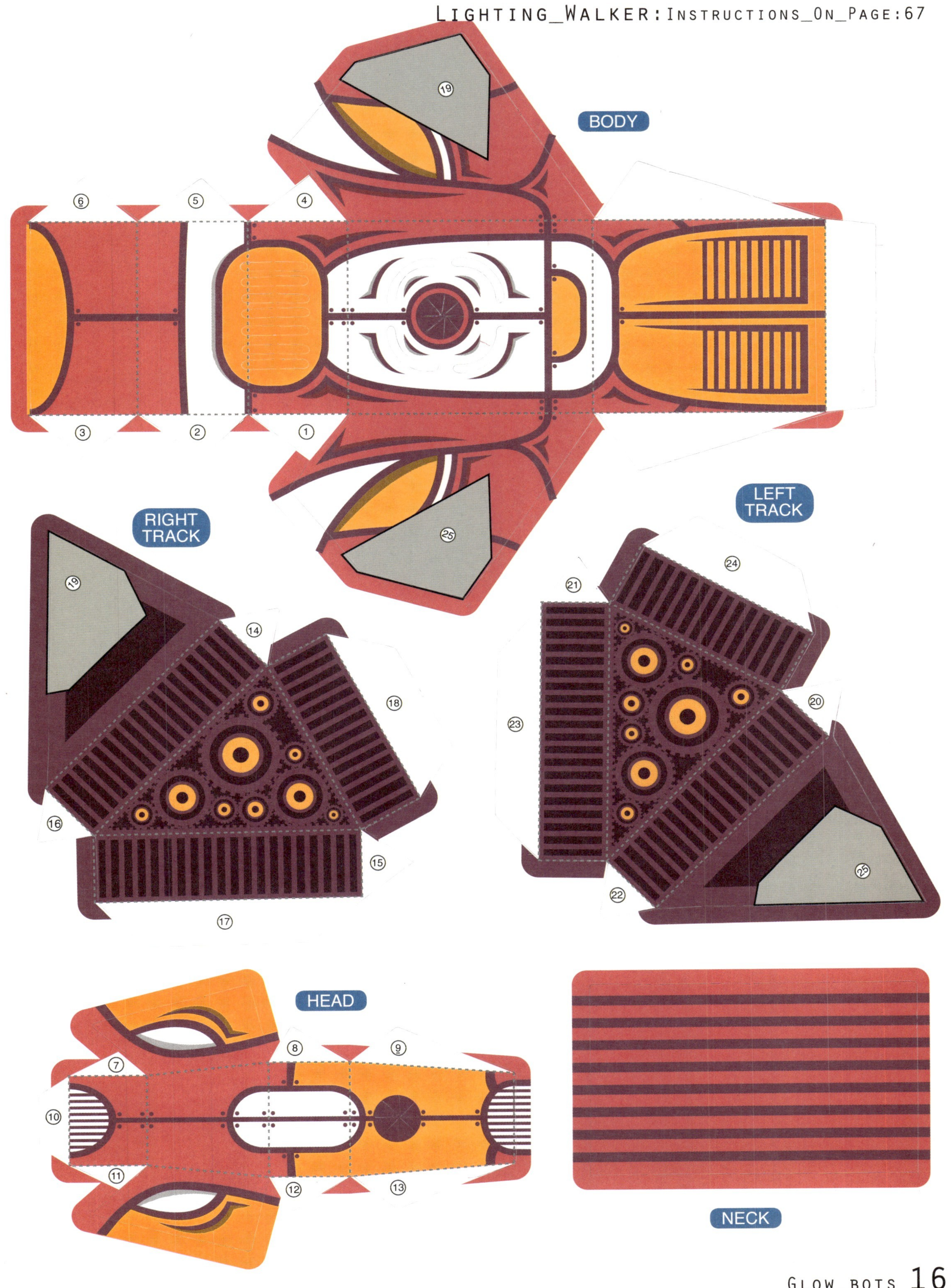
BODY
6
5
4
3
2
1
19
25
RIGHT TRACK
19
14
18
16
15
17
LEFT TRACK
24
21
23
20
22
25
HEAD
7
8
9
10
11
12
13
NECK

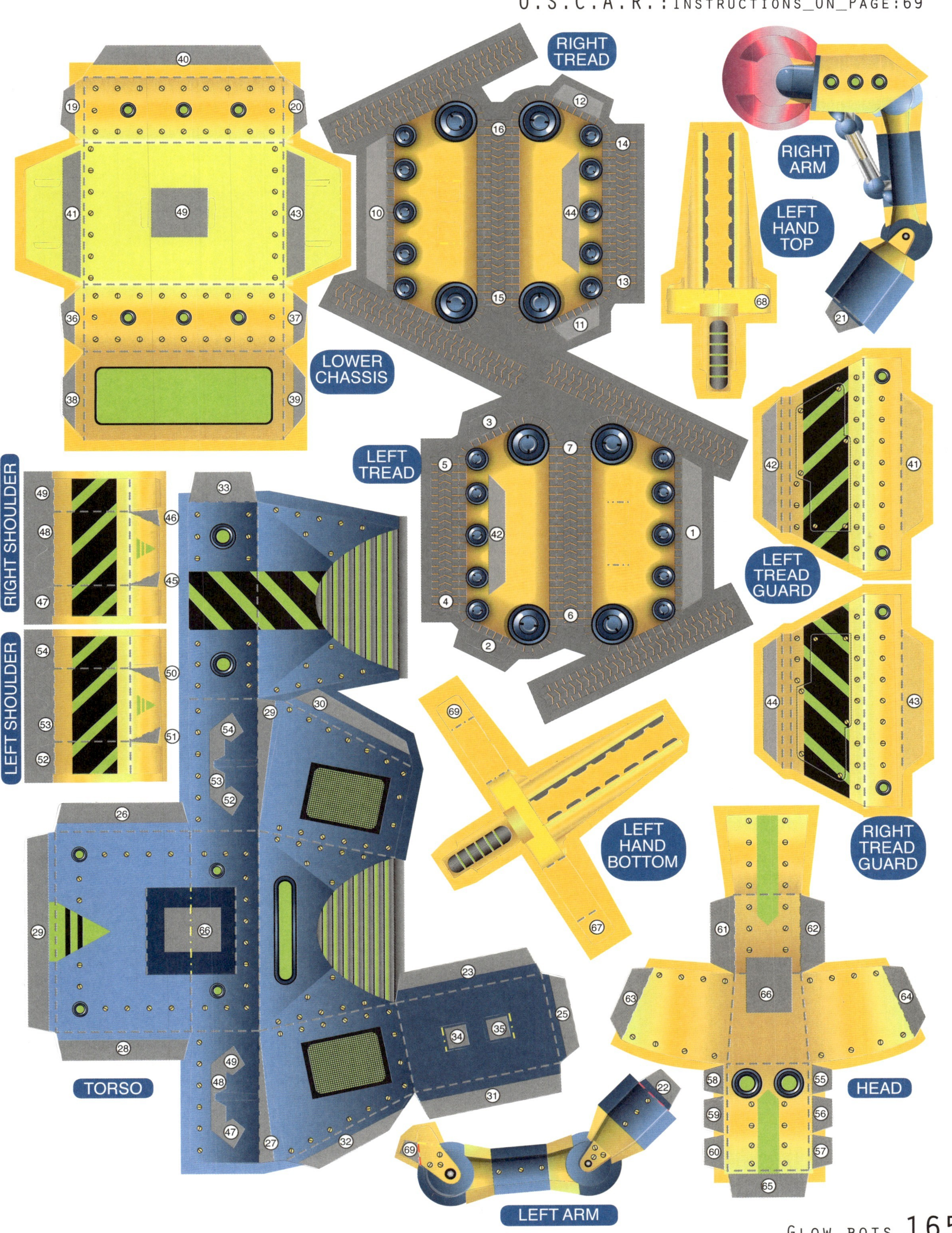
RIGHT TREAD
LOWER CHASSIS
RIGHT ARM
LEFT HAND TOP
LEFT TREAD
LEFT TREAD GUARD
RIGHT SHOULDER
LEFT SHOULDER
LEFT HAND BOTTOM
RIGHT TREAD GUARD
TORSO
HEAD
LEFT ARM

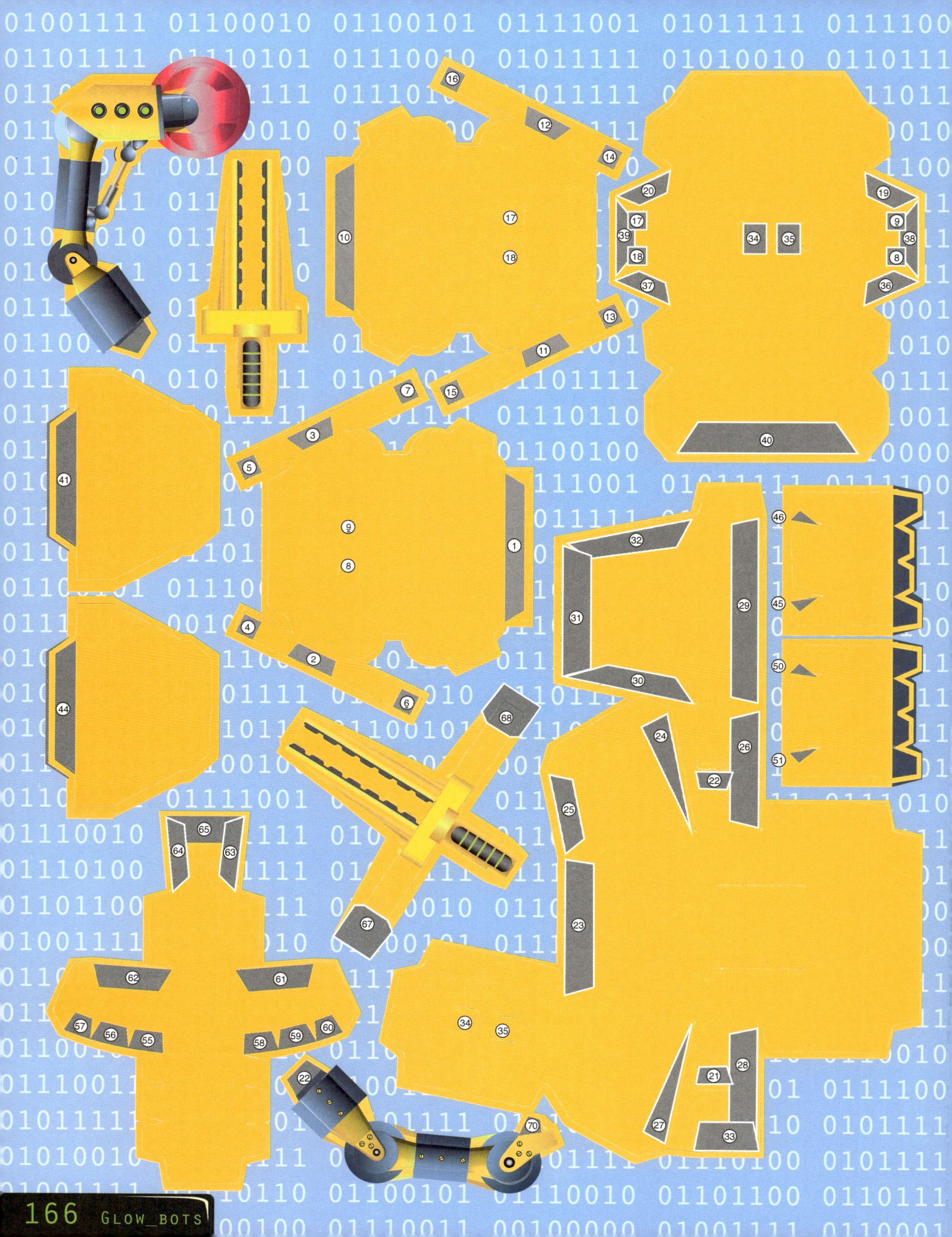

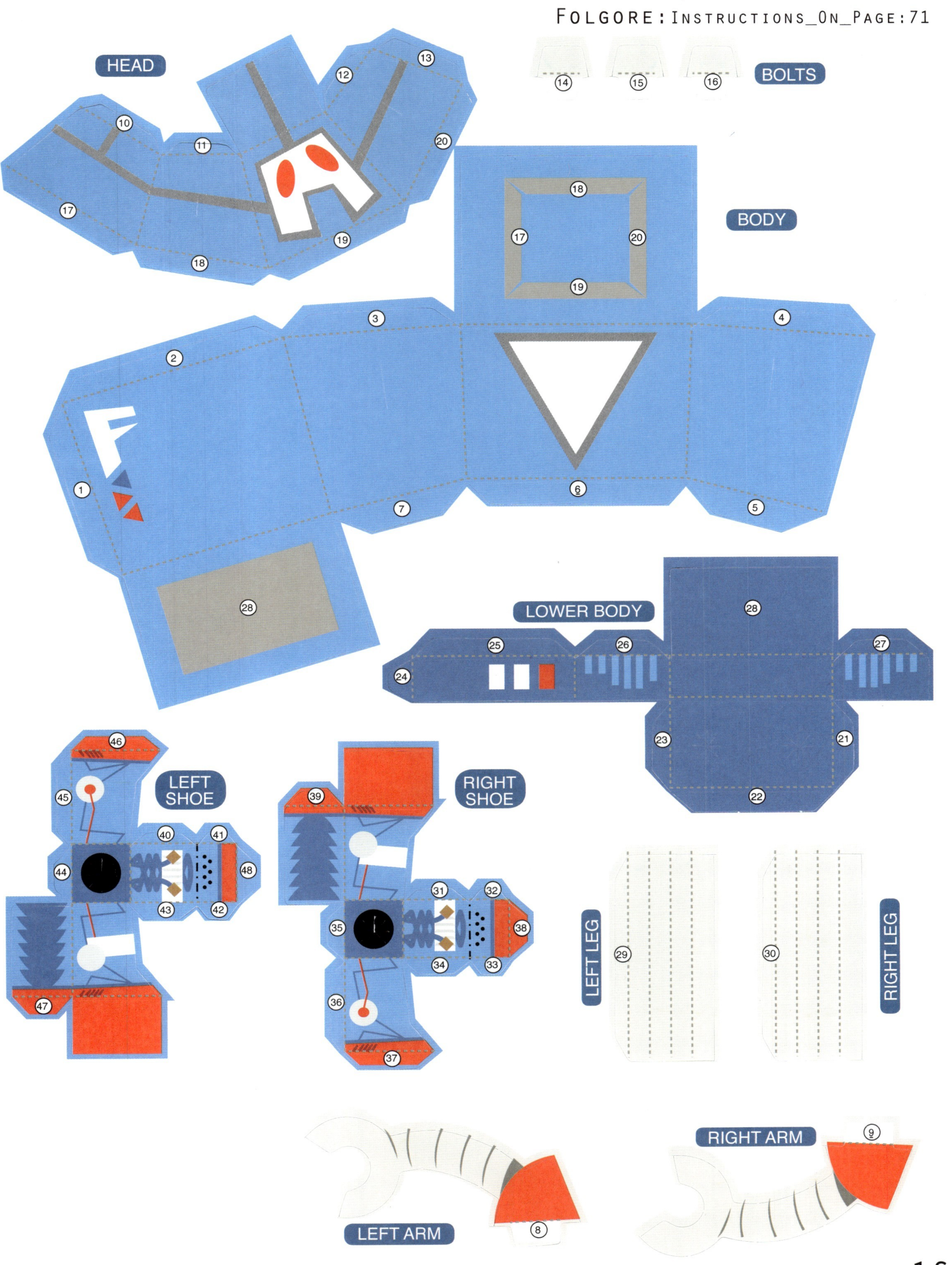
HEAD
BOLTS
BODY
LOWER BODY
LEFT SHOE
RIGHT SHOE
LEFT LEG
RIGHT LEG
LEFT ARM
RIGHT ARM

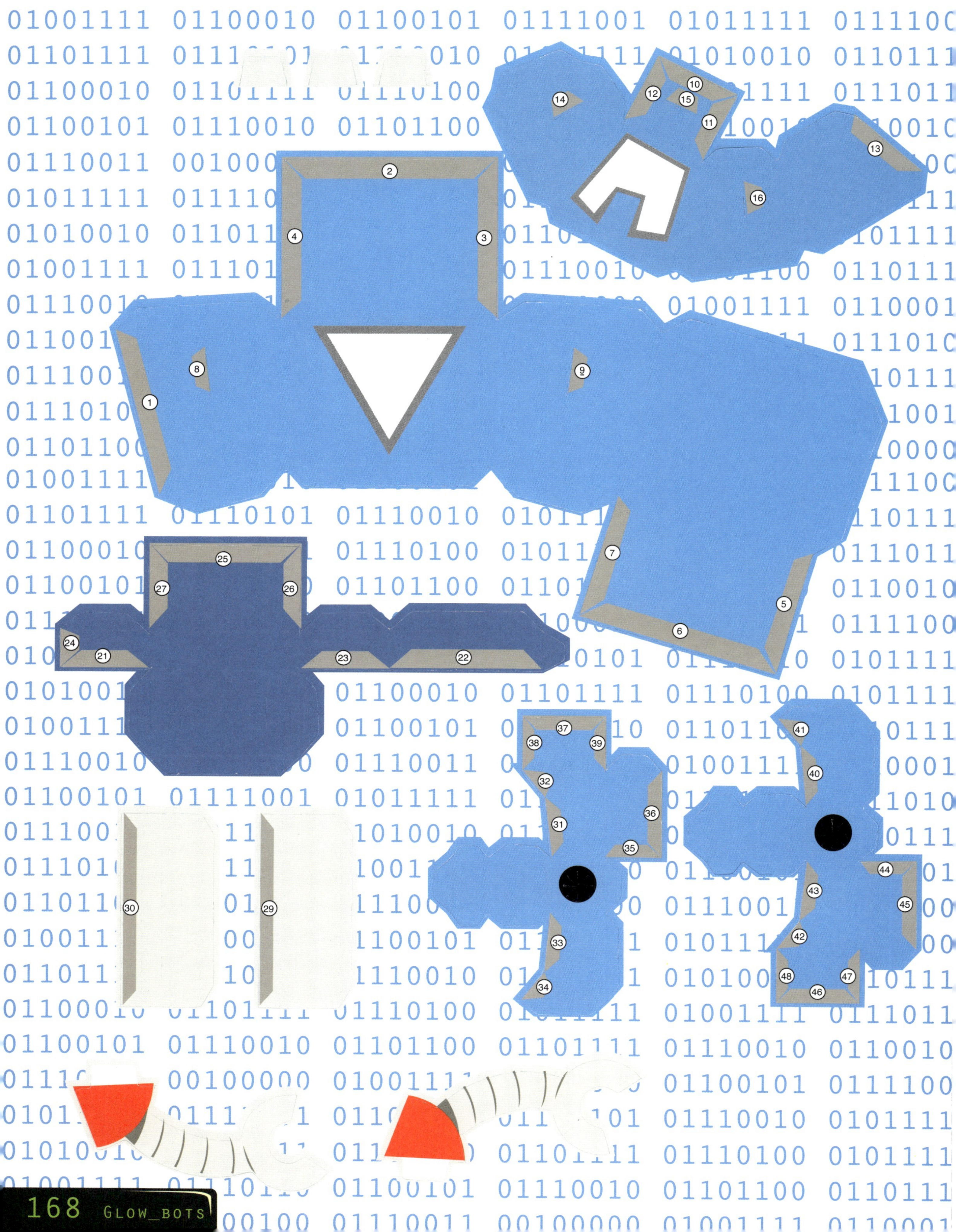

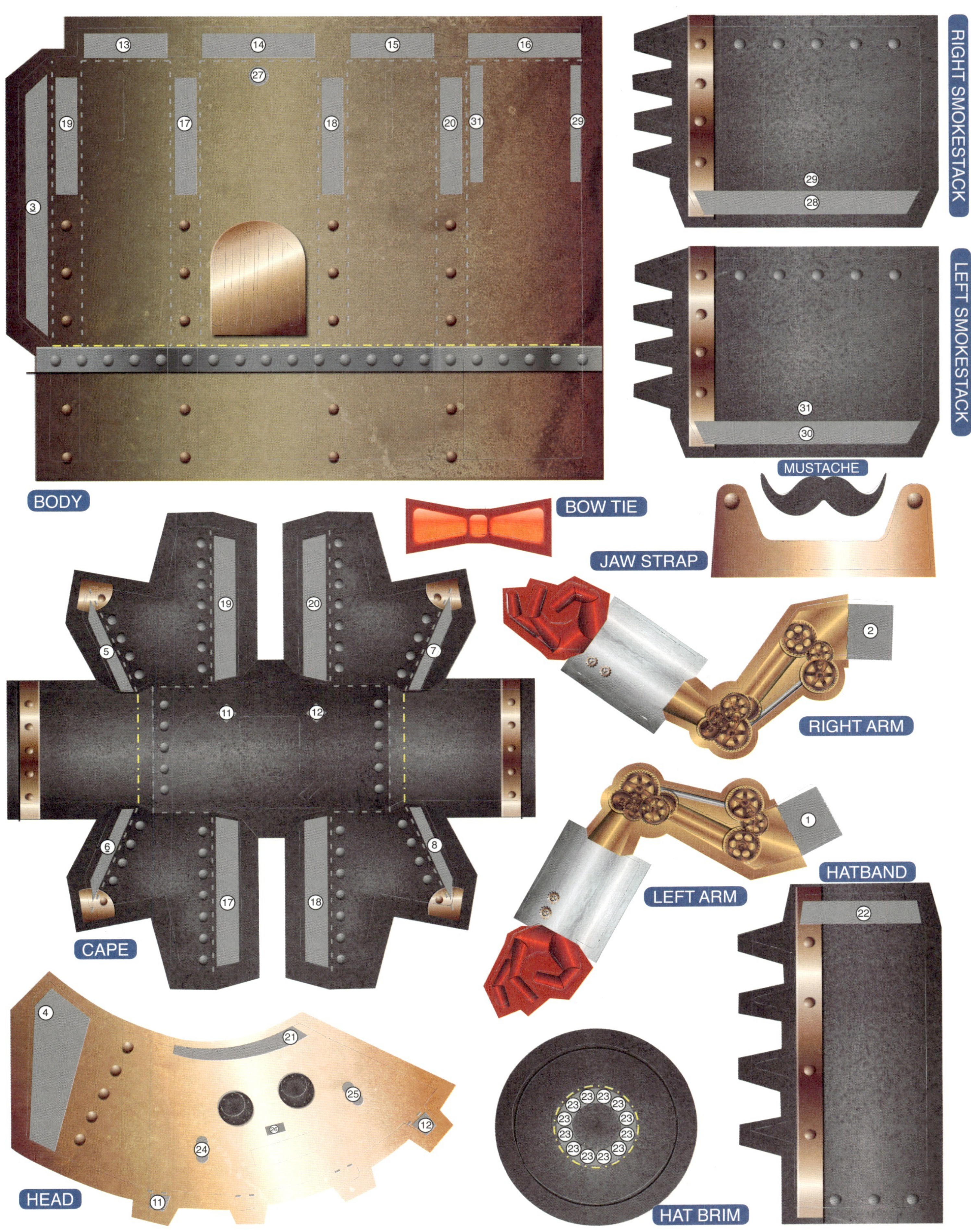
BODY
RIGHT SMOKESTACK
LEFT SMOKESTACK
MUSTACHE
BOW TIE
JAW STRAP
RIGHT ARM
LEFT ARM
HATBAND
CAPE
HEAD
HAT BRIM

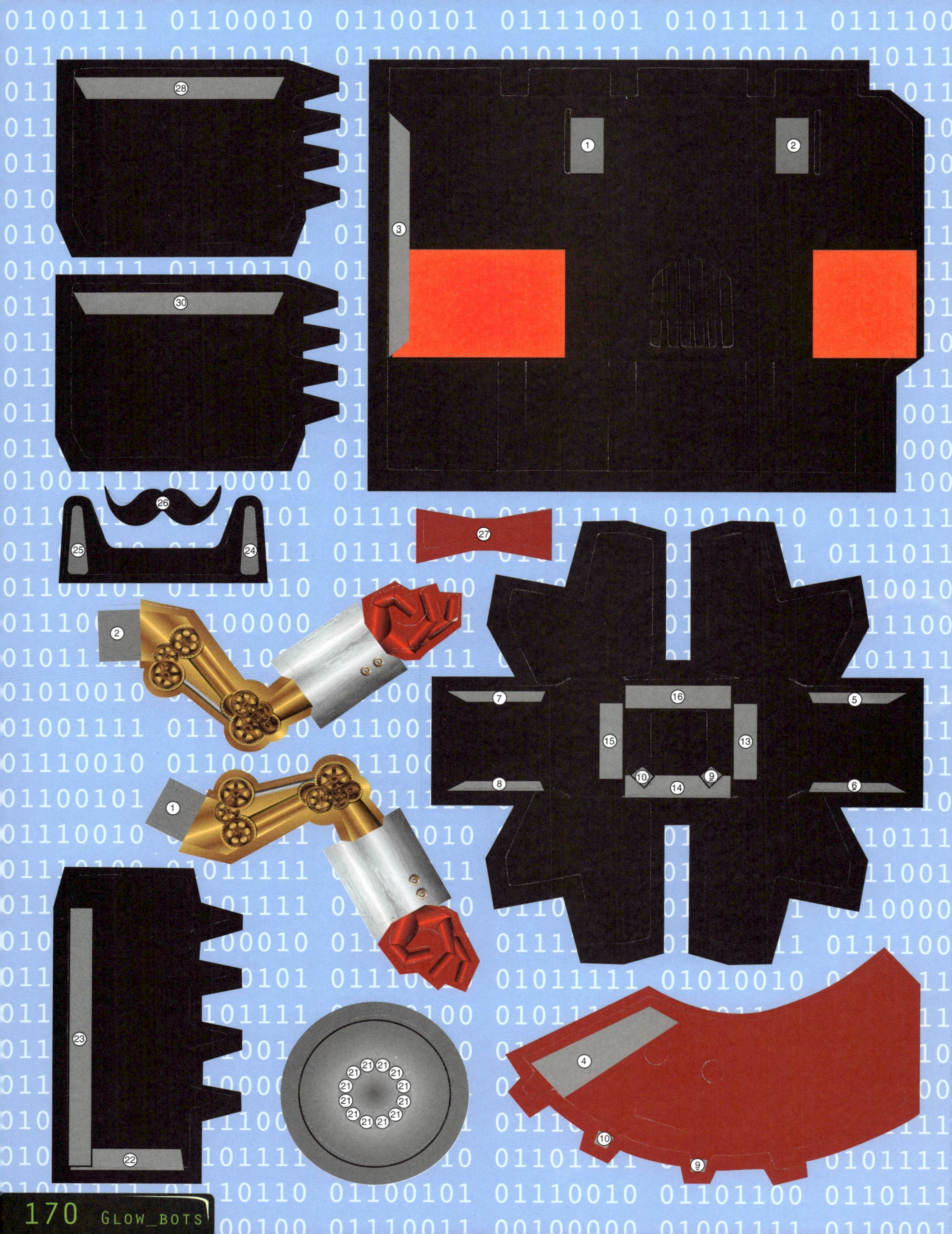

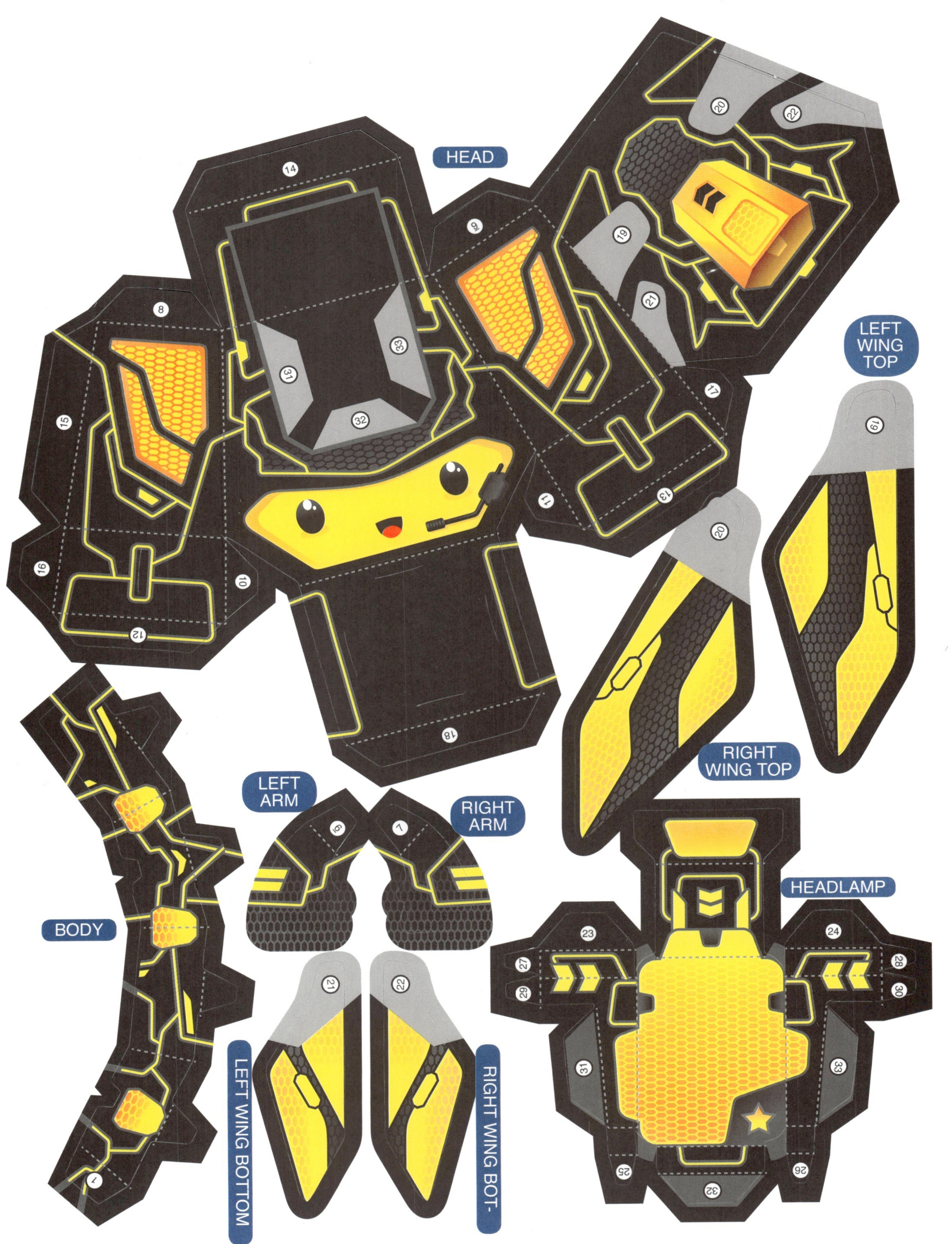
HEAD
LEFT WING TOP
RIGHT WING TOP
LEFT ARM
RIGHT ARM
HEADLAMP
BODY
LEFT WING BOTTOM
RIGHT WING BOT-

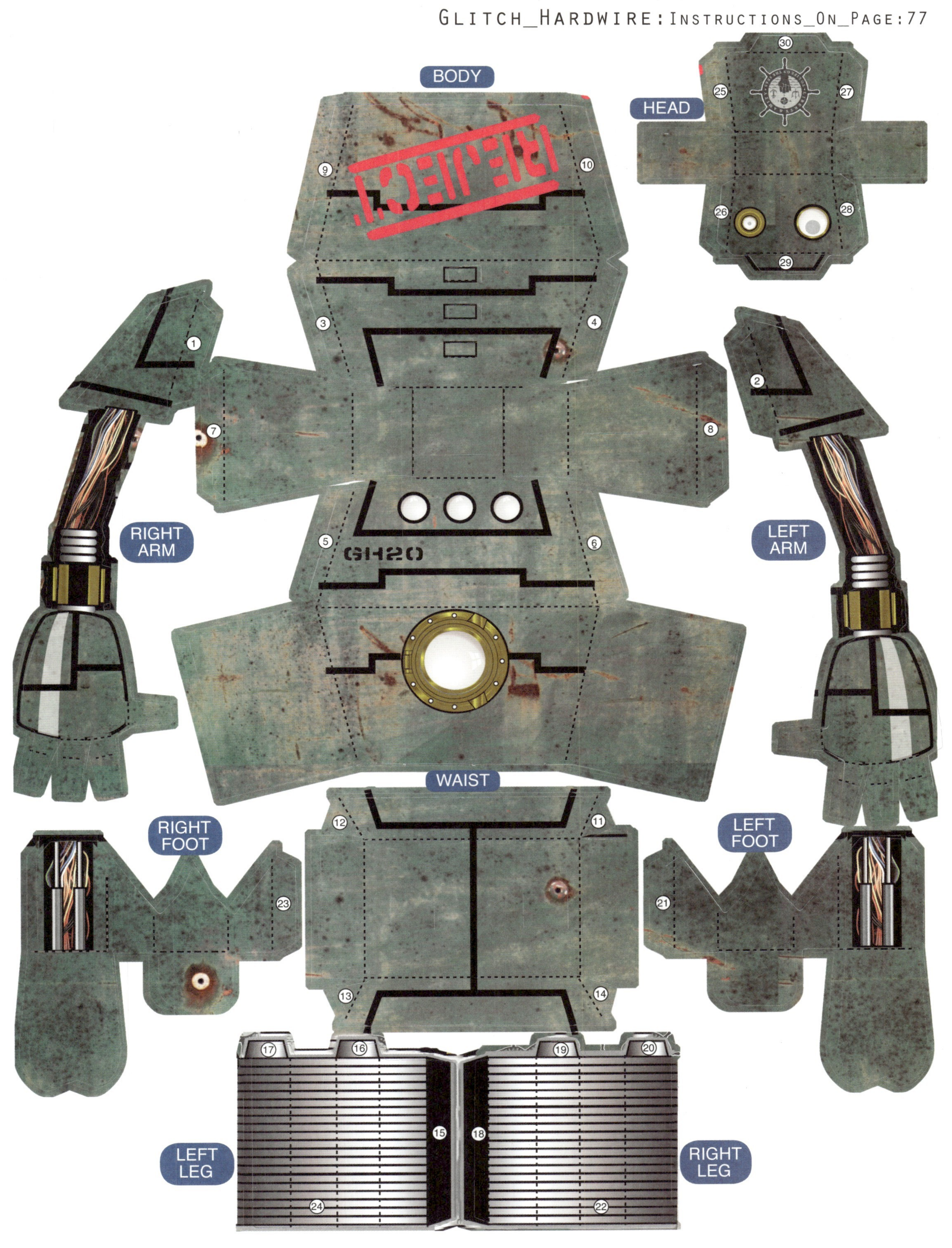
BODY
HEAD
RIGHT ARM
LEFT ARM
WAIST
RIGHT FOOT
LEFT FOOT
LEFT LEG
RIGHT LEG
GH20

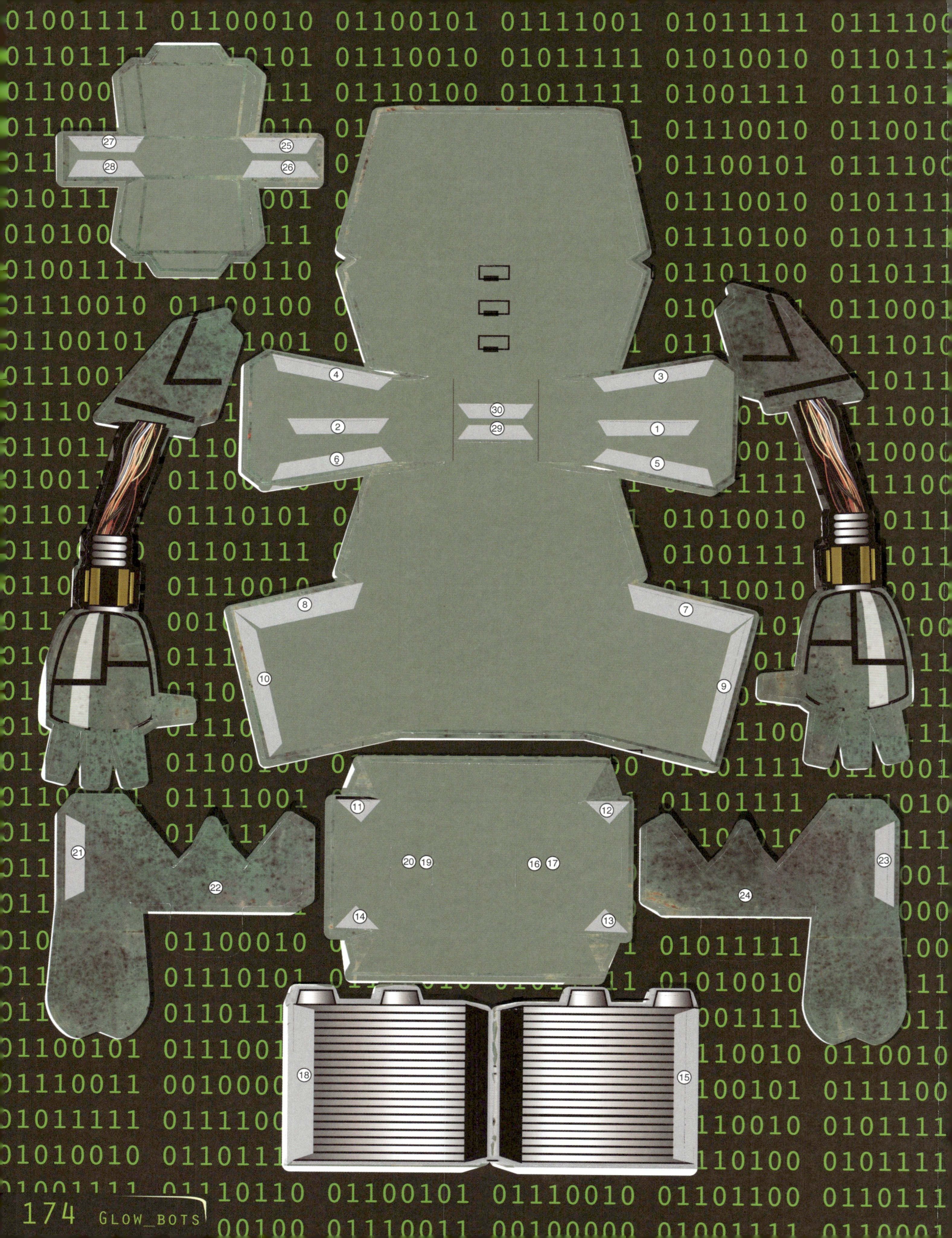

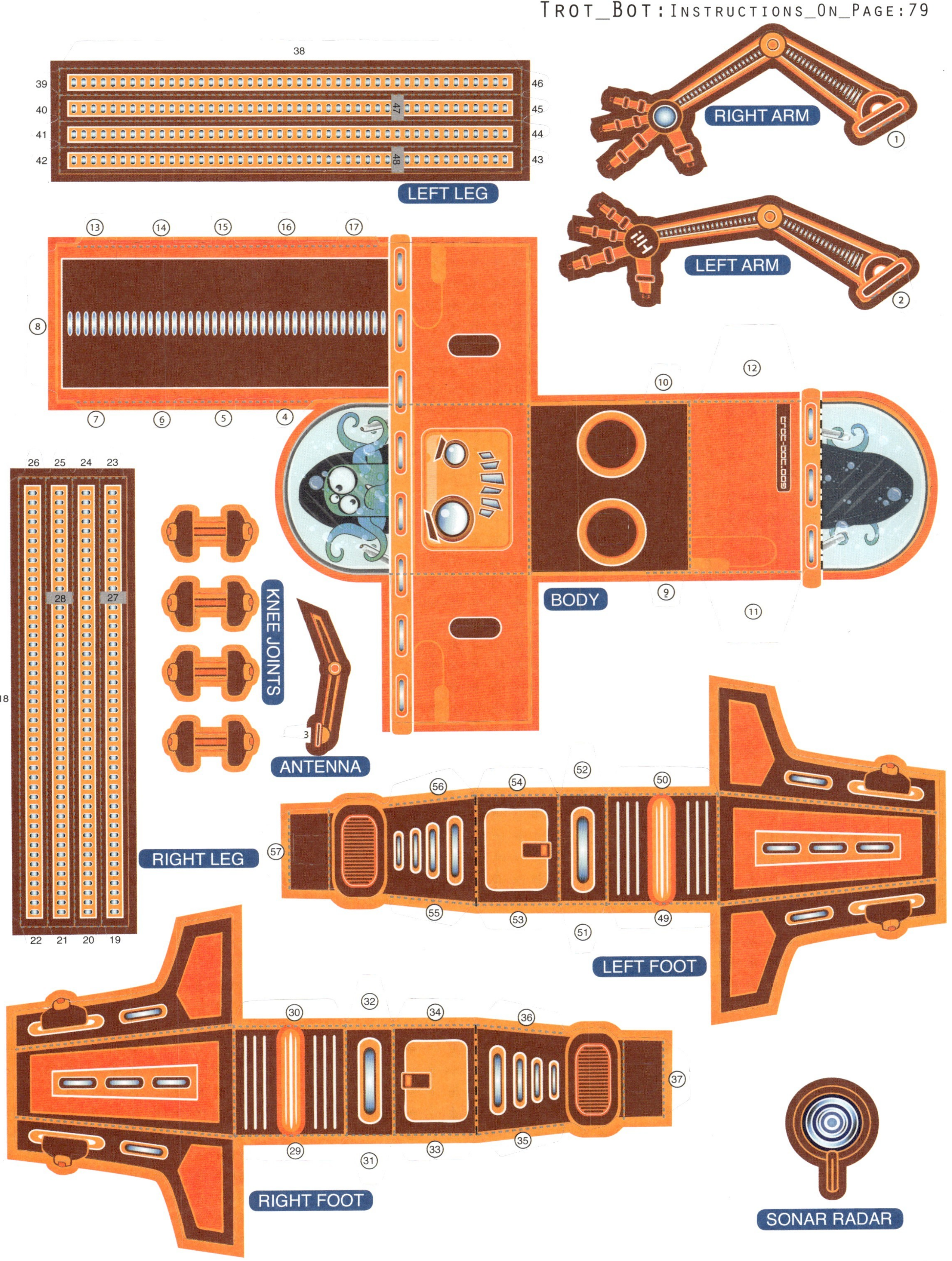
LEFT LEG
RIGHT ARM
LEFT ARM
BODY
KNEE JOINTS
ANTENNA
RIGHT LEG
LEFT FOOT
RIGHT FOOT
SONAR RADAR

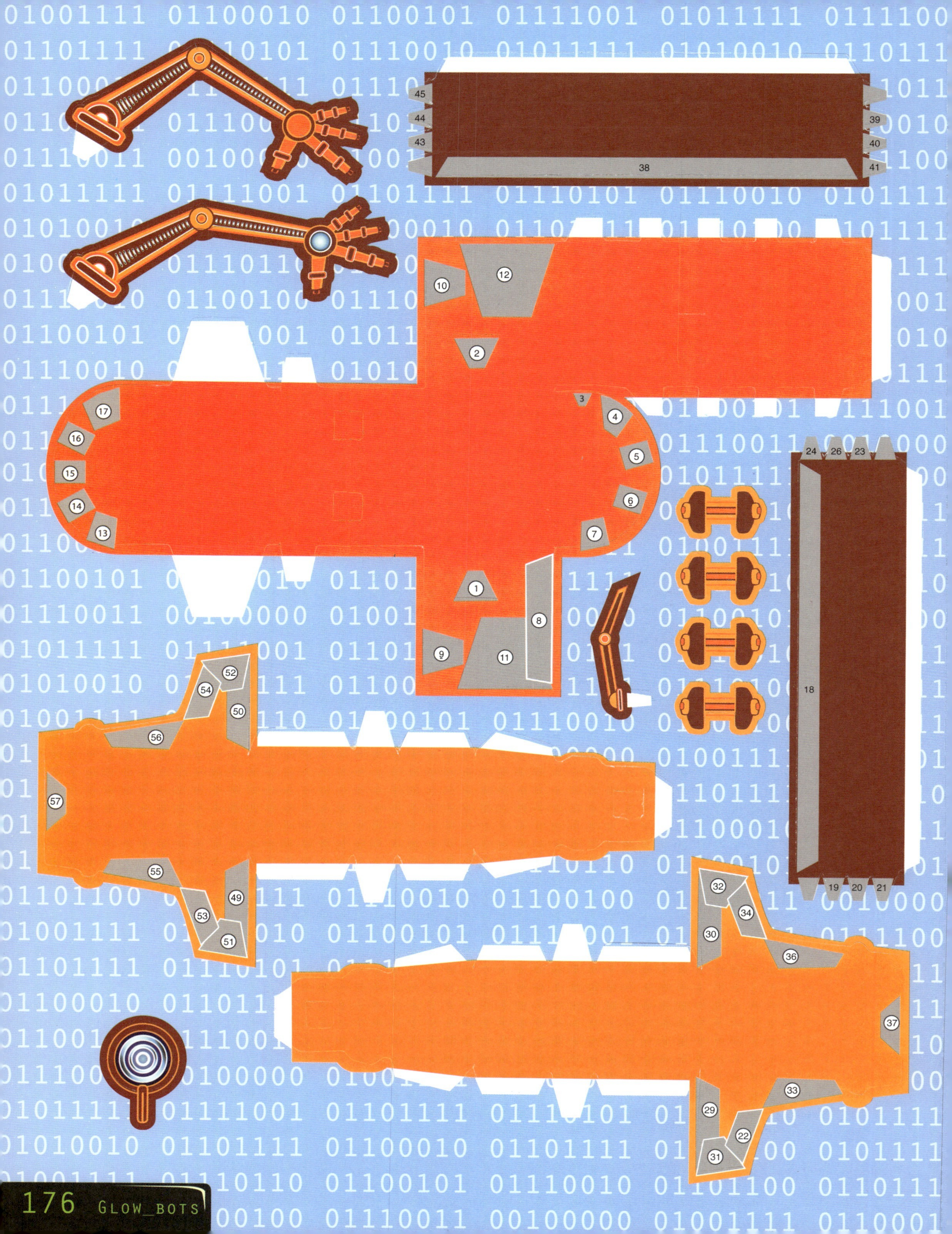

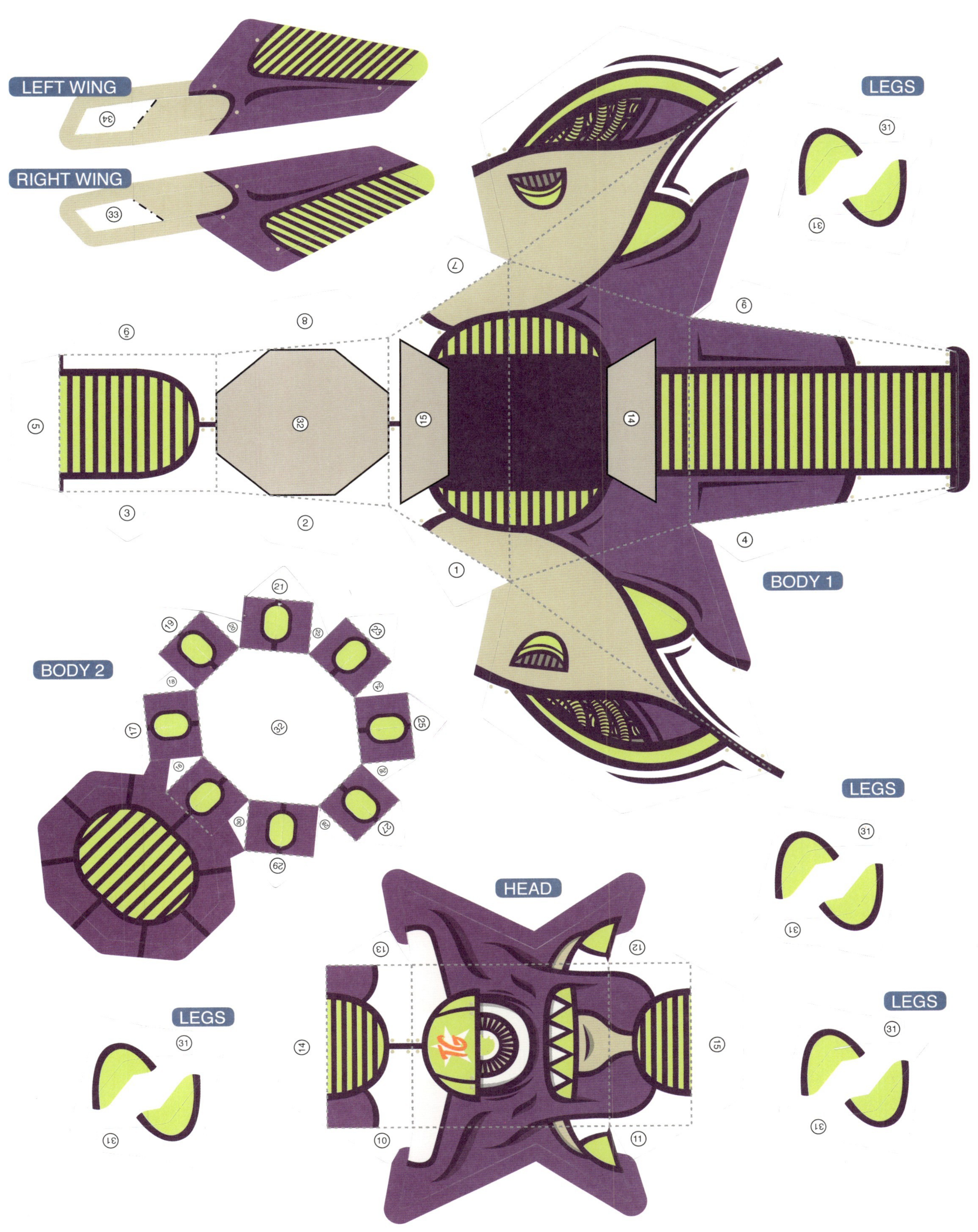
LEFT WING
RIGHT WING
LEGS
BODY 1
BODY 2
LEGS
HEAD
LEGS
LEGS

SPRING 2

(17)

(16)

SPRING 1

(25)

EXHAUST

(22) (23) (20) (24) (21) (22) (19)

(15)

LEGS

(14) (13) (12) (8)

ENTRY

(11) (10) (9) (18)

FOOT

(6) (3) (4) (7) (5) (2) (1)

NO STEP AREA

(15)

BODY

SMOKEY!

(30) (29) (28) (27)

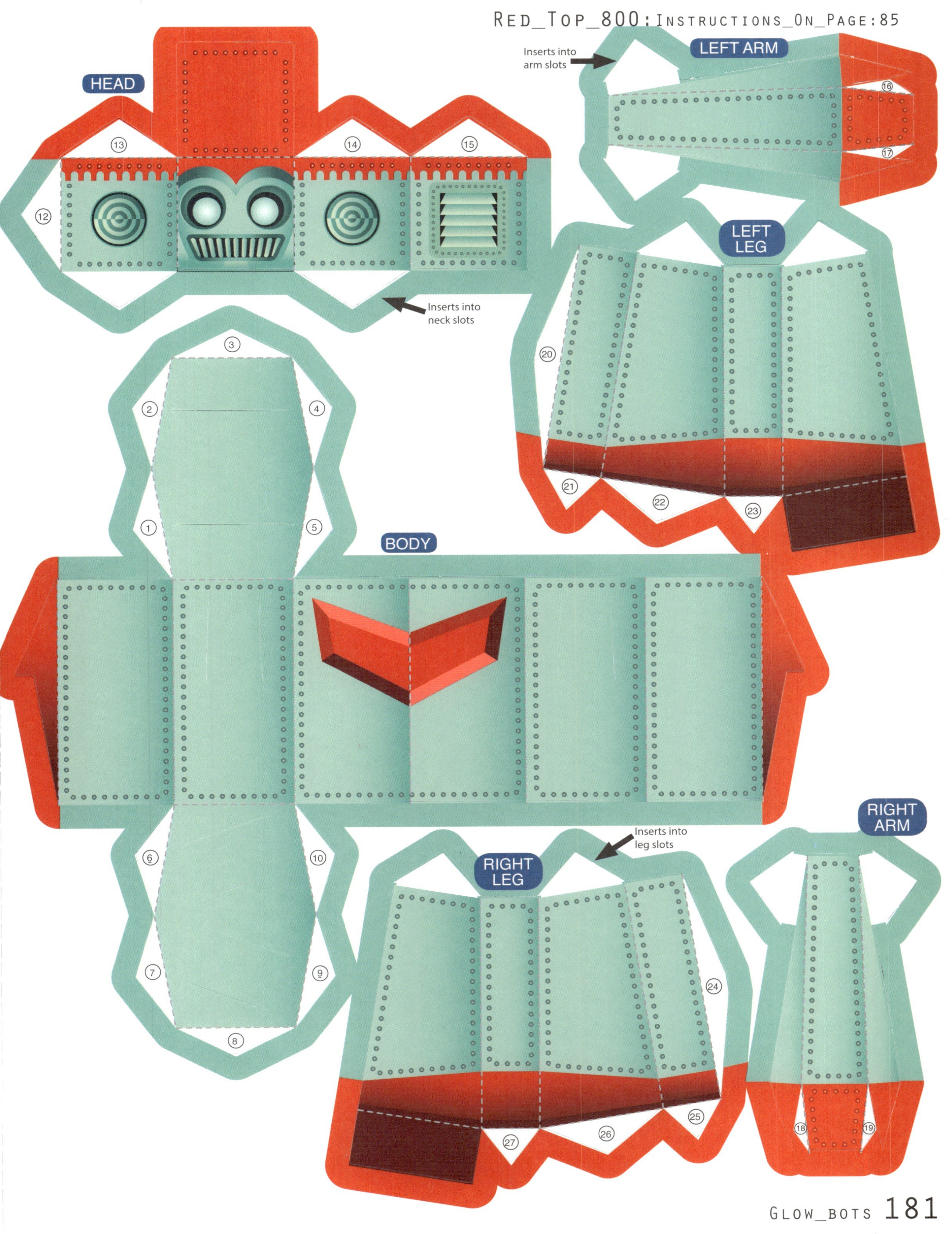

HEAD
13
14
15
12
Inserts into neck slots
LEFT ARM
Inserts into arm slots
16
17
LEFT LEG
20
21
22
23
BODY
3
2
4
1
5
6
10
7
9
8
RIGHT LEG
Inserts into leg slots
24
25
26
27
RIGHT ARM
18
19

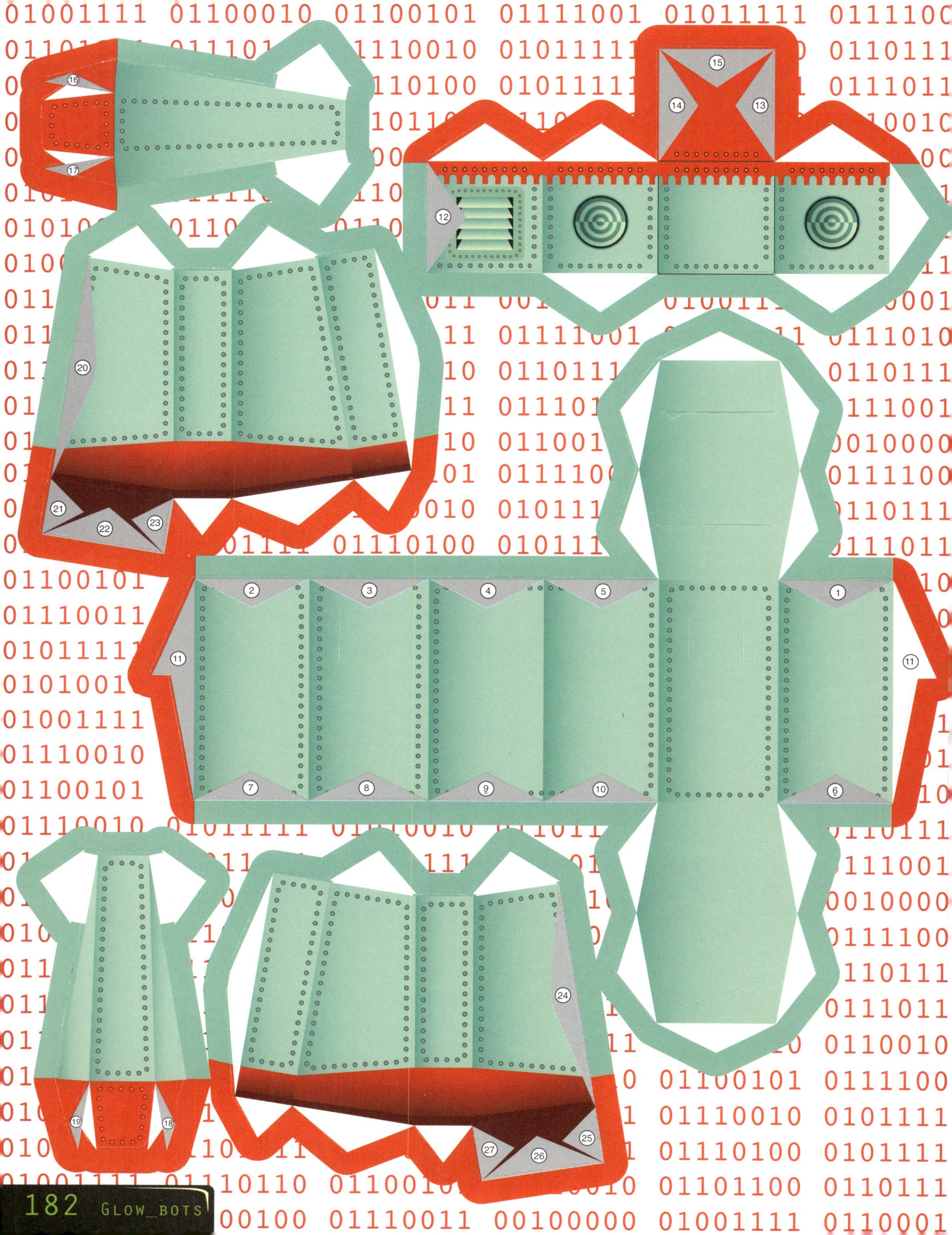

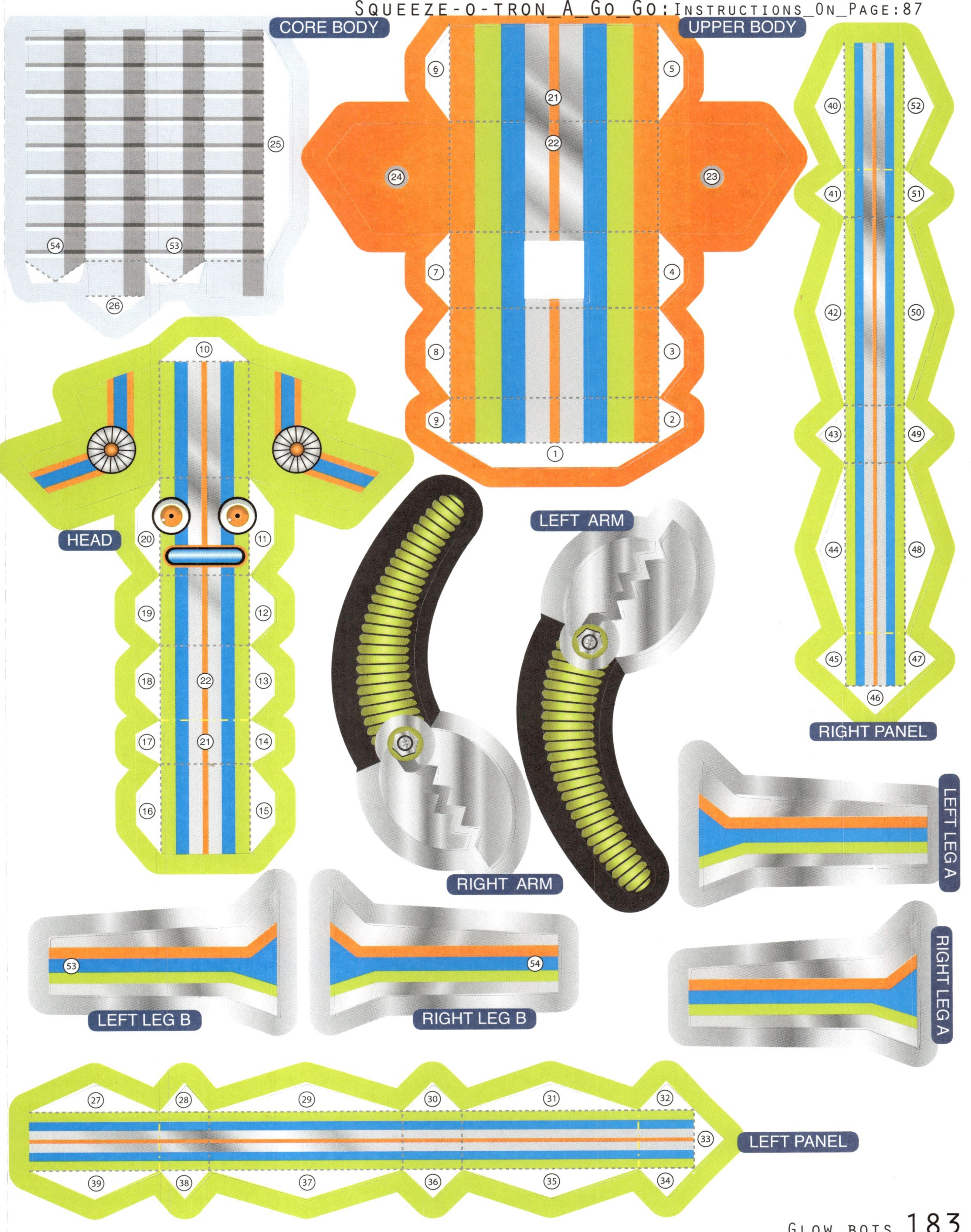
CORE BODY
UPPER BODY
HEAD
LEFT ARM
RIGHT ARM
RIGHT PANEL
LEFT LEG A
LEFT LEG B
RIGHT LEG B
RIGHT LEG A
LEFT PANEL

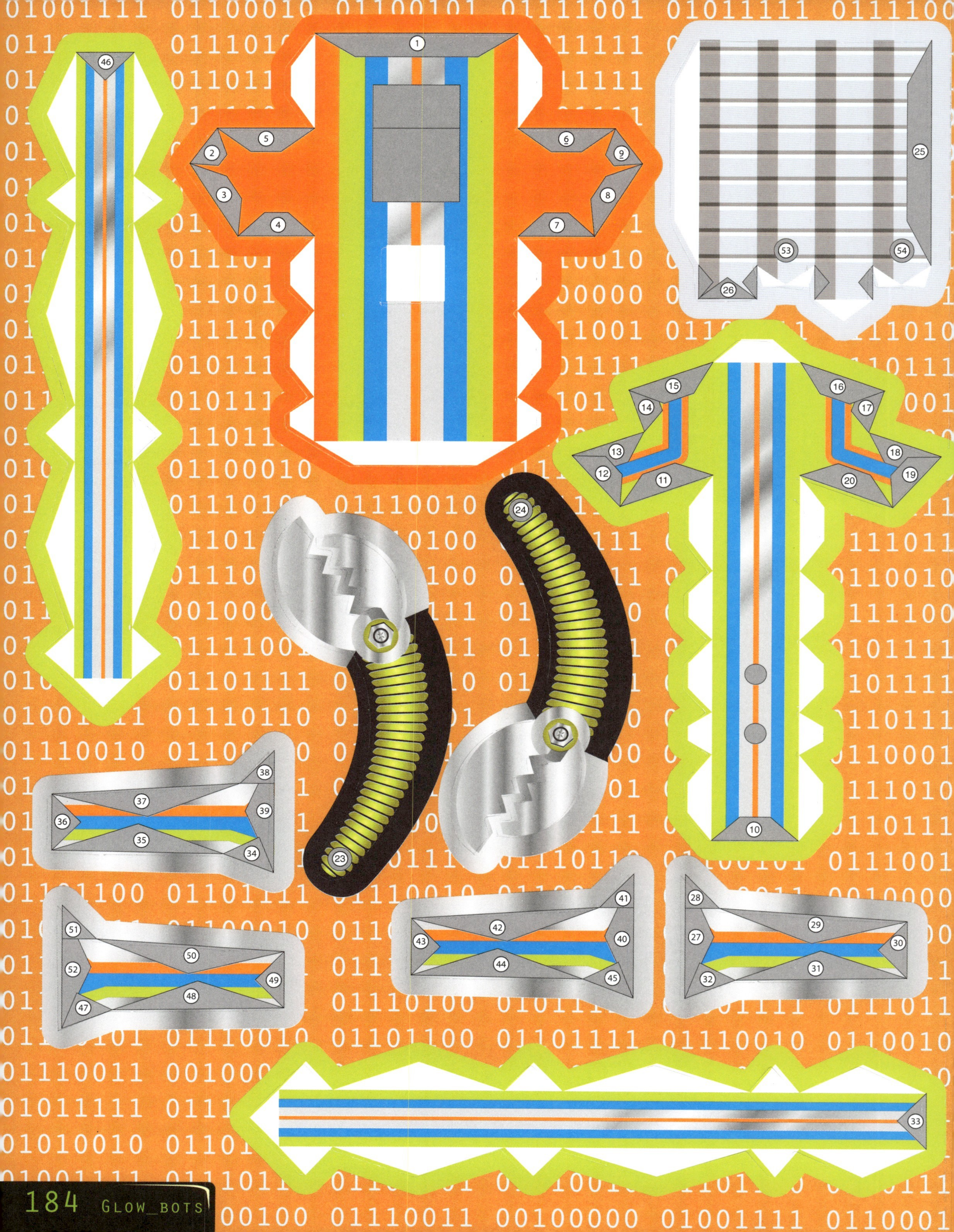

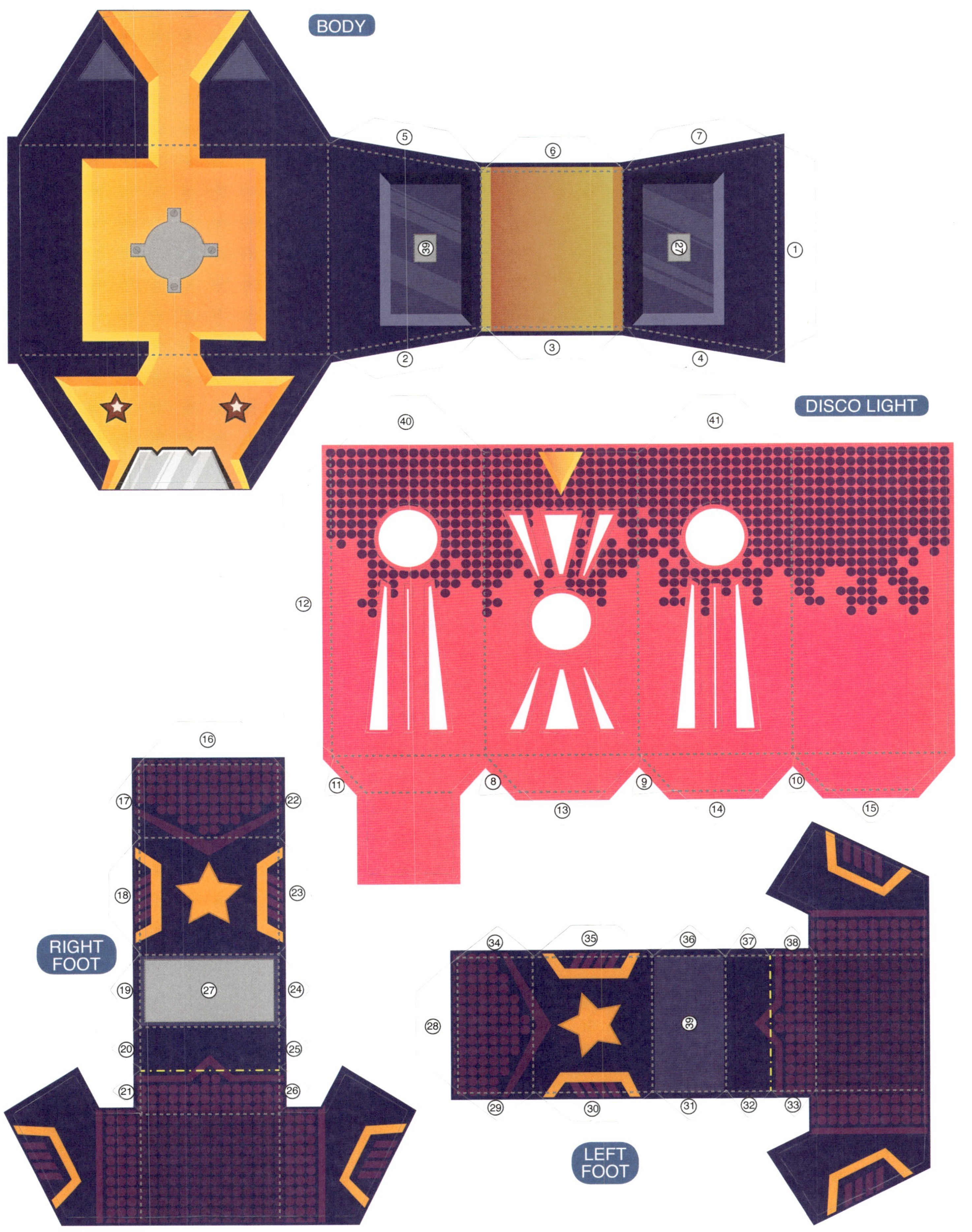
BODY
DISCO LIGHT
RIGHT FOOT
LEFT FOOT

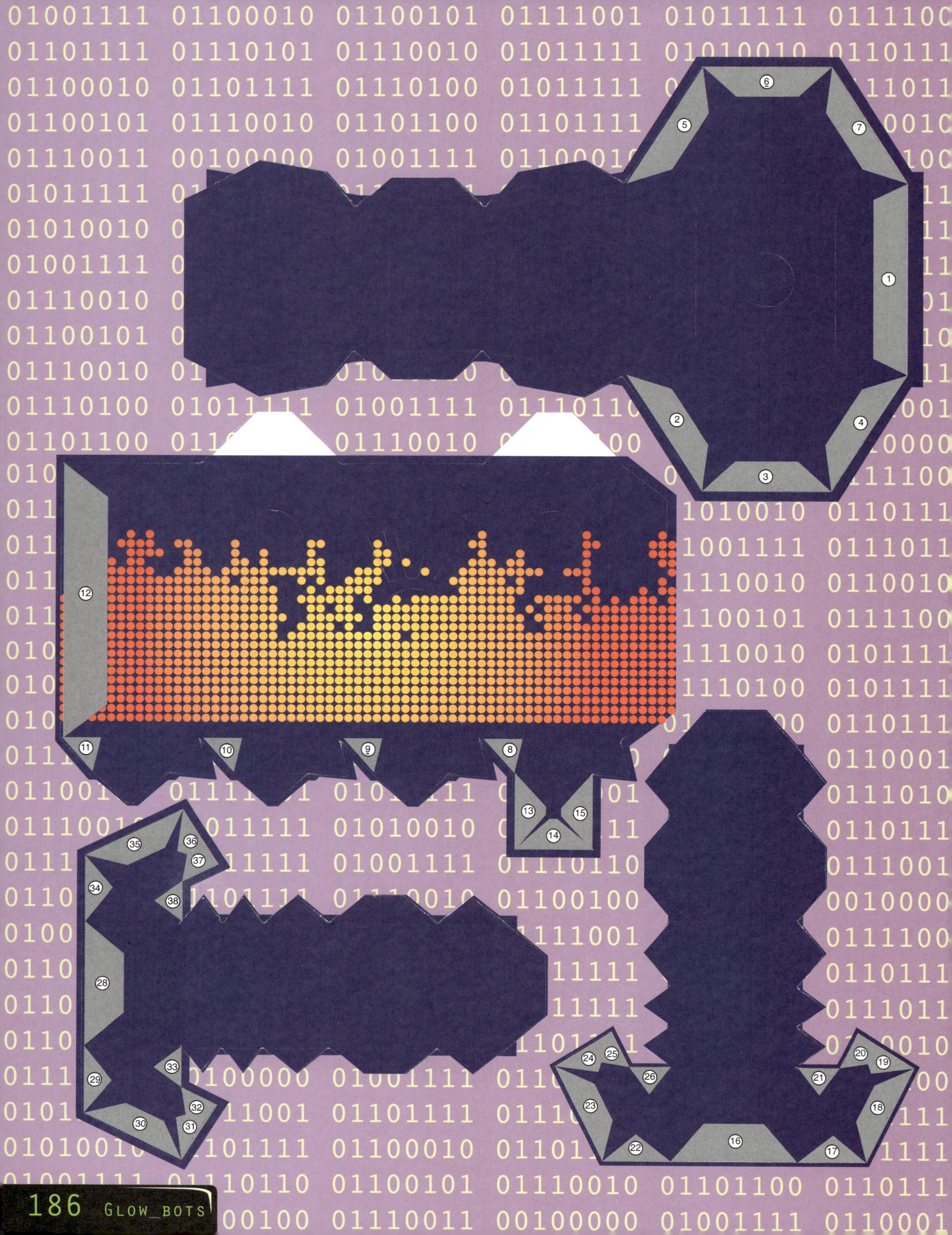

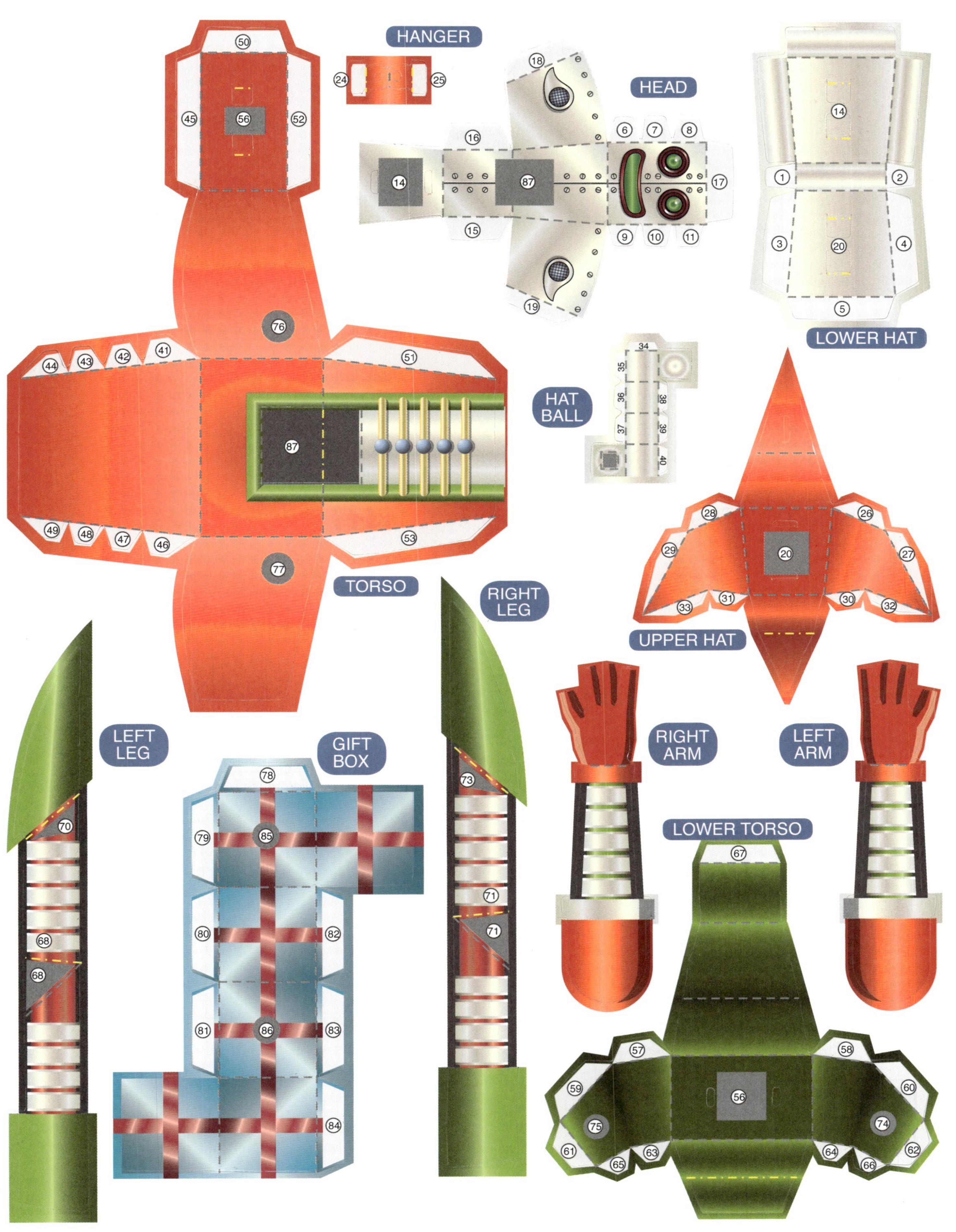

HANGER
HEAD
LOWER HAT
HAT BALL
TORSO
RIGHT LEG
UPPER HAT
LEFT LEG
GIFT BOX
RIGHT ARM
LEFT ARM
LOWER TORSO

Daisujin p.1
Glow-Go p.7
S.S. Tubmarine p.11
Drillrr p.9
Blitztrail p.15
Big Fun p.17
B.A.A.R.T p.13
Garlic p.19
Mega Byte p.21
WavForm p.27
HUGZ p.29
Disinfectoid pg.33
ERR-07 p.35
ED-03 p.37
Ardore p.39
TaTiki p.43
KeiKoko p.41

Traxx p.45
Evv p.47
Moon Walker pg.51
Hydro Bulb p.53
Spence-o-nator p.55
Yujein p.57
Dairobo p.61
IQ 4.0 p.65
Lighting Walker p.67
Sparxy p.63
O.S.C.A.R. p.69
Folgore p.71
Glitch Hardwire p.77
Red Top 800 p.85
Lighting Bee 2 p.75
Trot Bot p.79
Lighting Fly p.81
Ch1pp3r p.83
Squeeze-O-Tron A GoGo p.87
Spinach p.89